The Landscape of Reform

The Landscape of Reform

Civic Pragmatism and Environmental Thought in America

Ben A. Minteer

The MIT Press
Cambridge, Massachusetts
London, England

MIT Press books may be purchased at special quantity discounts for business or sales promotional use. For information, please email special_sales@mitpress.mit.edu or write to Special Sales Department, The MIT Press, 55 Hayward Street, Cambridge, MA 02142.

This book was set in Sabon by SNP Best-set Typesetter Ltd., Hong Kong. Printed on recycled paper and bound in the United States of America.

Library of Congress Cataloging-in-Publication Data

Minteer, Ben A., 1969–
The landscape of reform : civic pragmatism and enviromental thourht in America / Ben A. Minteer.
     p. cm.
Includes bibliographical references and index.
ISBN 0-262-13461-6
1. Environmentalism—United Satates. 2. Enviromental ethics—United States. I. Title.
GE197.M57   2006   333.72—dc22   2005053428

10 9 8 7 6 5 4 3 2 1

Contents

Acknowledgments

For their helpful discussions and encouragement during the period in which the ideas in this book either first emerged or took on their final shape, I want to thank Barry Bozeman, Jim Collins, Jan Dizard, Andrew Light, Don Loeb, Bob Manning, Curt Meine, Bryan Norton, Philip Pauly, Bob Pepperman Taylor, Steve Pyne, and Paul Thompson. I would also like to acknowledge the suggestions of three anonymous reviewers for MIT Press who provided many thoughtful criticisms of an earlier draft of the manuscript. While the virtues of this volume must be shared with all of these individuals, its vices are, I'm afraid, mine alone. Clay Morgan at MIT Press was an enthusiastic supporter of this project from the very beginning, and I thank him for his good advice and steady guidance. I would also like to thank Mort Munk and Jane Maienschein, both in the School of Life Sciences at Arizona State University, for providing me with much-needed research time to complete this project. Finally, my wife, Elizabeth Corley, has my heartfelt appreciation for her unwavering support, as well my admiration for bearing with me throughout this process.

Earlier versions of two of the chapters in this book have appeared previously in print. A version of chapter 3 was published as "Regional Planning as Pragmatic Conservationism," in *Reconstructing Conservation: Finding Common Ground*, Ben A. Minteer and Robert E. Manning, eds. (Washington, DC: Island Press, 2003), pp. 93–113. An earlier treatment of chapter 4 was published as "Wilderness and the Wise Province: Benton MacKaye's Pragmatic Vision," in *Philosophy and Geography*, vol. 4 (2001), pp. 187–204. This work has been significantly revised and expanded for inclusion in this book, and I am grateful to the publishers for allowing me to use this material here. Finally, I would like to thank the Special Collections Library at Dartmouth College for permission to use material from the MacKaye Family Papers, as well as the library of the University of Wisconsin-Madison for allowing me to quote from the Aldo Leopold Papers.

When a way of thinking is deeply rooted in the soil, and embodies the instincts or even the characteristic errors of a people, it has a value quite independent of its truth; it constitutes a phase of human life and can powerfully affect the intellectual drama in which it figures.

George Santayana

Our village life would stagnate if it were not for the unexplored forests and meadows which surround it.

Henry David Thoreau

1
Civic Pragmatism and American Environmental Reform

Environmentalism's Lost "Third Way"

The American environmental tradition is often depicted as torn between two diametrically opposed moral visions. On one side lies anthropocentrism, with its penchant for viewing the environment through the lens of human interests (usually cast in the language of economic good). On the other lies ecocentrism, with its unbending defense of the intrinsic value or inherent worth of nature—especially wild species and ecosystems. This moral schism is most obvious in the well-worn distinction between shallow or reform environmentalism and the radical environmental worldview of deep ecology. According to deep ecologists, shallow environmentalism is a piecemeal approach to environmental problems, hamstrung by its policy incrementalism and a superficial focus on the promotion of human health and environmental amenities. Deep ecology, on the other hand, offers a bold egalitarianism of species, a sweeping critique of modern techno-industrialism, and a far-reaching environmental policy agenda based on biocentric and ecocentric principles.[1]

The stories that have been told about the historical development of American environmental thought have certainly tended to reinforce a dualistic understanding. For example, historians and philosophers often trace the alleged rupture in the moral foundation of American environmentalism to the showdown between John Muir and Gifford Pinchot over the damming of the Hetch Hetchy Valley in Yosemite National Park in the early part of the twentieth century. In the traditional version of this debate, Muir—founder of the Sierra Club and one of history's great wilderness advocates—is embraced as a hero by later environmentalists for his rhapsodizing about the spiritual and aesthetic qualities of wild nature and his take-no-prisoners defense of the Hetch Hetchy Valley from the dam builders. The more utilitarian-minded Pinchot—first head of the U.S. Forest Service and a staunch defender of the efficient and equitable development of natural resources—is tarred as the anti-wilderness, pro-development villain of this morality play, defending the dam and a "highest use" conservation philosophy that appeared to have little regard for the nonmaterial values of the landscape.[2] The Muir–Pinchot row over the damming of Hetch Hetchy, and its subsequent interpretation by scholars, has done much to solidify the most infamous incarnation of the environmentalist dualism: the divide between "conservation," referring to the "wise" or sustainable use of natural resources, and "preservation" (or in some cases, simply "environmentalism"), denoting the protection of environmental systems from the insults of human use.

While the dualistic narrative captures a real conflict running though the history of environmental thought and policy reform, I think that the anthropocentrism versus ecocentrism framework, especially in its more dogmatic varieties, has tended to oversimplify what is in fact a complex and rich moral tradition, one that is not nearly as bifurcated as the received account would have us believe. In particular, the black-and-white nature of this narrative has had the effect of foreclosing the possibility of a more tempered and philosophically pluralistic approach to environmental ethics and politics; that is, the option of a pragmatic alternative running between the zealous "humans first!" and "nature first!" camps.

In this book I seek to restore this lost pragmatic, or third way tradition to the intellectual landscape of American environmentalism, a philosophical path that has been almost completely obscured by the overgrowth of the anthropocentric–ecocentric legend. I believe that this alternative tradition was most powerfully advanced by a small group of conservationists and planners in the first half of the twentieth century. They are Liberty Hyde Bailey, a horticultural scientist and rural reformer who was a leading figure in the agrarian wing of Theodore Roosevelt's conservation movement; Lewis Mumford, an urban theorist, cultural critic, and regional planning thinker active in the Regional Planning Association of America (RPAA) during the interwar period; Benton MacKaye, a forester and conservationist (and Mumford's RPAA colleague) who proposed the Appalachian Trail in the 1920s; and finally Aldo Leopold, the forester-philosopher and author of the environmentalist classic *A Sand County Almanac*.[3]

Of this group, only Leopold is regularly acknowledged in contemporary environmentalist discussions. In the standard reading, Leopold is lionized for giving us a new land ethic, an orientation toward the natural world that is often presented as a kind of fusion of Muir's older ecocentric (or, more accurately, biocentric) environmentalism with the more mature scientific insights of mid-twentieth-century community ecology (along with a dash of Pinchot's managerial practicality). Leopold's land ethic, speaking as it does to the "rights" of and "love" for nonhuman nature, became for many a moral manifesto when it was rediscovered by environmental advocates, professionals, and academics in the 1960s and 1970s. Today the land ethic (and the book in which it appears, *A Sand County Almanac*) is widely held to be the secular equivalent of holy writ within environmentalist circles.

In this volume I hope to challenge this understanding of the tradition by offering a different take on Leopold's significance, but also by showing Bailey, Mumford, and MacKaye to be important and unduly neglected environmental thinkers that deserve much more attention than they have received. One of the benefits of a focus on these lesser-known figures in the narrative is that it introduces other landscapes, ideals, and models of the human–nature relationship into the intellectual history of environmentalism. Historical and philosophical studies of the roots of American environmentalism have traditionally been consumed by the ideas of natural resource conservationists like Pinchot and iconic wilderness advocates like Muir and Leopold. As a result, and with very few exceptions, we have not heard voices such as Bailey's speaking to rural and agrarian conservation issues. Nor has the tradition of regional planning of Mumford and MacKaye often been incorporated into the histories and philosophical studies of conservation and environmentalism.[4] I think this is unfortunate, especially given the significance of these threads in the larger story of the development of American environmental reform in the first decades of the twentieth century.

Although I describe it more fully in the individual chapters, one of the noteworthy features of the third way tradition in environmental thought is its embrace of a pluralistic model of environmental value and action that accommodates both the prudent use *and* the preservation of nature, rather than demanding that we must always choose between these commitments.[5] It is a way of thinking, in other words, that accepts the interpenetrating character of intrinsic and instrumental values in experience, the basic continuity of means and ends in environmental thought and practice. As such, the third way tradition is a strand within environmentalism that cannot be accurately characterized as either narrowly anthropocentric or ecocentric. Rather, it incorporates critical elements of both sensibilities in a more holistic, balanced, and practical vision of human environmental experience.

Furthermore, this pragmatic strain in environmental thought views humans as thoroughly embedded in natural systems. Yet this recognition does not lead to the conclusion that humans have carte blanche with respect to the natural world, or that there is no moral limit to the dominion of human will over the landscape. Instead, the third way view supports a wider and more integrative perspective in which human ideals and interests (including economic interests, but also other nonmaterial social, cultural, and political values) are understood to be wrapped up in the natural and the built environment, and are secured and promoted through deliberate and broad-based planning and conservation efforts. While respectful of wilderness geographies and values, this tradition nevertheless represents a retreat from pure preservationist forms of environmentalism to views that accommodate ecologically benign and adaptive forms of technological enterprise and sustainable community development on the landscape.

Most significantly, the philosophies of Bailey, Mumford, MacKaye, and Leopold form a politically grounded and civic-spirited tradition in environmental thought. I argue that these thinkers were deeply concerned about the health of American political culture and the civic capacity of the community in the face of industrial and urbanizing forces in the first half of the twentieth century. Even though they were often occupied—especially Bailey and Leopold—with the moral character of our relations with the natural world (in some cases going so far as to express a commitment to the intrinsic value of the environment), they also viewed citizens' attitudes toward nature as playing a pragmatic or instrumental role in the criticism and transformation of American social and political experience. Their land conservation and regional and wilderness planning efforts were at the same time attempts to assert environmental values, especially the ideal of a "balanced" or "healthy" landscape, and to advance vital public commitments as essential parts of the good life within a modern democratic community. Instead of focusing narrowly on the transformation of individuals' environmental consciousness (which seems to be the goal of many ecocentrists today), environmental reform in the hands of Bailey, Mumford, MacKaye, and Leopold therefore took on the shape of a more ambitious moral and political enterprise. It was seen as a powerful tool that could help advance the ends of civic regeneration and social improvement.

A Return to Pragmatism

In my attempt to illuminate this overlooked tradition in environmental thought, I will employ some of the resources of classic American philosophy, especially the work of John Dewey (and to a lesser extent, Josiah Royce). As mentioned earlier, and as I discuss in more detail in the chapters that follow, I believe this third way in environmental thought displays many of the marks of philosophical pragmatism. In some cases I think this intellectual influence is fairly direct and overt; in others it is more implicit, yet still palpable and always intriguing. Since pragmatism plays such a key part in my reading of this alternative strain of environmentalism, I should say a few words about it before we go any further.

While its influence in American philosophical circles waned considerably by the 1940s (when it was partly eclipsed by logical positivism), pragmatism has experienced something of a scholarly resurgence in recent decades, thanks to the work of a diverse group of high-profile "neopragmatist" philosophers, such as Richard Rorty, Richard Bernstein, Hilary Putnam, and Jurgen Habermas. It has also made inroads into several other academic fields, including literary, film, and cultural criticism;[6] law,[7] and political theory.[8] Pragmatism has even enjoyed a return to the public eye (Dewey was, after all, the quintessential public philosopher of his time), at least if we can take the enthusiastic reception of Louis Menand's Pulitzer Prize-winning historical biography of the pragmatists, *The Metaphysical Club*, as any indication.[9]

A philosophical school that can count thinkers as diverse as Charles Sanders Peirce, WVO Quine, Richard Rorty, and Cornel West among its ranks probably resists any simple and concise definition. Still, we can think of pragmatism as being marked by a set of core methodological and normative commitments.[10]

Perhaps the most salient feature of pragmatism is its instrumentalist character and the emphasis it places on the realm of practice (as opposed to the sphere of the ideal). Pragmatism is not a mirroring philosophy that seeks to reflect ideas said to exist outside of human culture, nor does it claim to register an objective, preexperiential understanding of nature. It is rather an active, constructive (or reconstructive) philosophy, one that arises from practical experience and takes shape as individuals—and communities—confront problems, learn about their (and others') values and beliefs, and adjust and progressively improve their natural and built environments. To paraphrase Ian Hacking, pragmatism suggests less the image of the philosopher's armchair than it does the craftsman's workbench. Ideas, as well as values and moral principles, are not abstractions; they are tools for social experimentation with the goal of bettering the human condition and enhancing our cultural adaptation to the environment. Among other things, this emphasis on instrumental action and social practice suggests that new knowledge and novel values can emerge from reflective and well-planned human activity on the landscape. Indeed, such activities have the potential to expand human experience and generate cultural wisdom in a manner that can improve our ability to achieve valued social goals, as well as deepen our appreciation of our natural and built environments.

Pragmatism is also known for its acceptance, if not hearty embrace, of the condition of pluralism; i.e., that individuals are differently situated and are shaped to a significant degree by dissimilar traditions and experiences. Any claim to a universal or singular "good" is thus illusory to most pragmatists. This commitment to pluralism (including both its metaphysical and ethical varieties) prompts in turn the acknowledgment of the fallibility of our beliefs and moral commitments. It requires an openness to revision and change as we come into contact with the views of others and accept that new evidence and further discussion may show our beliefs to be mistaken and our values to be ill-considered or to have unacceptable implications.[11] In the environmental case, a growing body of social scientific research on public opinion has shown that citizens embrace a range of moral stances toward the environment, including both anthropocentric and ecocentric positions.[12] In light of this evidence, the notion that we should be searching for a final and universal ethical principle (or even a small set of ultimate principles) to govern all of our problematic environmental situations seems misguided to pragmatists. Such a view not only sweeps aside real moral diversity, it also fails to acknowledge that values can and do change in the context of public debate and deliberation over environmental problems and policies.[13]

Another core element of the pragmatist approach is the centrality of experience in all types of knowing and valuing. Human transactions with the social and physical environment are for pragmatists the ultimate generator of knowledge and value, and the ongoing process of direct experience is the only authoritative source of moral and political guidance. Experience, in other words, is uniquely regulative. Furthermore, since all value and knowledge arise through this transactional process, pragmatists believe that it is pointless to make rigid distinctions between means and ends, instrumental and intrinsic values. The basic continuity of experience also leads pragmatists to reject the dichotomy between fact and value, yet this is done without simply collapsing value expressions into factual statements. Instead, pragmatists view facts about human experience as offering empirical support or evidence for moral claims about what is, in fact, good or right (or bad or wrong), evidence that is always capable of being overturned in light of additional experience.[14] Once more, it follows from this way of thinking that culture is fundamentally entwined with the surrounding environment. Environmental values are experienced as human values; they are the products of the transactions between humans and nature in particular social situations and ecophysical contexts.[15] I believe this pragmatic conception of experience runs through the third way tradition in environmental thought discussed in this book.

Finally, within pragmatism there is a high regard for the epistemic, moral, and political worth of the community.[16] On logical grounds, pragmatists like Charles Sanders Peirce and John Dewey embraced the notion of community because of their belief in its ability to provide an institution capable of solving complex scientific and social problems. They believed that, working in concert, a diverse association of "inquirers" (which could include experts, citizens, or both) was better positioned to identify facts, construct solutions to problems, and root out crippling errors than were individuals operating by themselves and saddled with their idiosyncratic perspectives and biases. In Dewey's understanding, this idealized view of cooperative inquiry was manifest in what he called the method of "social intelligence."[17] This process, patterned after the method of inquiry successful in the sciences and technical professions, in Dewey's writing was linked to the political culture of democracy. A democratic social order, characterized by openness, toleration, freedom of expression, and so on, would permit social intelligence to function most effectively; i.e., it would facilitate free and cooperative inquiry and the collective resolution of social problems.[18]

Community held more than purely cognitive value for the pragmatists, however (especially for more socially and politically oriented thinkers in the tradition, like Dewey). It was also a core moral concept, embodying a communicative and social ideal in which individuals participated in collective experience, contributing to the development of shared values and the direction of group affairs toward a locally defined notion of the common good. The community in turn provided the critical social and educational environment in which individuals could fully mature and flourish, both as individuals and as democratic citizens. For pragmatists of Dewey's persuasion, democracy rested upon this intertwined social and moral vision. It was a vision, moreover, that he believed required a vigorous defense in an age of rampant market individualism.

In the *Public and Its Problems*, for example, Dewey argued for the retrieval of a participatory, face-to-face politics and a renewed understanding of the common good. These values, he lamented, were being eroded by the corrosive culture of an unplanned industrialism and overly materialistic individualism. As we will see in the chapters that follow, the third way environmentalist thinkers shared Dewey's concerns about the growing threats to community life and the corrosion of a sense of the public interest in modern America. Although their ideas differed in a number of ways, I believe that Bailey, Mumford, MacKaye, and Leopold were of one mind in the hope that ambitious environmental reform would reinvigorate communities and strengthen citizens' sense of their collective stake in a healthy landscape and a vibrant social life.

As it has in other academic circles, pragmatism has recently surfaced in a number of fields within environmental studies, including environmental philosophy,[19] environmental law,[20] environmental economics,[21] and environmental policy and management.[22] Even though I will touch on several themes and questions in this book that have consumed the attention of environmental philosophers, my discussion here is pitched more generally than this. I want to show that a strong current of what might be called civic pragmatism (marked by an emphasis on instrumental action and experience, a recognition of value pluralism, and a focus on revitalizing community and cultural affairs) runs through the American environmental tradition. I also want to illustrate how this third way tradition resonates in certain efforts at environmental reform being advanced today, movements that speak to a wider cultural view of the impact of pragmatism on American environmental thought.

Finally, I want to suggest a role for this civic pragmatist approach in the construction of a more balanced and better-adapted environmentalist culture. My discussion of pragmatism, in other words, is generally not as concerned with the more technical and specialized questions of knowledge and value that have largely dominated its career within environmental philosophy.[23] Rather, I want to understand how the alternative environmentalism set forth by Bailey, Mumford, MacKaye, and Leopold—a tradition that is in general humanistic (but not narrowly utilitarian), attentive to the beauty and nonmarket value of nature, yet resistant to doctrinaire versions of ecocentrism—can lead to a transformed understanding of the relationship between our environmental values and our other moral and political commitments.

Plan of the Book

My approach is to uncover the tradition of civic pragmatism in environmental thought and practice by exploring the work of the four environmental reformers already introduced: Liberty Hyde Bailey, Lewis

Mumford, Benton MacKaye, and Aldo Leopold. I then consider how this third way in environmental thought is manifest on the landscape today by examining in detail two important and ongoing reform movements in land conservation and planning that I see as reflecting and extending this tradition of pragmatic environmentalism. I close the book with a few brief reflections on how this third way environmentalism challenges some of the current assumptions and preoccupations of the academic field that has spoken the most loudly about the moral character of human–environment relations: environmental ethics.

In chapter 2 I consider the work of Liberty Hyde Bailey, a horticultural scientist, agricultural administrator, and rural reformer who played a pivotal role in the Progressive Era Country Life Commission, the brainchild of Teddy Roosevelt and an attempt to bring a version of the conservation spirit to agriculture and the countryside. Bailey's emphasis on nature study in childhood and the transformative effects of immersive environmental educational activities such as planting and tending school gardens fed into efforts to reform American country life, an agenda that hinged in no small part on making rural environment and culture an attractive and valued realm in a rapidly industrializing and urbanizing nation. I argue that Bailey's educational goal is completely in step with that of pragmatist philosopher and educational reformer John Dewey, whose well-known advocacy of active, child-centered learning and the role of education in cultivating a democratic citizenry reverberates in Bailey's work. Like Dewey, Bailey viewed education (in this case, nature study) as the means for creating more public-spirited and civic-minded individuals. Bailey also hoped that such experiences would instill a love of nature and the farm landscape within a new generation of rural residents, a regard that would anchor them to the countryside and stem the flow of population into the early twentieth-century metropolis.

In a series of books with environmental themes written in the period beginning at the turn of the twentieth century to the onset of World War I, Bailey developed an environmental ethic that captured both a sense of the land's intrinsic value (the "holy earth") and a more traditional conservationist concern for resource sustainability and the well-being of future generations. Bailey's environmentalism was therefore both morally pluralistic—i.e., encapsulating both instrumental and intrinsic values of nature—and grounded in a broader pragmatist-inspired educational philosophy and a political goal of rural reform and civic revitalization. While his contribution to environmental thought and the historical development of conservation and environmentalism is therefore quite significant, Bailey is largely unknown within the contemporary environmental studies and environmental practitioner communities. Yet his influence may be felt today in several quarters of environmental reform, including movements for a sustainable agriculture and those promoting an overarching ethic of stewardship within public and private land conservation programs.

I continue to develop this third way environmental tradition in chapter 3 with an exploration of the work of Lewis Mumford in the period between the two world wars. Like Bailey, Mumford is fairly uncommon in environmentalist discussions; he is certainly much better known among urbanists and historians of technology. For the present discussion, my interest in Mumford is in his regional planning theory and his involvement in the Regional Planning Association of America in the 1920s and early 1930s. I attempt to show that an important part of Mumford's planning program was his effort to widen the American conservation vision to include a regional rather than a single-resource focus, and to diversify and strengthen its philosophical foundations beyond a narrow utilitarianism by appealing to deeper cultural and political values.

Although Mumford had some unflattering things to say about pragmatism in his classic work of cultural criticism, *The Golden Day*,[24] and squared off with John Dewey in the pages of the *New Republic* in the late 1920s, I argue that Mumford's approach to regional planning was thoroughly pragmatic; indeed, I suggest that he articulated what was in fact a Deweyan understanding of social intelligence in his discussion of the staging of the regional planning process. Furthermore, as with Bailey's nature-study efforts, Mumford also linked his environmental program (regional planning) to a larger civic agenda. The participation of citizens in Mumford's regional survey process would, he believed, teach them about the biophysical and cultural resources of their community and surrounding landscape, while at the same time building a common political identity and nurturing a wider civic pride. Mumford's participatory and democratic vision for the regional survey is thus another point of intellectual contact with Dewey's pragmatism, especially the political ideas Dewey advanced in works like the *The Public and Its Problems*.

Finally, while Mumford's writing during this period conveys what we might think of as a broadly humanistic environmental ethic (albeit one that included discernable organicist, i.e., nonanthropocentric elements), the intellectual significance of Mumford's regionalism, I believe, is best understood as a more expansive cultural form of environmentalism, one that speaks to a range of political and aesthetic concerns as well as to ethical questions surrounding the value of nature and the human community.

Mumford's friend and regionalist ally Benton MacKaye is the subject of chapter 4. MacKaye, a Harvard-trained forester who straddled the conservation and planning camps in the interwar period, was both a fascinating practical philosopher of the wilderness and a thoughtful and effective advocate of the regional planning agenda. These passions would converge in his most significant environmental legacy: the Appalachian Trail, a 2,100-mile-long recreational footpath running along the mountains from Maine to Georgia. In this chapter I argue that MacKaye's original justification for the Trail—it was to be an instrument for the social and political reform of the Appalachian region by building up the provincial forces of "indigenous" America to repel the physical and cultural advance of metropolitanism—reflects the influence of the social philosophy of Josiah Royce, an American philosopher who was one of MacKaye's teachers at Harvard. MacKaye's reformist hopes for the Trail also appealed to several older ideas in the American intellectual tradition, including a Thoreau-style turn to nature for a clearer view of social and economic questions, as well as the notion of an alternative provincial political founding that harkened back to the generation of the American Revolution.

Like Mumford, MacKaye's ethical orientation toward nature was generally humanistic. In his mind, environmental values were bound up with the intrinsic values of authentic (i.e., "indigenous") local communities living a balanced and human-scaled communal life in nature. This orientation, and MacKaye's focus on the cultural dimensions of wilderness conservation and the maintenance of vital communal and folk traditions in the hinterlands, makes him a thinker of great originality and contemporary relevance, especially in light of the recent wilderness debate that has cropped up among scholars and environmental advocates over the past decade or so.[25] MacKaye's attempt to unite issues that we would today describe as community planning or rural development with the protection of the American wilderness remains a unique contribution in the annals of conservation and environmental thought. His effort stands as a lesson—perhaps one forgotten by some ecocentric environmentalists—that a serious regard for the civic health of human communities does not preclude a concern for the integrity of wild places (and vice versa).

In chapter 5 I consider the work and thought of Aldo Leopold, MacKaye's fellow wilderness advocate and widely considered to be the father of environmental ethics. Leopold's reputation in environmental studies is, to put it mildly, secure. Generations of readers have been inspired by *A Sand County Almanac*, his towering contribution to the environmentalist canon. The challenge for anyone who takes on Leopold's legacy for contemporary environmentalism, unlike that for Bailey, Mumford, and MacKaye, is certainly not one of establishing relevance. It is the opposite: What could there possibly be left to say? Leopold has spawned a virtual cottage industry within environmental ethics and environmental history; *Sand County* and its philosophical crown jewel, "The Land Ethic," have figured prominently in environmental ethics discussions and debates since the early 1970s. Indeed, efforts to claim Leopold as either a nonanthropocentrist or an environmental humanist have become in many respects a struggle over the very soul of environmental ethics and the moral underpinnings of environmental policy, planning, and management.

Here I approach Leopold somewhat differently than he has been in the past. Instead of focusing solely on the more philosophical anthropocentrist versus ecocentrist debate and the issue of his stance on the "moral considerability" of nature, I treat Leopold as what we might today refer to as a public intellectual and reformer who spoke to the core normative political question of the public interest. I suggest that Leopold's developing notion of land health became for him a substantive definition of the public interest, and that we can understand his endorsement of the intrinsic value of nature in works like *A Sand County Almanac* as (at least in part) a pragmatic move designed to motivate land owners, and citizens generally, to practice sound conservation and promote a healthy landscape, which would in turn produce a number of valued cultural, aesthetic, and economic goods.

I also argue that the notion of land health serves an additional pragmatic, especially Deweyan purpose in Leopold's work. It offers a means by which a disparate public can recognize its common interest in a fertile and biologically diverse landscape and the civic values it supports, an instrumental precondition for intelligent social action within a recognized political community. This claiming of Leopold as a public thinker, I suggest, is further justified by his rhetorical efforts to reform conventional views of American material progress and technological development. He consistently advocated a view of the public interest that asserted the cultural and aesthetic values of nature over acquisitive individualism, commercial boosterism, and the accumulation of ever more numerous gadgets and technological devices at the expense of the health of the land.

Building from the third way tradition of Bailey, Mumford, MacKaye, and Leopold, I turn in chapter 6 to a discussion of current practice, focusing on two important attempts at land-use reform: Natural Systems Agriculture and New Urbanism. I believe that these practical movements both illustrate and further develop the civic pragmatist environmental tradition constructed in the preceding chapters. For nearly three decades Natural Systems Agriculture (also known as perennial polyculture) has been promoted by Wes Jackson and his collaborators at The Land Institute in Salina, Kansas, as a more sustainable and ecologically benign alternative to chemical- and energy-intensive industrial agriculture. I examine the main features of Jackson's program and his ethical justifications for developing a new agricultural paradigm that seeks to mimic wild ecosystems. These rationales, I argue, turn out to be both anthropocentric and nonanthropocentric in content. Moreover, Jackson's agricultural vision, like that of the four historical figures discussed in the earlier chapters, is tied to a larger social reform agenda devoted to preserving American communal traditions and democratic values from the moral corruption, social atomism, and ecological destructiveness of the market and the consumer impulse.

In the second half of chapter 6 I provide an analysis of the intertwining environmental and social philosophies of New Urbanism, a movement composed primarily of architects and planners seeking to remedy the negative environmental, physical, social, and civic effects of suburban sprawl. I suggest that the New Urbanist charter and the overall design philosophy advanced by many of its proponents represent an intriguing convergence of environmental and social ends, and that New Urbanism also carries forward the third way tradition of a pragmatist-inspired environmentalism with its value pluralism, its strategic and conceptual inclusiveness, and its emphasis on community building and the restoration of a human-scaled environment conducive to a fuller and more vibrant civic life in an increasingly urban environment.

In the concluding chapter I briefly summarize the main themes of the book and discuss how the third way tradition suggests a different path than that currently being taken by most writers on environmental ethics, the field that has taken responsibility for interpreting and advancing the moral discourse of environmentalism today. I argue for a rethinking of the field's mission and advocate the adoption of a more civic style of environmental ethics that comports both with the third way tradition explored in this book and with the growing number of citizen-led environmental movements on the American scene.

The "landscape" of this book's title is both metaphorical and conventionally literal. It is, on the one hand, the intellectual territory navigated by the third way environmental thinkers whose work and ideas I discuss in the following pages. It is also the physical landscape itself, which, in addition to being an object of moral concern and the locus of past and present conservation and planning efforts, also serves in this alternative tradition as a vehicle for criticizing our social and political practices and a means for proposing alternative visions of the good life in a democratic community.

I have also chosen the term *landscape* (over the more widely used *nature* in environmentalist discourse) deliberately. John Brinckerhoff Jackson has pointed out that it is a semantically rich and resonant word, one that "underscores not only our identity and presence, but also our history."[26] Indeed, landscape suggests a more cultural understanding of the environment that encapsulates social goods and experiences. It therefore also signifies, I believe, an implicit acceptance of responsible human agency in nature, rather than dismissing human will and activity out of hand, a move that has become commonplace in the more zealous versions of ecocentric environmentalism. Staying with this theme, I close this introduction with the words of Simon Schama (from his spellbinding book, *Landscape and Memory*), which I think also serve as an appropriate preface to the chapters that follow:

All our landscapes, from the city park to the mountain hike, are imprinted with our tenacious, inescapable obsessions. So that to take the many and several ills of the environment seriously does not, I think, require that we trade in our cultural legacy or its posterity. It asks instead that we simply see it for what it has truly been: not the repudiation, but the veneration, of nature.[27]

2

Nature Study, Rural Progressivism, and the Holy Earth: The Forgotten Contribution of Liberty Hyde Bailey

Liberty Hyde Bailey, Jr.—horticulturalist, agricultural administrator, educational theorist, conservationist, and rural reformer—occupies an important, though little-known position in the history of American conservation and environmental ethics.[1] Bailey's contribution is admittedly difficult to gauge on any quick reading since his thought both embodies and departs from the typical commitments we associate with the heyday of Progressive conservation. Like the more celebrated leaders of the early American conservation movement, for example, Bailey often adopted heroic rhetoric celebrating the "conquest" of wild nature and the efficient use of the earth's resources for human benefit. On the one hand, this is not surprising, especially given Bailey's involvement in the Roosevelt-appointed Country Life Commission, which sought to bring a version of the conservation agenda to the countryside. Yet Bailey also wrote *The Holy Earth*, a probing and, as its title suggests, overtly spiritual reflection on the values of the natural world.[2] Bailey's ideas in this book (and in other works around the same period) are therefore intriguing elements in the story of conservation and the development of American landscape philosophy, even if his work has not been recognized by environmental philosophers and historians. Moreover, Bailey developed an interesting pragmatic educational and civic philosophy, embodied in his program of "nature study," that both mirrored and elaborated on many of the reformist approaches of American philosopher and educational theorist John Dewey. As a result, Bailey's work marks a critical early intersection of pragmatist and conservation thought in the Progressive period. He is therefore an important figure in the third way environmental tradition.

Bailey the Horticulturalist

Born in 1858, Liberty Hyde Bailey, Jr. grew up in the rural environs of South Haven, Michigan, located on the eastern shore of Lake Michigan. This bucolic setting doubtless fed into Bailey's precocious interest in natural history, especially taxonomy, and an early exposure to Charles Darwin's *Origin of the Species* left him completely fascinated by the theory of natural selection. When he was 14 years old, Bailey discovered the work of one of America's great Darwinians of the time—Harvard botanist Asa Gray—through the latter's *Field, Forest, and Garden Botany*.[3] This book, which, in an interesting chain of events, Bailey would later edit into a revised edition in 1895, had a profound impact on the budding scientist, and Bailey soon was off collecting and identifying the flora in the fields around his South Haven home. This early exposure to key scientific texts, the time spent with his father in the family's apple orchard, and Bailey's taxonomic excursions in his midwestern landscape instilled an enthusiasm for natural science and learning that he would never lose. Indeed, it was an enthusiasm that, as one of the premier scientific educators in the United States, he would later pass on to a generation of students.[4] Moreover, these childhood experiences also sparked an early conservation impulse in Bailey as he became concerned about the abuses caused by wasteful and short-sighted exploitation of resources, especially the rampant deforestation that was taking place in the Midwest and in other areas of the country at the time.[5]

In 1877, Bailey enrolled in the Michigan State Agricultural College (MAC), one of the nation's first state agricultural colleges. At MAC (later Michigan State University), Bailey studied under the noted botanist William James Beal, a former student of Asa Gray and the illustrious Louis Agassiz at Harvard. After graduation in 1882, Bailey returned to South Haven, where he tried to figure out what he should do next. Always interested in journalism, he took a job as a reporter with a Springfield, Illinois, newspaper. Bailey warmed to his new vocation and began to move up the paper's ranks. He was about to be promoted to city editor when he received an unexpected, and, as it turned out, fortuitous letter from Beal. Beal wrote that the famed Asa Gray was looking for an assistant to help sort and classify a large collection of plants bequeathed to the Harvard herbarium by the renowned Kew Gardens in England. Gray had asked Beal to recommend an assistant who had the "makings of a botanist in him," and Beal suggested Bailey for the 2-year position. Bailey happily accepted the offer to work under the legendary botanist, and he moved to Cambridge in early 1883.[6]

Upon his arrival, Bailey's major responsibilities at the Harvard herbarium involved sorting and arranging the new Kew collection into several sets (one was to go the Missouri Botanical Garden in St. Louis, the other to the U.S. National Museum in Washington, D.C.). Eventually, Bailey's work on the collection so impressed Gray that he told the young botanist he could keep the set of remaining duplicate specimens for his own.[7] The 2 years working under Gray at the herbarium were a significant period in Bailey's professional and intellectual development. Well beyond the "Darwin wars" fought with his Harvard colleague Agassiz in the early 1860s, Gray was nearing the end of a long and distinguished career as the country's leading botanist and was one of the most fervent defenders of the theory of evolution.[8] As we will see, Bailey would bring a strong evolutionary perspective to his own environmental philosophy.

In 1885, Bailey was offered a professorship of horticulture and landscape gardening at his alma mater, Michigan Agricultural College. He accepted the position despite Gray's disappointment that he was choosing a career in horticulture rather than botany. To Gray and other scientific botanists of the time, horticulture was seen as an unscientific, ornamental art—a gardener's business—and one that lacked a sufficiently rigorous grounding in experimental science.[8] Bailey was not deterred, however, largely because he believed that horticulture could become a respectable science along the lines that Gray and his colleagues understood. At MAC Bailey quickly distinguished himself with his horticultural research, particularly his fruit hybridization experiments, and he began to build a reputation as an excellent and creative teacher. The college awarded him an MS degree in 1886.[9]

After only a few years in Michigan, however, Bailey was lured to Cornell University in Ithaca, New York, which hired him as a professor of practical and experimental horticulture. He spent the next 25 years at Cornell, the last ten of these as dean of the agricultural college. During this time Bailey became the leading horticulturalist in the country and an international authority on the subject, helping, in the process, to raise the field from its association with the "gardening" craft to a distinct and highly professional science resting on a solid foundation in experimental botany.[10] At Cornell, Bailey published at a nearly superhuman rate, averaging roughly a book a year, including his landmark multivolume works, *Cyclopedia of American Agriculture* and *Cyclopedia of American Horticulture*, as well the books on environmental themes discussed later in this chapter.[11] In addition to his administrative and scholarly activities, he was also actively involved in civic improvement efforts in Ithaca, offering his advice on a number of issues relating to the preservation of the area's aesthetic values.[12]

Bailey's intellectual leadership in horticultural science was matched by his educational and administrative efforts as Cornell's agriculture dean, in which he helped direct the physical and institutional expansion of the College of Agriculture and the steady growth of the university's agricultural extension programs.[13] It was also during his years as a Cornell professor, administrator, and "agricultural ambassador" that Bailey became active in the American Country Life movement, first as editor of the magazine *Country Life in America*, and later as the chairman of the Country Life Commission. Since this activity marks a critical point in the development of Bailey's environmental philosophy—my primary interest here—we need to examine this part of his intellectual biography in some detail before moving on to consider the philosophical underpinnings of his environmental writing during this period.

The Country Life Commission

Created in 1908, the Commission on Country Life was a reformist effort devoted to "rural uplift" (i.e., the revitalization of farming life in a rapidly urbanizing and industrializing society), and for a short time it served as the agrarian wing of the Roosevelt conservation movement. Yet the commission was only the most politically visible expression of what was in fact a larger popular movement already under way by the time Theodore Roosevelt called it into being. Beginning roughly at the turn of the twentieth century, the Country Life movement brought together a diverse assortment of academicians, businessmen, bureaucrats," journalists, and rural clergy concerned about the social and economic conditions of the American countryside during a period of unprecedented cultural, social, and technological change. Despite its designation and the rural focus of its reform efforts, the leadership of the Country Life movement was, as historians have pointed out, composed mostly of nonfarmers. They were a group of middle-class (and often urban-based) intellectuals, a demographic in line with the broader Progressive movement. This is no surprise, given that many of the leading figures associated with the Country Life movement (such as Theodore Roosevelt and Gifford Pinchot) were well-known names in Progressive circles. While generally of one mind about the need for social and institutional reform in the countryside, the Country Life leaders were in fact driven by a variety of goals and motives, some of which were in conflict.

A large segment of the movement, for example, was animated by fairly typical Progressive utilitarian commitments, including the drive for technological diffusion, scientific management, and increased efficiency and productivity in the countryside. Others, however, and Bailey may be counted among them, were more concerned with the intellectual, aesthetic, and social character of country life. Country Life reformers of this bent focused especially on educational issues and the moral and spiritual conditions of communities in the countryside, including the need to promote a deeper and more effective cooperative spirit among rural residents. As we will see, in Bailey's case this concern also manifested itself in the promotion of nature study for schoolchildren and an argument for its significance in creating an environmental ethic among country dwellers, especially farmers.

In his influential social history of this period in rural reform, historian David Danbom has identified several distinct factions within the Country Life movement.[14] One group, commonly referred to as the "urban agrarians," included the more socially oriented thinkers such as Bailey, who were interested in revitalizing and marshaling the perceived moral resources of the agrarian life—virtues such as simplicity, honesty, and authenticity—against the vices of the modern industrial city, which was viewed as overly complex, hopelessly corrupt, and artificial. For many (including Bailey) this was partly an effort to preserve the vanishing Jeffersonian ideal of a rural agrarian order in the modern industrial era.

Bailey stated this position quite bluntly: "The city sits like a parasite, running out its roots into the open country and draining it of its substance. The city takes everything to itself—materials, money, men—and gives back only what it does not want."[15]

At the same time, it is not exactly right to describe Bailey as a one-note antiurbanist or as a naive utopian about agrarian life. Bailey, like many other Country Life reformers, also recognized that there were real social and cultural deficiencies in rural America. And he acknowledged that the city would necessarily play a significant role in any meaningful and lasting rural reform program. As he wrote in 1911:

The country needs the city. It does not need the city man so much to teach the countryman farming, as to touch and elevate the general currents of all country life. The city man goes to the country with new and large ideas, active touch with great affairs, keen business and executive ability, generosity, altruism, high culture. May we not hope that he will also always go with sympathy? All these traits will arouse the country from its tendency to complacency and narrowness. This blend should perhaps produce the real American.[16]

Still, it is nevertheless true that Bailey and other Country Life reformers of the Jeffersonian persuasion subscribed to a version of the agrarian myth that saw lives lived close to the earth as especially supportive of a virtuous and harmonious social and political order. According to this view, the farmer could play an important conservative and stabilizing role in American politics, balancing the excesses of both powerful corporate interests and a restless urban working class. Unlike these other groups, Bailey suggested, farmers were "steady, conservative, abiding by the law, and are to a greater extent than we recognize a controlling element in our social structure."[17] The goal, it seems, was to avoid the undesirable excesses and deficiencies of rural and urban life, while advancing the best combination of both in a revitalized social and environmental order. As we will see in the following chapters, this ideal union of country and city was not only on the minds of Bailey and many of his fellow Country Lifers, it also motivated the efforts of decentralist regional planning theorists such as Lewis Mumford, Benton MacKaye, and their allies.

In addition to Bailey and the urban agrarians, another notable camp within the Country Life crusade was composed of amateur and professional social scientists who saw, not virtue and moral rectitude and certainly not political salvation, but rather an alarming degeneracy in American country life—a cultural, moral, and social backwardness manifest in deplorable physical conditions, intellectual impoverishment, rural isolation, and frail social and political institutions. As Danbom notes, despite their differences, the urban agrarians and antiagrarians were united in their firm commitment to rural reform and the fundamental reconstruction of social institutions.[18] Rounding out the Country Life movement was an eclectic assortment of government bureaucrats, rural clergy, and urban businessmen; the latter were motivated by the desire for a stable and productive agricultural enterprise that could be achieved through improved rural conditions.[19]

Bailey had for several years contributed to the Country Life movement indirectly through his educational work, his editorship of *Country Life in America*, and his writings on various rural and agricultural issues. Beginning in 1907, however, his involvement in this effort became considerably more formal and significant. In May of that year, he delivered a presidential address to a meeting of the Association of Agricultural College Experiment Stations that would thrust him into the center of Country Life reform activities. Titled "The State and the Farmer," Bailey's talk (which was expanded into a book bearing the same title the following year), focused on the need to revivify and reorganize rural institutions through the cooperative efforts of the agricultural colleges, the experiment stations, and state governments.[20] Among Bailey's distinguished audience was President Roosevelt, who was apparently so impressed by his remarks that the following year he asked Bailey to become the chairman of a new presidential Commission on Country Life. After some initial reluctance (owing mostly to a crowded schedule and the fear of entangling the university in presidential politics), Bailey agreed, and the new commission was soon formed.[21]

The commission, like the Country Life movement itself, was composed mostly of nonfarmers. In addition to Bailey, most notable among the members were the rural sociologist Kenyon L. Butterfield; Walter Hines Page, editor of the progressive *World's Work* magazine; and Henry Wallace, editor of *Wallace's Farmer* and a leading midwestern agrarian.[22] Adding to its conservationist bona fides, the commission also included Gifford Pinchot, the head of the U.S. Forest Service and Roosevelt's close advisor on all conservation matters. Not surprisingly, Roosevelt charged the commission with a bold and ambitious three-part agenda. They were to assess and report the prevailing conditions of American country life, identify the best means at hand for remedying existing problems in the countryside, and recommend the best methods of "organized permanent effort" in subsequent rural inquiry and reform work.[23]

The commission's final report (written by Bailey) was submitted to Roosevelt in January 1909. In this document, the commission enumerated a set of deficiencies in rural society, all of which played a role in the lack of social and economic organization in the countryside. Among these were farmers' dearth of knowledge about their regional environmental conditions, the shortage of appropriate educational instruction for agricultural life in the rural schools, the relatively weak economic power of the farmer compared with established business interests, the inadequacy of rural roads and transportation systems, the serious problem of soil depletion, and the need for effective rural leadership.[24]

In response to these problems, the commission made three main recommendations. First, they suggested that a comprehensive survey and planning process for country life should be conducted so that informed and intelligent action might be taken to improve conditions in the countryside. Second, they proposed that a nationalized system of extension work, carried out by state colleges of agriculture, was needed to help local communities improve their technical knowledge of the farming enterprise. Third, the commission called for the organization of local, state, and national conferences on rural progress so that educational, religious, and other rural associations could be united into a common movement for reconstructing American country life.[25]

Given its close association with Roosevelt, as well as the profiles of its members, it is not a surprise that the Country Life Commission Report reads as a classic Progressive statement, sounding many common early twentieth-century reformist themes. There is, for example, an almost giddy enthusiasm for science and its unlimited potential for improving all areas of rural life. This is most noticeable in the commissioners' promotion of a scientific survey of rural conditions as a critical preliminary step in improving country life across the nation. The commissioners recommended a sweeping natural and social scientific inventory of the countryside, including topography, soil, climatic conditions, waterways, and forests, as well as a study of existing transportation and communication systems, local industry, general social and economic conditions, historical data, and an assessment of "community experience."[26] Bailey hoped that through this survey process "great numbers of earnest, competent women and men on the farms" would be identified as natural leaders in the reconstruction of agricultural life.[27]

Another core Progressive idea captured in the report is found in the commissioners' brief for a reconstructed educational system that would play a key role in the redirection of rural social and economic life. "Everywhere there is a demand that education have relation to living," the report said, adding that "all difficulties resolve themselves in the end into a question of education."[28] The commissioners believed that the rural schools needed to connect their curriculum to common agricultural pursuits—to the farmer's daily life in the country. This would not only improve the efficiency and skill of rural producers, it would also help to make an agricultural life more vital and attractive to rural residents. The result, Bailey and his fellow reformers believed, would be a stemming of the flow of the population out of the countryside into the towns and cities. The report also suggested that country schools could be used as social centers for community gatherings and civic activities. Bailey held the educational component of rural reform in particularly high regard, advocating a program of nature study for rural and urban schoolchildren that he believed would have a profound and lasting effect on the future of rural life. I will discuss this further later.

Finally, the report also restated widespread Progressive concerns about the need to build a community spirit in the face of the rapid industrialization taking place in the countryside. Greater social organization and a more robust community sentiment were necessary to improve the farmer's economic condition, but they were also, the commissioners thought, required to ensure that rural residents' spiritual needs for fellowship and higher ideals of community and personal leadership were fulfilled. Echoing the approach of Washington Gladden, Walter Rauschenbusch, and other preachers of the "Social Gospel," the report promoted a call to service on behalf of the good of the community and stressed the social role of the rural church, which the commissioners believed possessed a unique ability "to build up the moral and spiritual tone" of the community.[29] Like the Social Gospel reformers, the Country Life commissioners were concerned about the growing materialism and "money hunger" among urban and rural populations. Intellectual, social, and moral ideals must not, they cautioned, be overshadowed by economic and remunerative pursuits.[30]

In spite of the commission's efforts, however, the report did not have much of a future. Roosevelt himself was quite pleased with the document, and after he received it in early 1909 he sent it to Congress with a cover letter lauding the work of the commission and stressing the urgency of the rural situation. He also asked the Congress to provide sufficient funds to support the printing and dissemination of the commission's findings. His request was flatly denied, and the commission was directed to cease its operations. Apparently many in Congress were still harboring some anger over Roosevelt's decision to create the commission in the first place (a decision that took place without their consent). They were also clearly not concerned about accommodating the wishes of an end-of-term president.[31] Cut off from financial and political support during a critical period of incubation, the report died a quick death.

Still, the Country Life movement as a whole did see some limited success. In several cases the Country Lifers managed to promote a more modern business spirit among farmers, and they were able to stimulate the organization of cooperative associations designed to advance farmers' economic interests. On the educational front, Bailey's reforms made some inroads in the elementary school curriculum, and the passage of the Smith-Lever Act of 1914 solidified federal support for agricultural extension work through the nation's land-grant universities.[32] Despite these bright spots, however, the far-reaching changes envisioned by the commissioners and other Country Life thinkers did not come to pass. Historian David Danbom attributes this failure to a variety of factors, including the excessive optimism of the Country Lifers and their fundamental inability to understand the values and needs of rural people. He also suggests that farmers and rural residents were actively resistant to changes they saw as imposed on them by urban society, reacting negatively to Country Life reform proposals that they viewed as an unwanted urban intrusion on rural life and its traditions.[33]

Nature Study, the School Garden, and John Dewey

As his writing and activities outside of the Country Life Commission suggest, Bailey had a profound influence on the commission's reform agenda. At the same time, it is clear that the commission's report did not, and probably could not, capture many of the nuances of Bailey's own thinking about the virtues of the rural life and the aesthetic, spiritual, and moral qualities of nature. Indeed, an examination of Bailey's writing on these and related subjects in a series of books written shortly before and after the work of the commission reveals a more complex picture of his philosophical orientation toward both the land and rural society. In works such as *The Nature-Study Idea*,[34] *The Outlook to Nature*, and especially, *The Holy Earth*, Bailey displays a commitment to educational reform, civic improvement, and environmental values that goes well beyond the language of the commission's report.

In this section I would like to focus on Bailey's educational ideas, particularly his promotion of nature study and the school garden as a reform program that reflected many of the elements of the Progressive approach to education, especially that championed by John Dewey. In the following section, I will consider Bailey's evolving (and philosophically eclectic) environmental ethic, including its culmination in his most sustained reflection on human–nature relations, *The Holy Earth*.

As we have seen, educational reform occupied a central position in the Country Life Commission's strategy for rural improvement. Many Country Life reformers, however, were skeptical of hanging their hopes for improved agricultural efficiency and productivity in the countryside on the hook of educational reform, seeing it as too idealistic and impractical.[35] Bailey's personal championing of nature study in elementary schools and his unyielding faith in the ability of education to solve all manner of social ills therefore set him apart from the more utilitarian-minded members of the Country Life set. The Cornell Nature-Study Movement, which included not only Bailey but educators like Anna B. Comstock and John W. Spencer, grew out of the university's agricultural extension work. Its goal was to train both rural and urban elementary schoolteachers to bring nature into the curriculum, which its proponents believed would build interest and excitement for the natural world, hone the students' powers of observation, and expand their poetic faculties. In this effort Bailey and his colleagues prepared a series of educational leaflets and publications to assist grade-school teachers in developing their nature-study programs.[36]

Noting that his own interest in nature study centered on its value "as a means to improve country living,"[37] Bailey, in his 1903 book, *The Nature-Study Idea*, made a case for the importance of the direct and unmediated study of nature, horticulture, and agriculture in promoting and revitalizing rural life:

Farming introduces the human element into nature and thereby makes it more vivid in the child's mind. . . . The children in the schools are taught much about the cities, but little about the farming country. The child should be taught something from the farmer's point of view. This will broaden the child's horizon and quicken his sympathies.[38]

Bailey believed that the study of nature would connect the student and the school to the affairs of the wider community, introducing rural young people to the attractions and appeal of farming life, which he hoped would encourage them to remain in the countryside and become happy and successful rural producers. Yet he also hoped to engage urban youths in the often overlooked elements of nature surrounding them in their cities, with the goal of fostering a more appreciative view of the countryside among urban residents. As he wrote, nature study "sets our thinking in the direction of our daily doing. It relates the schoolroom to the life that the child is to lead. It makes the common and familiar affairs seem to be worth the while."[39] Bailey thought that students' development of a serious interest in the "objects and affairs of the country" would go a long way in combating feelings of rural isolation and a longing for the excitement and variety of urban life.[40]

Yet Bailey believed that the nature-study program had other significant rewards beyond the potential to keep young people on the farm. It was also a revolt from the prevailing "dry-as-dust science-teaching."[41] Much of the worth of nature study, Bailey suggested, was owed to the fact that it could not be "reduced to a system, is not cut and dried, cannot become part of rigid school methods."[42] As a young boy growing up in the Michigan countryside, he had first-hand knowledge of the value of an early immersion in nature and of its ability not only to teach scientific habits of observation but also to instill a personal appreciation and an ethic of care for the landscape. Nature study, in "putting the child into intimate and sympathetic contact with the things of the external world," promoted the "development of a keen personal interest in every natural object and phenomenon."[43] He further believed that such affection for one's natural surroundings was an essential part of the good life in modern society. "If one is to be happy," Bailey wrote, "he must be in sympathy with common things. He must live in harmony with his environment."[44] Human interests and goods were thoroughly enmeshed in the parts and processes of the natural world, and fullness of experience could not be achieved by following the purely utilitarian strategy so dominant in urban industrial life. "No man is efficient," Bailey suggested, "who is at cross-purposes with the main currents of his life; no man is content and happy who is out of sympathy with the environment in which he is born to live."[45]

Bailey obviously understood nature study in bolder terms than as one more subject to be worked into the curriculum, or as yet another means to improve the technical knowledge and economic efficiency of a new generation of farmers. It was, he suggested, a concept that could be traced back to Socrates and Aristotle; a "pedagogical ideal" in which natural history was employed as a method to reinvigorate the school and rural life.[46] At once an ancient and yet completely new philosophy of education, Bailey believed that the nature-study movement in the schools would produce a revolution in teaching and living:

Nature-study is not merely the adding of one more thing to a curriculum. It is not coördinate with geography or reading or arithmetic. Neither is it a mere accessory, or a sentiment, or an entertainment, or a tickler of the senses. . . . It has to do with the whole point of view of elementary education, and therefore is fundamental. It is the full expression of personality. . . . More than any other recent movement, it will reach the masses and revive them. In time it will transform our ideals and then transform our methods.[47]

Bailey's enthusiasm for the nature-study program, especially its focus on, as he put it, "doing and accomplishing,"[48] echoes that of John Dewey, who was developing a strikingly similar argument within Progressive education circles during this same period.[49] Like Bailey, Dewey was highly critical of the rigidity and mechanical nature of traditional education of children. Also like Bailey, Dewey argued for a more active and experiential educational environment, one that broke out of the recitation-based and textbook-bound instructional method. Instead, every educative process, Dewey claimed,

should begin with *doing something*; and the necessary training of sense perception, memory, imagination and judgment should grow out of the conditions and needs of what is being done. The something done should not be of the nature of an arbitrary task imposed by a taskmaster; but something inherently significant, and of such a nature that the pupil appreciates for himself its importance enough to take a vital interest in it. This is the way the child gets all the first training of his powers and all his first knowledge of the world.[50]

Dewey viewed the nature-study movement as offering just this sort of active and absorbing approach to the natural world and to science generally. In his 1915 book, *Schools of To-Morrow*, written with his daughter Evelyn, Dewey surveyed a number of schools in which the "new education"—progressive, student-centered, and experimental—was being put into practice, schools in places such as Gary, Indiana; Riverside, Illinois; and Greenwich, Connecticut. He enthusiastically reported the growth of nature-study activities across the country, noting approvingly that in these programs, "The attempt is to vitalize the work, so that pupils shall actually get a feeling for plants and animals, together with some real scientific knowledge, not simply the rather sentimental descriptions and rhapsodizings of literature."[51]

Dewey's practical views on education were in many respects the outgrowth of his pragmatic epistemology (although he eschewed the latter term), which emphasized the active and constructive character of "knowing"—a fallible, but self-correcting process of inquiry—over alternative views that identified "knowledge" with the possession of fixed beliefs or truths held independently of investigation, experimentation, and judgment. For Dewey, belief and thought were to be seen in an instrumentalist light, that is, as a means for clarifying and resolving specific questions and problems that arise in the course of daily life. In his 1909 essay, "The Bearings of Pragmatism Upon Education," he drew a direct line between this instrumentalist stance toward knowledge and the educational process. A pragmatic approach to educational instruction, he wrote, would grow out of the real needs and opportunities of student activities and practices. As a consequence, information would not be "amassed and accumulated and driven into pupils as an end in itself, but would cluster about the development of activities."[52] A pragmatic form of student instruction would reinforce the contingent nature of all ideas, truths, and theoretical positions, showing them to be working hypotheses rather than unquestionable and unchanging certainties.[53]

Bailey's approach to nature study, then, shared with Dewey's educational program an emphasis on the importance of activity and experiential methods in the learning process. The sympathy between their thinking does not stop there. In addition to providing the elements of a child-centered, "learning-by-doing" educational philosophy (for which he is perhaps now most popularly known), in a series of writings over a period of many years, Dewey assailed the long-standing divide separating the school (and the child) from the affairs of the community. As he wrote in his 1899 book, *The School and Society*:

From the standpoint of the child, the great waste in the school comes from his inability to utilize the experiences he gets outside the school in any complete and free way within the school itself; while, on the other hand, he is unable to apply in daily life what he is learning at school. That is the isolation of the school— its isolation from life. When the child gets into the schoolroom he has to put out of his mind a large part of the ideas, interests, and activities that predominate in his home and neighborhood.[54]

Dewey's alternative, liberal, educational ideas would consequently focus on the personal growth and creativity of the child within an explicit social context. A perceptive observer of the dramatic social changes produced by the modernizing forces of science, urbanism, and industrialism at the turn of the century, Dewey argued that for education to have any meaning for life, it must itself undergo an equally great transformation.[55] Every school, he suggested, should become "an embryonic community life, active with types of occupations that reflect the life of the larger society, and permeated throughout with the spirit of art, history, and science."[56]

In this model, children would not only learn within a dynamic and experiential setting, they would also be taught the value of participation in and service to the life of the community. Dewey thought that such an environment would allow students to gain the skills, knowledge, and motivation required to become intelligent and active democratic citizens. The growth of the individual child and the health of the community would thus be mutually reinforcing:

If the school is related as a whole to life as a whole, its various aims and ideals—culture, discipline, information, utility—cease to be variants, for one of which we must select one study and for another another. The growth of the child in the direction of social capacity and service, his larger and more vital union with life, becomes the unifying aim; and discipline, culture and information fall into place as phases of this growth.[57]

Ideally, the school would become, as Dewey put it, a "social centre"; a place where adults and children could "share in the intellectual and spiritual resources of the community" through social, recreative, and intellectual activities.[58]

This civic dimension of the school, so pronounced in Dewey's writing (especially his landmark book, *Democracy and Education*[59]), was also grasped by Bailey. For Bailey, one of the most powerful components of the nature-study program was the idea of the school garden. There were, he wrote, two main purposes for the school garden: (1) the physical improvement and aesthetic adornment of the school's landscape and (2) the direct instruction of children within the nature-study curriculum.[60] Furthermore, the construction of school gardens, which he suggested required the active participation of citizens in addition to students and teachers, was, Bailey thought, a way to stimulate and organize public spiritedness and neighborhood pride in the school grounds within the larger community. He also believed that this kind of landscape improvement effort could provide a catalyst for further discussion and deliberations over issues bearing on civic life and the public good.

Once established, Bailey envisioned the school garden as a key tool in the direct instruction methods of nature study, a kind of "outdoor laboratory."[61] In the process, and by virtue of the cooperative nature of its construction and its public setting, the garden would link the schoolhouse with the surrounding neighborhood, doing its part to tear down the walls between the school and the wider community.[62] Bailey described the multiple educational, ethical, and civic functions of the school garden with characteristic optimism:

[The school-garden] supplants or, at least, supplements mere book training; presents real problems, with many interacting influences, affording a base for the study of all nature, thereby developing the creative faculties and encouraging natural enthusiasm; puts the child into touch and sympathy with its own realm; develops manual dexterity; begets regard for labor; conduces to health; expands the moral instincts by making a truthful and intimate presentation of natural phenomena and affairs; trains in accuracy and directness of observation; stimulates the love of nature; appeals to the art-sense; kindles interest in ownership; teaches garden-craft; evolves civic pride; sometimes affords a means of earning money; brings teacher and pupil into closer personal touch . . . sets ideals for the home, thereby establishing one more bond of connection between the school and the community.[63]

These were certainly ambitious aims for a humble garden. Bailey did not stop there, however. He also saw the school garden and the method of nature study reaching out to embrace the wider landscape, including that of the public park. "There must be a greater interest in parks and public gardens," he wrote, observing that "These institutions have now come to be a part of our civic life . . . [the park] should have an intimate relation with the lives of the people. The greater the number of parks the better for the children."[64] Evoking the work of Andrew Jackson Downing and especially Frederick Law Olmsted, Bailey envisioned these efforts as part of grand new aesthetic of the countryside.

Some day we shall construct great pictures out-of-doors. We shall assemble the houses, control the architecture, arrange the trees and the forests, direct the roads and fences, display the slopes of the hills, lay out the farms, remove every feature that offends a sensitive eye; and persons will leave the galleries, with their limitations and imitations, to go to the country to see some of the greatest works of art that man can assemble and produce.[65]

Bailey's great enthusiasm for the school garden was shared by John Dewey. "No number of object-lessons, got up *as* object-lessons for the sake of giving information, can afford even the shadow of a substitute for acquaintance with the plants and animals of the farm and garden acquired through actual living among them and caring for them," Dewey wrote in *The School and Society*.[66] The benefits of the school garden, the philosopher believed, were its relative ease of accessibility for urban as well as rural schoolchildren, and, in more substantive terms, its ability to introduce students in the city to nature and to some of the richness of the countryside. "The vegetable garden is the obvious starting point for most city children," Dewey wrote; "if they do not have tiny gardens in their own backyards, there is a neighbor who has, or they are interested to find out where the vegetables they eat come from and how they are grown."[67]

Dewey did not just extol the school garden in his writings about educational philosophy and practice. During his early years as a young professor at the University of Chicago, he established in the mid-1890s what became known as the University "Laboratory School" (or the "Dewey School"). At the peak of its development, the school provided instruction for 140 students and was staffed by nearly three dozen teachers and graduate assistants.[68] The Chicago Lab School would, Dewey hoped, offer the means to field test his evolving philosophy of education. It would also provide a training ground for democracy by creating an environment in which each student actively participated in the development of the school's community life.[69] Nature study, gardening, and other outdoor and indoor living skills were an important part of the school's curriculum:

The child comes to school to do; to cook, to sew, to work with wood and tools in simple constructive acts; within and about these acts cluster the studies—writing, reading, arithmetic, etc. Nature study, sewing, and manual training, so-called, are by no means new features in education; what perhaps is the novel and distinctive feature of the primary school of the University is that these things are not introduced as some studies among others, but as the child's activities, his regular occupations, and the more formal studies are grouped about these occupations, and, as far as possible, evolved naturally from them.[70]

The school garden thus played a significant role in this educational "experiment." Dewey scholar Larry Hickman, for example, has noted how the Laboratory School's garden was an especially useful tool for introducing the students to a variety of subjects, including botany (as the students learned to recognize edible plants and their relationships), history (through the teaching of the history of plant domestication and the use of herbs and fibers), and economics (where the students learned about food production and distribution).[71]

In *Schools of To-Morrow*, Dewey and his daughter wrote that the school garden also possessed an additional civic value: it could be a useful mechanism for making important connections to the surrounding neighborhood. In Chicago, for example, the school garden served a diverse set of social, political, and economic ends:

The work is given a civic turn; that is to say, the value of the gardens to the child and to the neighborhood is demonstrated: to the child as a means of making money or helping his family by supplying them with vegetables, to the community in showing how gardens are a means of cleaning up and beautifying the neighborhood. If the residents want their backyards and empty lots for gardens, they are not going to throw rubbish into them or let other people do so. Especially in the streets around one school has this work made a difference. Starting with the interest and effort of the children, the whole community has become tremendously interested in starting gardens, using every bit of available ground. The district is a poor one and, besides transforming the yards, the gardens have been a real economic help to the people.[72]

The school garden's influence, therefore, could indeed radiate out into the wider community, creating, in the process, a new ethic of landscape aesthetics and health that also had the potential to yield real economic dividends in supplying food to the poorer urban neighborhoods. In addition, Dewey and his daughter saw school gardens and the other activities of nature study as political and economic instruments for stemming the great influx of rural residents into the city. These educational reform efforts could, they suggested, create an environment in which "our young people grow up with a real respect for the farmer and his work, a respect which should counteract that overwhelming flow of population toward congested cities."[73] This was just the kind of educational and social influence that Bailey and other nature-study reformers were hoping for, and captured especially Bailey's hopes that nature study could play an important role in revivifying rural society in a metropolitan age.

Furthermore, I think it is true that Dewey, as did Bailey, saw the potential of school gardens and nature-study programs to build a deep appreciation for the natural world, a regard triggered by the close observation and scientific study of plants, trees, and animals, as well as the direct sensory immersion of the student in natural elements and environments. On the one hand, the knowledge gained from the various nature-study activities (such as the school garden) would be its own end, expanding the students' understanding of natural history, botany, and agriculture and turning them on to further scientific methods and questions. Nature study could also, Dewey and Evelyn wrote, work to "cultivate a sympathetic understanding of the place of plants and animals in life and to develop emotional and aesthetic interest."[74] Such an interest could in turn be expected to lead to the formation of a positive attitude toward plants, animals, and the rest of nature, forming a nascent environmental ethic among schoolchildren.

Dewey was obviously very impressed with the nature-study efforts under way at a number of schools throughout the country. While he was greatly interested in the pedagogical aspects of the movement and its ability to open the young student's mind to science and the methods of intelligent inquiry, I think it's also the case that Dewey recognized and appreciated the potential of nature study to cultivate an emotional, aesthetic, and even ethical attachment to the natural world among schoolchildren. "Reverence for the natural, the physical, conditions of human well-being," Dewey wrote in 1909, "is perhaps the chief moral accomplishment of the study of science."[75] Contrary to those observers who insist upon painting the great pragmatist philosopher as a narrow-minded positivist, Dewey's enthusiasm for nature study was obviously much more than a case of fanatical science worship.

To summarize, Bailey (and Dewey) saw in the study of nature and the school garden the means to generate serious and widespread educational, civic, and moral reform. Students, teachers, and citizens would become involved in public issues, and a deep pride in the landscape and the community would be cultivated. Bailey also believed that the direct instructional method in the classroom, in the garden, and in the field and forest, would introduce them to the diversity, beauty, and poetry of the natural world. This in turn would inspire them to take a greater interest in horticulture and agriculture, and consequently to develop a higher regard for the values of the rural life. The renewed appreciation for life in the country would also, Bailey hoped, keep young people contented and productive on the farm, quelling their desire to flee to the cities and conserving the rural lifestyle, culture, and landscape.

Despite the progressive nature of many of his ideas, Bailey's rural philosophy was in many respects also a highly sentimental vision. Perhaps as a consequence, and notwithstanding some significant accomplishments of nature-study enthusiasts in the first decades of the twentieth century, Bailey's more idealistic and frankly philosophical approach to the study of nature was not very effective in gaining support in either rural or urban communities. In the countryside, for example, farmers typically dismissed what Ann M. Keppel refers to as Bailey's "undifferentiated and sympathetic" program of nature study as irrelevant to their real needs. Farmers were instead much more interested in vocational education, training that was perceived to have a more practical and direct bearing on agricultural practices.[76] In the cities, Bailey's approach met with a similar response. Urban teachers sought to embrace more formal and structured pedagogical techniques than Bailey's self-consciously liberal approach to nature study, especially those techniques deemed more translatable to the student's urban life.[77]

Nevertheless, I believe we can see in Bailey's advocacy of nature study and the school garden the elements of a wider educational and social philosophy, one that bore as well the distinct marks of Progressive ideas about the value of child-centered, active learning and a Deweyan-style argument for the need to connect the school to the civic life of the community. These commitments set Bailey apart from the more utilitarian proponents of the Country Life movement, who were more occupied with economic and technical concerns, such as an increase in agricultural efficiency. While Bailey was certainly in favor of such efforts, he was, as we have seen, also attuned to more expansive social, aesthetic, and moral considerations within country life and the rural environment. To gain a more complete picture of Bailey's environmental thinking, however, we need to take a look at his high-water mark in environmental philosophy, *The Holy Earth*, for it is here that we encounter Bailey's most sustained reflections on the value of nature and the scope of human responsibility within it.

Bailey's Environmental Thought

As I mentioned in the introduction to this chapter, the conventional either-or categories used to describe American environmental thought—e.g., conservation or preservation, anthropocentric or nonanthropocentric, utilitarian or aesthetic, and so on—do not offer much help when it comes to placing Bailey in the moral and intellectual tradition of environmentalism. It is precisely because Bailey voiced commitments on both sides of these conceptual pairings (in some cases, transcending them), that he is a difficult thinker to pin down. For example, Bailey held many of the attitudes and philosophical commitments we typically associate with the early Progressive conservation movement of the Roosevelt–Pinchot variety. Consider the following remarks (from Bailey's 1911 book, *The Country-Life Movement in the United States*):

We have scarcely begun even the physical conquest of the earth. It is not yet all explored. . . . There are mountains to pierce, sea-shores to reclaim, vast stretches of submerged land to drain, millions of acres to irrigate and many more millions to utilize by dry-farming, rivers to canalize, the whole open country to organize and subdue by means of local engineering work, and a thousand other great pieces of construction to accomplish, all calling for the finest spirit of conquest and all contributing to the training of men and women. There is no necessity that the race become flabby.[78]

Here Bailey nearly outdoes Roosevelt, the great avatar of the "strenuous life," in his celebration of the heroic march of progress across the landscape. Yet it is not too difficult to square Bailey the Rooseveltian conservationist (with all the rhetorical trimmings) with the humble naturalist extolling the school garden and the more contemplative art of studying nature. Despite the muscular language, it is clear from the context of this discussion that Bailey is not prescribing the conquest or subjugation of the earth as much as he is attempting to generate interest in and appreciation for what he took to be the noble work of farming life, which he feared was increasingly being viewed as little more than drudgery best left behind as rural citizens flocked to the cities. "Farming will attract folk with the feeling of mastery in them, even more in the future than in the past, because the hopelessness, blind resignation, and fatalism will be taken out of it."[79] Even when he chose to use this kind of grand Rooseveltian language, then, Bailey should not be seen as promoting the route of nature by civilization. He was simply trying his best to embolden and stiffen the backs of a rapidly diminishing farm population.

Also, the "mastery" Bailey had in mind was not to be displayed in the kind of wasteful and ecologically destructive practices that degraded precious fertility of the soil. Bailey's Darwinian commitments, which were no doubt powerfully reinforced during his apprenticeship with Gray at the Harvard herbarium, led him to view adaptation, rather than physical conquest, as the ultimate scientific and moral measure of human practices. "A good part of agriculture," he suggested, "is to learn how to adapt one's work to nature, to fit the crop-scheme to the climate and to the soil and the facilities. To live in right relation to the natural conditions is one of the first lessons that a wise farmer or any other wise man learns."[80] Poor, ecologically unsustainable farming practices were maladaptive, since they destroyed what Bailey felt was ultimately the most critical natural resource: the soil. Bailey was concerned, moreover, that conservationists were not paying sufficient attention to this foundational element in their reform efforts. As he wrote in 1911:

To my mind, the conservation movement has not sufficiently estimated or emphasized [the soil] problem. It has laid stress, I know, on the enormous loss by soil erosion and has said something of inadequate agricultural practice, but the main question is yet practically untouched by the movement,—the plain problem of handling the soil by all the millions who, by skill or blundering or theft, produce crops and animals out of the earth.[81]

Believing that "The greatest of all resources that man can make or mar is the soil," Bailey proposed that the safeguarding of the nation's soil resources effectively represented the Country Life "phase" of the larger conservation movement.[82]

The Country Life and conservation movements, while sharing an overt economic concern in their advocacy of the wise and efficient use of resources, were for Bailey ultimately moral and social enterprises oriented toward sustaining a sufficient material foundation for citizens, especially those living in the future.[83] "No man has a right to waste, both because the materials in the last analysis are not his own, and because some one else may need what he wastes," Bailey asserted, concluding that "A high sense of saving ought to come out of the conservation movement. This will make directly for character-efficiency, since it will develop both responsibility and regard for others."[84] Conservation could therefore be an effective tool for developing a greater sense of care and responsibility for one's fellow citizens.

Bailey's philosophy of rural conservation, just like his views on nature study and the school garden, entailed a strong civic dimension. The resources of the planet were not the privilege of the select few, but were a common heritage shared by all citizens. "A man has no moral right to skin the earth," he argued, observing that the farmer's primary moral obligation to society was to make wise and efficient use of his land.[85] In turn, society—if it was to fulfill its part of the moral contract envisioned by Bailey—owed an "equal obligation to him to see that his lot in society is such that he will not be obliged to rob the earth in order to maintain his life."[86] The nation needed to make a significant social and economic investment in farming life, and this investment would be repaid by an economically productive, ecologically sustainable, and socially stable agricultural enterprise. In good Jeffersonian fashion, Bailey's hardworking, thrifty, and socially responsible farmer would provide the needed moral ballast for an urbanizing society. "No nation can long persist that does not have this kind of citizenry in the background," he warned.[87]

If Bailey attempted to turn the conservation agenda more toward the rural environment and the care of the soil, and sought to widen its civic vision by evoking the moral bonds between the farmer and society within and across generations, he also contributed an interesting and important environmental ethic to the larger conservation mission. While the most sustained and focused expression of his environmental ethical views would take place in *The Holy Earth*, seeds of Bailey's later ideas may be found in some of his earlier writings, including *The Nature-Study Idea* and *The Outlook to Nature*. In *Nature-Study*, Bailey wrote disparagingly of the tendency for people to adopt a shallow and anthropocentric view of nature's beauty, one in which, for example, cut (ornamental) flowers were prized more than living plants, and where the deeper forms and functions of nature were ignored because of a myopic anthropocentrism:

This habit of looking first at what we call the beauty of objects is closely associated with the old conceit that everything is made to please man: man is only demanding his own. It is true that everything is man's because he may use it or enjoy it, but not because it was designed and "made" for "him" in the beginning. This notion that all things were made for man's special pleasure is colossal self-assurance. It has none of the humility of the psalmist, who exclaimed, "What is man, that thou art mindful of him?"[88]

Here, Bailey seems to be groping toward an articulation of nature's intrinsic value, a view of natural objects and systems that recognizes their non-use qualities. Such language is, of course, a hallmark of preservationist environmental thinkers in the tradition, including the great wilderness defender John Muir, as well as earlier Romantic figures such as Thoreau (albeit in a qualified form). Like these writers, Bailey clearly found great beauty and nonmaterial good in the natural world. Furthermore, rather than expunging all value from nature, Bailey thought science revealed a world worthy of our interest and care, one in which the deepest beauty was found in the way organisms revealed their fitness to the environment.[89]

In *Nature-Study*, Bailey also introduced a distinct spiritual dimension to his discussion of environmental attitudes, an aspect that would take on greater significance in his writing in subsequent years (culminating in *The Holy Earth*). This element appears most notably in his discussion of hunting and the humane treatment of animals, in which Bailey lamented in particular the wanton killing of the American bison. "The lower creation is not the plaything of man," he wrote, arguing that the true sportsman did not equate hunting with killing.[90] Instead, the real value of hunting was found in its naturalistic qualities. "It is primarily a means of enjoying the free world of the Out-of-doors. This nature-spirit is growing, and there are many ways of knowing the fields and woods. The camera is competing with the trap and gun."[91] Bailey made it clear that he was not to be taken as being patently opposed to hunting; rather, he noted that this was a question that each citizen had a right to decide for himself. "I wish only to suggest that there are other ideals," he offered diplomatically.[92] While respectful of hunting as a rural tradition, Bailey nevertheless believed that the movement away from taking animal life would eventually come with an evolving spiritual outlook that led humans away from needless killing and the destruction of the animal community, a position that calls to mind Thoreau's discussion of "higher laws" in *Walden*.

Appearing 2 years after *Nature-Study*, Bailey's *The Outlook to Nature* would find him exploring further the spiritual side of human–nature relations. There he wrote of the importance of adopting a reverential attitude toward nature, an attitude that was the "result of our feeling toward the materials of life,—toward the little things and the common things that meet us hour by hour. One stimulates it in himself only as he feels that the earth is holy and that all the things that come out of the earth are holy."[93] As Bailey made clear, however, this reverential attitude did not preclude making use of the earth's resources, nor did it imply a strict preservationist policy that barred humans from making a productive living from the land. "A man may conquer the earth and yet feel that he has taken no advantage that does not belong to him because he is a man, and may hold the highest reverence for the rights and welfare of everything that exists."[94] For Bailey, a reverence for the earth and its creatures could exist alongside the active development, even control, of the landscape.

If Bailey's "ecospiritual" reflections on the underlying foundations of environmental concern are partly audible in his earlier work, *The Holy Earth* plays these themes at full volume. "Our relation with the planet must be raised into the realm of spirit," he exuberantly declared on the book's second page. Picking up his earlier thoughts about the common possession of land and the social obligations surrounding its use, Bailey now grounded this discussion in a deeper religious context:

We come out of the earth and we have a right to the use of the materials; and there is no danger of crass materialism if we recognize the original materials as divine and if we understand our proper relation to the creation, for then will gross selfishness in the use of them be removed. This will necessarily mean a better conception of property and of one's obligation in the use of it. We shall conceive of the earth, which is the common habitation, as inviolable. One does not act rightly toward one's fellows if one does not know how to act rightly toward the earth.[95]

Once again, Bailey recognized no contradiction between the commitment to a sacred earth and the view that humans were fully entitled to the use of its natural resources. "Crass materialism" would be checked and constrained by a feeling of responsibility for a value-laden world, an "inviolable" one. It is important to emphasize, too, that Bailey's spiritualized environmentalism retained an overt social dimension. The proper treatment of a holy earth Bailey thought, would provide a moral foundation for right action among one's fellows. That is, an environmental, "earth" ethic would also lead to improved social intercourse among citizens.

Such a view of the sacred earth was not, Bailey believed, inconsistent with his belief, bolstered by his years as a botanist and experimental horticulturalist, in evolutionary naturalism. As he put it, "The earth sustains all things. It satisfies. It matters not whether this satisfaction is the result of adaptation in the process of evolution; the fact remains that the creation is good."[96] Like his mentor Asa Gray, Bailey found little difficulty in subscribing to both divine creation of the cosmos and the Darwinian understanding of the evolution of life through natural selection. In his earlier *Outlook to Nature*, for example, Bailey had argued for the compatibility between religion and evolution. In *Outlook*, he claimed that science and evolutionary thought, far from vanquishing the religious view of the origin of the universe, would in fact emancipate religion from the calcified convictions of the past. In doing so, it would bring a distinctly progressive and rationalizing spirit to religious teachings: "Evolution stands for the quest of truth as distinguished from adherence to dogma. It affirms that the origin of the forms of life is a natural phenomenon and is governed by law."[97] Religion cannot afford to be afraid of such truth, he wrote, in "the natural science sphere or any other sphere."[98] Accordingly, Bailey rejected the special creation expounded by thinkers like Agassiz that posited an interventionist creator meddling with the direction of life on earth. "The means and methods of creation are not a part of revelation," Bailey asserted, further noting that he found "nothing in Scripture to make [him] disbelieve evolution."[99] In his view, evolution did not attempt to explain the fundamental act of creation, only its organic development. This allowed Bailey to believe in the existence of a divine creator at the same time he was a practicing scientist firmly committed to the evolutionary worldview.

Bailey's philosophical approach in *The Holy Earth* might best be described as justifying what we would now refer to as a stewardship-based environmental ethic; a moral approach grounded in the recognition of human dominion over a sacred earth. As such, for Bailey, "dominion" did not mean human omnipotence; his was not the sort of "despotic" reading of Genesis later to become infamous in environmental circles.[100] Bailey stressed instead the responsibilities entailed by this divine bestowal of dominion, writing that the earth and its resources were to be treated with due care and respect:

One cannot receive all these privileges without bearing the obligation to react and partake, to keep, to cherish, and to cooperate. We have assumed that there is no obligation to an inanimate thing, as we consider the earth to be: but man should respect the conditions in which he is placed; the earth yields the living creature; man is a living creature; science constantly narrows the gulf between animate and inanimate, between the organized and the inorganized; evolution derives the creatures from the earth, the creation is one creation. I must accept all or reject all.[101]

The evolutionary view, Bailey noted, implied a continuity between humans and other living organisms, and reinforced the material links bonding us to the physical world. All was, in his understanding, a part of the larger creation. As stewards of the earth, humans are placed in a special caretaking role and are accountable to present and future generations: "Dominion does not carry personal ownership. There are many generations of folk yet to come after us, who will have equal right with us to the products of the globe. It would seem that a divine obligation rests on every soul. Are we to make righteous use of the vast accumulation of knowledge of the planet?"[102]

Bailey's notion of stewardship was quite naturally infused with his own conservation sensibility carried over from the Country Life movement, which condemned inefficiency and waste and promoted the sustainable use of natural resources. Arguing that human dominion on the planet had been mostly destructive, Bailey wrote that society had failed to demonstrate the basic "care and thrift of good housekeepers."[103] Instead,

The remnants and accumulation of mining-camps are left to ruin and decay; the deserted phosphate excavations are ragged, barren, and unfilled; vast areas of forested lands are left in brush and waste, unthoughtful of the future, unmindful of the years that must be consumed to reduce the refuse to mould and to cover the surface respectably, uncharitable to those who must clear away the wastes and put the place in order; and so thoughtless are we with these natural resources that even the establishments that manufacture them—the mills, the factories of many kinds—are likely to be offensive objects in the landscape, unclean, unkempt, displaying the unconcern of the owners to the obligation that the use of the materials imposes and to the sensibilities of the community for the way in which they handle them.[104]

This was, of course, largely an anthropocentric view, but Bailey's idea of conservation stewardship also accommodated more nonanthropocentric elements, ideas that, as we saw above, there were hints of in his earlier writing. In *The Holy Earth*, he is more direct:

We are parts in a living sensitive creation. The theme of evolution has overturned our attitude toward this creation. The living creation is not exclusively man-centered: it is *biocentric*. We perceive the essential community in nature, arising from within rather than from without, the forms of life proceeding upwardly and onwardly in something very like a mighty plan of sequence, man being one part in the process. We have genetic relation with all living things, and our aristocracy is the aristocracy of nature. We can claim no gross superiority and no isolated self-importance. The creation, and not man, is the norm.[105]

In a surprising turn of phrase given its early vintage, Bailey's reading of the moral implications of evolution, a reading conditioned by his growing spiritual commitments, apparently led him to the doorstep of a biocentric, or life-centered worldview. If so, Bailey would stand with John Muir as one of the earliest advocates of a nonanthropocentric position in the tradition of American environmental thought.

Nevertheless, I believe that it is not exactly right to claim Bailey as a biocentrist, at least in any pure or philosophically consistent sense. His is certainly not the same species of biocentrism that we associate today with environmental philosophers like Paul Taylor and the deep ecologists. While it is undeniable that early nonanthropocentric ideas figure prominently in many passages in *The Holy Earth* (such as the one cited here), and that Bailey had expressed similar ideas in his earlier writing, we have seen that he also clung, at the same time, to a number of more squarely anthropocentric views. If Bailey's mature environmental ethic in *The Holy Earth* was shaped by his underlying commitments to a divine creation and the moral equivalence with nature that he read from the process of organic evolution, it was also, as I have noted, infused with the anthropocentric conservationism that marked his earlier participation in the Country Life Commission. That Bailey drew from such humanistic justifications for conserving nature *and* biocentric ideas in *The Holy Earth* suggests that he did not adopt an exclusivist or pure nonanthropocentric stance. Consequently, I think Bailey is best seen as a pluralist when it comes to environmental values, since he openly embraced claims of both instrumental and intrinsic values in his writing and resisted the reduction of these claims to any single and universal moral principle.

Moreover, any reading of Bailey as an unequivocal biocentrist also must somehow take into account that in his heart he was an agrarian and not a wilderness thinker. Given the harsh criticisms of agriculture voiced by many "wilderness-first" preservationists in recent decades, the phrase "biocentric farmer" probably would strike some environmentalists today as incongruous, if not oxymoronic. I think it is telling, though, that this would not have sounded so strange to Bailey. He saw no contradiction, for example, between the idea of a divine nature, one that was "good in itself," and admiration for the work of the (properly moral) tiller of the soil. Bailey thought that the farmer was in fact essential to maintaining a close moral sympathy between people and the planet, especially during a time of rapid urbanization and industrialization.[106] Good farming, in his view, adapted to nature and took care to protect the soil's precious fertility, both for the good of the earth and the well-being of future citizens. As we will see in a later chapter, there are intriguing parallels between Bailey's position here and that of contemporary neoagrarians like Wes Jackson, who has inherited the Bailey legacy within the movement for a sustainable agriculture.

I think Bailey's distance from purer forms of biocentrism may be seen, too, in his intriguing mention of Muir near the end of *The Holy Earth*. There, Bailey praised Muir for his contributions to the understanding of nature and natural history, but in doing so he did not focus so much on Muir's biocentric philosophy or his wilderness advocacy as he did on the social and political lessons taught by Muir's lifetime of close contact with the environment. Suggesting that such intimate experience with nature "tends to make one original or at least detached in one's judgments and independent of group control," Bailey noted that Muir's distance from organized institutions, from "big business" and "group psychology," provided him with an essential integrity and independence of thought and judgment that was much needed in society, especially in an era of great social regimentation and homogenization.[107] Here, too, I think we see Bailey's refusal to decouple his environmental ethical views from wider political issues and commitments.

Given all this, I believe that we should understand Bailey's environmental ethic as thoroughly bound up with his political thinking, especially his concerns about the vitality of democratic citizenship and the state of American civic life in a rapidly urbanizing and industrializing society. As he wrote in *The Holy Earth*: "Merely to make the earth productive and to keep it clean and to bear a reverent regard for its products, is the special prerogative of a good agriculture and a good citizenry founded thereon."[108] While we have seen that this civic emphasis appears in many places in his environmentally oriented work, Bailey's thoughts in this area are developed more fully in several short books published on the heels of *The Holy Earth* and written under the cloud of a world war: *Ground-Levels in Democracy*;[109] *Universal Service, the Hope of Humanity*;[110] and *What Is Democracy?*.[111]

In *Ground-Levels*, the retired Cornell dean wrote that the agricultural experiment stations he had invested so much of his energies in during his academic and administrative career were "factors of tremendous significance to any self-governing people" and that by advancing the scientific spirit throughout rural America, they were also "laying the very foundations of democracy."[112] It was another good Deweyan point. Even more intriguing is Bailey's argument later in the book that the study of agricultural and rural subjects, as "culture studies," provided an essential training for citizenship.[113] He had struck a similarly pragmatic and progressive tone in his discussion of the social and educational potential of the agricultural college some years earlier in *The State and the Farmer*:

> The colleges of agriculture are essential because they are leading the way to a really useful training for country life. Our agricultural problem is one of constant readjustment to conditions, and this readjustment can progress only through the diffusion of greater intelligence. Knowledge and education lie at the very foundation of the welfare of the open country. Information and knowledge, however, and even education, do not of themselves constitute reform or progress. We need legislation and broad redirection of social and economic forces; but education lies behind and at the bottom of all these movements and without it no lasting progress is possible.[114]

Like more well-known and contemporaneous Progressive thinkers such as Dewey and Herbert Croly, Bailey was deeply concerned about the health of the American political community in the early decades of the twentieth century. As a consequence, he saw a reformed, conserving rural society as offering hope for a more engaged, public-spirited, and ultimately more intelligent and virtuous democratic polity. In *What Is Democracy?*, for example, Bailey presented a definition of democracy that highlighted the role of participation in a renewed civic life and revealed his understanding of the deeper moral foundations of the democratic idea: "Democracy is primarily a sentiment—a sentiment of personality. It is the expression of the feeling that every person, whatever his birth or occupation, shall develop the ability and have the opportunity to take part. Its motive is individualism on the one hand and voluntary public service on the other,—the welfare and development of the individual and of all individuals."[115] Similar to Dewey's reconstruction of liberalism to embrace the social nature of the self and the life of the community, Bailey's notion of democracy sought to reconcile individualism with a more collective notion of the common good. On the one hand, Bailey argued that the unique personality and genius of the individual, inasmuch as it was the natural variation from which all future social and intellectual progress would evolve, needed to be protected from "the modern processes of standardization, resulting from the machinery habit, whereby all the wrinkles of society are ironed out."[116] At the same time, however, the individual had to be taught and motivated to voluntarily participate in the affairs of the community in the pursuit of the shared, or greater good. The ultimate purpose of education in a democracy, Bailey concluded in good Progressive fashion, was to "train citizens to excellence and to cooperation."[117]

Considered as a whole, Bailey's strong democratic and civic convictions, his pluralism of environmental values, his Progressive educational philosophy, and his zeal for the application of science (and "intelligence") to all realms of human experience—all of which were embedded within a program of rural reform and conservation—mark him as an early link in the chain of civic pragmatist thinkers in American environmental thought. Bailey's ethical ruminations on the landscape were ultimately connected to a more extensive set of moral and political values surrounding the virtues of country life and the necessity of nurturing young people to become farmer-conservationists and land stewards who would improve and sustain rural civilization amidst the intense modernizing forces of twentieth-century America. "The countryman must be able to interest himself spiritually in his native environment as his chief resource of power and happiness," Bailey believed, and only this interest and appreciation would allow the development of a "virile and effective rural society."[118] Nature and landscape become instrumentalized (though in a nonmaterialistic way) in Bailey's vision. The adoption of a proper set of attitudes and practices with respect to the earth and its products (including a sense of the intrinsic value of nature) provides citizens with the moral clarity and critical powers necessary to resist social homogenization and political apathy in an increasingly urban and industrial order.

Conclusion

Pulling the thematic threads of this chapter together, and working backward, I would suggest that Bailey's pluralistic environmental ethic is thus best seen as part of his broader vision of rural reform in the first two decades of the twentieth century. That is, I believe that Bailey's environmental thought as presented in *The Holy Earth*, *The Outlook to Nature*, and other works during this period should be viewed against a larger social and political backdrop in which the adoption of an attitude of reverence for the earth was seen as producing both good farmers and good citizens. Bailey's turn to nature—to the "holy earth" as an antidote to the aesthetic, moral, and political ills of modern industrial society (urban blight, corruption, avarice, and the like)—evokes a venerable tradition in American environmental thought. Like Jefferson, for example, Bailey held a Romantic notion of agrarian life, viewing it and the farmer as uniquely virtuous and superior to the world of the urban dweller and the manufacturer. However, perhaps unlike Jefferson, Bailey recognized that the farmer could be corrupted; the rural producer could be wasteful, short-sighted, and a poor steward of the land. Hence Bailey's profound confidence in educational reform, particularly his views about the corrective and transformative aspects of nature, the school garden, and agricultural extension efforts in the countryside. In hindsight, this boundless faith in education and nature as the key to revitalizing and advancing American country life seems idealistic, perhaps even somewhat naive. Nevertheless, it was a commitment that Bailey shared with John Dewey and many of the leading urban Progressive reformers of the time.

Today, Bailey's ethic of stewardship is not only alive in the work of neoagrarians like Wes Jackson and Wendell Berry, it also echoes across a number of canyons in contemporary environmental thought and practice. On the academic front, Bailey's indirect influence may be discerned in the expansive literature exploring the sources of the stewardship tradition in environmental ethics and ecotheological writing.[119] Stewardship ideas of a more secular (and less scholarly) variety have cropped up in international conventions like the 1992 Rio Earth Summit and in the missions and programs of a host of conservation and environmental organizations, including The Land Stewardship Project and The Forest Stewardship Council. The U.S. National Park Service has explicitly embraced the cause of "conservation stewardship" through the establishment of its Conservation Study Institute and with the educational and outreach programs run at the institute's home, the Marsh-Billings-Rock-efeller National Historical Park in Woodstock, Vermont.[120] While the arguments and programs currently advanced under the "stewardship" banner are often quite diverse, Bailey's work is clearly an important historical source of the "caretaker" ethic in the air today.

All told, I believe that Bailey's was a remarkable vision, especially given the dominant utilitarian and technocratic ethos of the conservation movement during this period. While he did not leave us with the literary equivalent of *Walden* or *A Sand County Almanac*, Bailey nevertheless produced an important and, in many respects, groundbreaking series of environmental books in the first two decades of the twentieth century. At the very least, I would argue that *The Holy Earth* deserves to be viewed as a minor classic of the genre. In the end, Bailey offers a new and interesting voice for the third way tradition, providing us with a pragmatic, civic-minded, agrarian-environmental philosophy in the Progressive Era. I think it is a voice that should sound much more familiar to us than it does.

3

Lewis Mumford's Pragmatic Conservationism

Despite the contribution of more nuanced thinkers like Liberty Hyde Bailey, historical accounts of American environmental thought usually depict the conservation movement as dominated by the institutionalization of a Gifford Pinchot-style utilitarianism in natural resource administration and policy. As a conceptual foundation for modern environmentalism, however, Pinchot's stance is often roundly criticized for its inappropriately narrow instrumentalist view of nature and for its reliance on an efficiency-oriented, "wise use" model of resource development. As I mentioned earlier, John Muir, Pinchot's antagonist in the tradition, fares much better in these historical treatments, mostly because his aesthetic-spiritual preservationism resonates more soundly with the commitments of ecocentric environmentalists today. The "professional" conservation movement, however, is thought to contribute only an ecologically uninformed and morally suspect "resourcism" to the American environmental story. According to this plot line, which I alluded to in the first chapter, we would have to wait for Aldo Leopold to push environmentalist thinking beyond these inadequate moral foundations with his groundbreaking land ethic in the 1930s and 1940s.[1]

An earlier generation of environmental historians may be credited with advancing this view of the conservation tradition. In particular, influential accounts by Samuel Hays, Roderick Nash, and Stephen Fox have generally reinforced the utilitarian and technocratic reading of classic conservation thought.[2] In recent years, however, a new wave of historical scholarship has begun to steadily challenge this conservationist orthodoxy. In various ways, these new contributions have offered a more complex and socially oriented interpretation of traditional conservation norms and practices.[3] In parallel fashion, intellectually sympathetic revisions of the philosophical commitments and policy attitudes of conservation principals such as Pinchot and Muir have sharpened our understanding of the political and moral motives driving conservation advocacy at the national levels.[4] Despite these important efforts, it is still true that most scholars of the history of American environmental thought continue to paint conservation during the early part of the century and the period between the world wars in a solid utilitarian color.

In this chapter I want to continue to fill in the third way tradition in environmentalism begun with our discussion of Bailey in chapter 2. In particular, I examine the regional planning vision of Lewis Mumford, which I believe also reflects the influence of John Dewey's pragmatism, especially his unified method of inquiry and strong democratic vision. In addition to these intriguing philosophical underpinnings, Mumford's regionalist view also represents a novel and historically unappreciated attempt to expand the foundations of conservationist thinking beyond its narrow single-resource focus and its more well-known utilitarian commitments during this period. Mumford's resulting program is thus what might be called a pragmatic conservationism. It is pragmatic both in its embrace of the full sweep of the various contexts of human environmental experience and in its methodological approach and Deweyan democratic agenda.

I think that this account has a number of implications for our understanding of the roots of contemporary environmentalism. Indeed, by linking Mumford's attempt to reconstruct conservation philosophy and practice through regional planning with Dewey's pragmatism, I hope to add another voice to the third way tradition in American environmental thought.[5] In doing so, I intend to challenge the belief that environmental thought during the interwar period was limited to a unidimensional utilitarianism. I also want to once again take issue with the position that the moral and cultural development of modern American environmentalism is best thought of as a story about the inevitable and seamless rise of an all-encompassing nonanthropocentrism, that of a metaphysical and ethical outlook on nature said to be expressed in its early form by nineteenth-century figures like Muir and later given a more scientifically sophisticated and philosophically palatable articulation in

Aldo Leopold's "land ethic" in the 1930s and 1940s (although as we will see in chapter 5, I do not think Leopold is best viewed as a nonanthropocentrist, even if he did have certain loyalties in this area).

My discussion is organized into several sections. In the first, I provide a brief overview of the intellectual antecedents and vision of the "communitarian" regional planning movement of the 1920s and 1930s, particularly the approach of the Regional Planning Association of America and its philosophical leader, Mumford.[6] After examining the intellectual precursors of this movement and Mumford's provocative attempt to reconstruct the conservation agenda along regional lines, I briefly consider Mumford's public debate with John Dewey in the pages of the *New Republic*, an episode that has tended to obscure recognition of their common interests and commitments. I follow this with a discussion of how Mumford's approach to regional planning was informed by a general pragmatic logic and a distinct democratic vision. I conclude by reflecting on some of the implications of Mumford's third way approach for rethinking the moral commitments and practical agenda of contemporary environmentalism.

One final prefatory note: Mumford was blessed with a long life, and his later work (i.e., that published after World War II) was often quite different in tone and substance than his regionalist writing and thinking in the 1920s and 1930s. In his postwar writing, for example, Mumford became deeply disillusioned with science and technology (especially in the wake of the atomic bomb), and he is therefore often remembered today for the pessimism and the doom-and-gloom of later works, such as *The Pentagon of Power*.[7] While I am sensitive to the problems created by establishing chronological boundaries on the study of Mumford's thought, I am nevertheless focusing in this chapter on his interwar work, particularly that relating to the theory of regional planning and undertaken during the reign of the Regional Planning Association of America (roughly, 1923–1933) and shortly thereafter. This is the time that marked Mumford's most intense collaboration with Benton MacKaye (the subject of the next chapter), as well as his most serious engagement with pragmatism. It was, furthermore, the time in which Mumford explicitly attempted to broaden the traditional agenda of resource conservation to incorporate larger regional, cultural, and geographic considerations.

His work during this period is therefore especially relevant to the intellectual history of the civic pragmatist tradition within environmental thought.[8]

The Rise of the Regional City

While the regional planning vision of Mumford and his colleagues during the interwar period was in many ways a novel philosophical enterprise and implied an innovative policy program, it also drew inspiration from several earlier sources, including the work of two giants in the history of planning: Ebenezer Howard and Patrick Geddes.

Ebenezer Howard preferred to think of himself as an inventor rather than a planner.[9] A shorthand clerk in London and not a design or planning professional, Howard was also an ardent urban reformer who saw in town and city planning the tools for directing social and moral progress in late nineteenth-century England. This commitment to improving the lot of citizens, especially the economically and physically distressed urban dweller, led him to author his groundbreaking "garden city" proposal in the 1890s. In doing so he advanced a design philosophy that would influence town planning in England and the United States well into the second half of the twentieth century. In his 1898 book, *To-Morrow: A Peaceful Path to Real Reform* (republished in 1902 as *Garden Cities of To-Morrow*), Howard unveiled an intriguing vision for the construction of cooperative, small-scaled urban commonwealths that would weld the social and environmental virtues of the country to those of the town while avoiding the vices of excess and deficiency associated with both settings.[10]

Howard's garden city would be relatively small (even by late nineteenth-century standards); its population would be capped at 32,000 inhabitants over a land area of 6,000 acres. Yet it would be a fully functional urban form, with residential, commercial, and industrial elements carefully planned and spatially distributed to promote a healthy and "balanced" biophysical environment. The city's heavy industries would be located away from the residential sector and placed at the edge of the city. Beyond this zone would be a several-thousand-acre rural greenbelt of forests, parks, and farms. These lands would supply agricultural goods to the city and would provide a natural barrier to keep the cities from sprawling farther into the countryside—an early version of an urban growth boundary. When a garden city reached its predetermined limits, the population would split off and form a new, planned garden city settlement. Eventually, multiple garden cities would be linked through high-speed transportation networks to form a "social city," a polycentric chain of garden cities that would collectively provide the opportunities and benefits of a large metropolitan center while possessing none of the social, economic, and environmental drawbacks that Howard viewed as hallmarks of the Victorian city.[11]

As Robert Fishman points out, Howard was in many respects a product of late nineteenth-century British radicalism—a group of primarily middle-class, non-Marxist communitarians who advocated a decentralized, egalitarian social order supported by dramatic reforms in land ownership, housing, and urban planning. Howard's garden city proposal was clearly driven by a social philosophy and a politics that sought to promote cooperative, noncompetitive relationships among citizens through urban planning and architectural design:

These crowded cities have done their work; they were the best which a society largely based on selfishness and rapacity could construct, but they are in the nature of things entirely unadapted for a society in which the social side of our nature is demanding a larger share of recognition—a society where even the very love of self leads us to insist upon a greater regard for the well-being of our fellows. The large cities of today are scarcely better adapted for the expression of the fraternal spirit than would a work on astronomy which taught that the earth was the centre of the universe be capable of adaptation for use in our schools. Each generation should build to suit its own needs.[12]

Even if Howard was somewhat fuzzy on the details of the garden city, as Mumford observes in his 1945 introduction to a later edition of *Garden Cities of To-Morrow*, Howard's contributions were not in technical planning. Rather, his genius was in understanding and depicting "the nature of a balanced community and to show what steps were necessary, in an ill-organized and disoriented society, to bring it into existence."[13]

The second major influence on the interwar regional planning movement was Patrick Geddes, one of the more brilliant and eccentric figures in the history of environmental thought. An idiosyncratic thinker and polymath, Geddes studied evolutionary theory under Thomas Huxley, Darwin's "bulldog", and later went on to apply an organic evolutionary model to social forms, including the development of cities. Specifically, Geddes developed a regionalist framework for understanding the nature and impact of the physical environment on human settlement and cultural life, a relationship he would operationalize with his diagrammatic model of the "valley section." In this effort, Geddes was strongly influenced by the German-trained French geographer Elisée Reclus, whose work taught the Scotsman the fundamental importance of the natural region in shaping social organization. To advance his regionalist investigations, Geddes proposed that an interdisciplinary survey method be employed to study regional geography and social life in preparation for town and city planning. Determined that the study of the human and natural conditions of the region proceed on solid scientific footing, Geddes borrowed French sociologist Frederic Le Play's social survey method and transformed it into the core planning tool for landscape and community exploration. For Geddes, the survey would be the primary method for incorporating the natural and social features of the region into the planning of settlements and communities.[14]

One of the most intriguing aspects of Geddes's conceptualization of the survey method was its political justification. In his view, the regional survey was to be a highly scientific and systematic activity, but it was also intended to be a thoroughly democratic endeavor. The general public, working alongside professional planners, would explore and compile an inventory of the historical, geographical, and economic circumstances of their community and its regional setting.[15] By taking part in this critical stage in the planning process, individuals would gain a greater awareness of their community's history and its current socio-biophysical conditions, including the structure and significance of its built and natural environment. This environmental sociological knowledge would in turn transform the inhabitants of a community into enlightened and civic-minded "regional selves." Indeed, Geddes saw the regional survey as a tool for a new and progressive form of democratic citizenship:

Our experience already shows that in this inspiring task of surveying, usually for the first time, the whole situation and life of the community in past and present, and of thus preparing for the planning scheme which is to forecast, indeed largely decide, its material future, we have the beginnings of a new movement—one already characterized by an arousal of civic feeling, and a corresponding awakening or more enlightened and more generous citizenship.[16]

Like Howard, Geddes was occasionally weak on the details of his program. Perhaps this is because he was, also like Howard, more of an "inventor" and visionary than a planning technician (even though he wrote dozens of plans over the years for town and city projects from Edinburgh to Tel Aviv).[17] As Helen Meller writes, if Geddes was never precise about the scientific criteria for delineating natural regions, for example, it was because he was more concerned with advocating the activity of the regional survey, especially for schoolchildren, than he was devoting his time to the formalistic "boundary question."[18] And if the environmental determinism on display in his valley section diagram and his late nineteenth-century brand of social evolutionism would fall out of fashion as the twentieth century rolled on, Geddes's regional outlook and methodological innovations would have a powerful influence on subsequent generations of planners and environmental thinkers.[19]

Among those inspired by Geddes's work was Lewis Mumford. Indeed, Howard's garden city and Geddes's regionalism would exert a great influence on Mumford and his colleagues in the 1920s and 1930s, an inspiration that would take wing with the formation of the Regional Planning Association of America in 1923. The RPAA was a loose-knit group of planners, architects, and social reformers that, in addition to Mumford and Benton MacKaye, included the architects Clarence Stein and Charles Whitaker, the planner Henry Wright, and the economist Stuart Chase, among others. The RPAA was an organizational reaction to a complex of social forces and environmental conditions that emerged in late nineteenth- and early twentieth-century America. These include, not unexpectedly, many of the same conditions that gave rise to the period's better-known conservation impulse, such as the growing recognition of the social and economic impacts of the overexploitation and destruction of natural resources. The RPAA was also concerned with a range of social and urban issues, among them the negative environmental and cultural costs of accelerating metropolitan growth and unplanned industrialization. The group saw these forces as only sharpening economic inequalities that had already taken their toll on citizens and their prospects for securing the "good life," a goal that included open access to decent and affordable housing.

Despite their varying professional backgrounds and interests, which naturally led to some differences regarding the association's philosophical bent and policy agenda, the members of the RPAA were united in their concern over the accelerating degradation of natural, built, and social communities by the steamrolling "metropolitan" forces of twentieth-century industrial capitalism. Their response to these forces drew creatively from Howard's garden city model and Geddes's regionalism. The RPAA sought a reconfigured and rescaled relationship between metropolitan forms and the surrounding natural region, one characterized by a carefully visualized functional and spatial balance among urban, rural, and wild landscapes. The association's promotion of human-scaled "regional cities" as alternative urban forms would in fact reproduce many of the design elements of Howard's garden city, including the planned constraints on city size and the creation of a surrounding greenbelt to buffer growth and provide food and outdoor recreation.[20]

In Mumford and the RPAA's vision we can also see the influence of the landscape architect and park planner Frederick Law Olmsted, Sr. Responding to the congestion and unhealthy living conditions of the nineteenth-century industrial city, Olmsted sought to improve and beautify the urban realm through the meticulous design of naturalistic public parks and other landscape features that could bring nature into the lives of city dwellers. He is of course best known for his work with architect Calvert Vaux on the plan for New York's Central Park, a masterpiece of landscape construction and artistic vision that gives the illusion of spontaneously formed nature in the midst of Manhattan.

Especially significant for the later regional city model is Olmsted and Vaux's plan for the "green community" of Riverside, Illinois, drawn up in the later 1860s. Their vision for Riverside (often referred to with the diminutive term "garden suburb") contained a long scenic "parkway" that would allow Chicago residents a common means to get out of the city and into more pastoral environs, and included curvilinear tree-lined streets, large public recreation grounds, and other parklike touches.

Olmsted thought that parks (and nature generally) had a great thera-peutic and regenerative effect on urban industrial society. The exposure to picturesque scenery and the open air, he believed, could improve human health and had a positive psychological impact on citizens. Fur-thermore, like Mumford and his other philosophical heirs in the RPAA, Olmsted believed that the creative and deliberate use of landscape and design could serve a larger reform agenda. The public space provided by parks in dense urban environments, he thought, performed an important conservative political function. In facilitating the mixing of social classes, it promised to reduce the tensions among citizens and quell potential social conflict.[21]

Despite the suburban tilt of some of Olmsted's work and the "village-in-nature" form of Howard's garden city idea, the RPAA's regional cities would not represent a flight from urban life; rather, they would be decen-tralized, genuine urban forms planned in accordance with the natural context of the region and facilitated by the controlled diffusion of indus-try that was afforded by the rising availability of the automobile, the construction of new transportation highways and hydroelectric dams, and the establishment of widespread rural electrification. These techno-logical developments—what Mumford, following Geddes, applauded as the hallmarks of the newly emerging "neotechnic" era—would allow the controlled migration (as opposed to unplanned sprawl) of swelling met-ropolitan populations out of the overcrowded cities into the smaller and more ecologically patterned regional forms.[22] The human scaling of the regional city would, the RPAA members hoped, encourage meaningful community building and allow the development of what Mumford and MacKaye saw as organic, "indigenous" values; values authentic to locally diverse and vibrant regional cultures.[23]

The RPAA housing projects at Sunnyside Gardens in Queens and at Radburn in New Jersey are the most tangible examples of the RPAA's planning legacy in the built environment, even if neither project comes close to full regional city proportions. Another enduring RPAA project is the Appalachian Trail, which was originally proposed by MacKaye in the *Journal of the American Institute of Architects* in 1921.[24] As we will see in the following chapter, MacKaye's original vision for the trail—it was to be an instrument of regional and communal reconstruction and

a defense of provincial America against encroaching metropolitanism—
is remarkable for its early linkage of traditional conservation of natural
resources with community and regional planning. While the more communitarian elements of MacKaye's plan never materialized, the Trail
today is a highly valued public recreational and cultural resource, one
that continues to draw the attention of both popular and academic
writers.[25]

Mumford's Regionalism as "New Conservation"

Lewis Mumford was the primary philosophical and literary force behind
the RPAA's regionalism, an agenda that also found a strong supporter in
his friend and colleague, MacKaye. A self-proclaimed "child of the city"
(New York), Mumford never received a college degree, even though
he attended several universities and later held visiting appointments at
Dartmouth, Stanford, and the Massachusetts Institute of Technology,
among other august institutions. The quintessential "public intellectual,"
Mumford spent his career writing for an educated yet general audience,
and over a 70-year career produced an impressive stream of books and
countless articles and short pieces. His "The Sky Line" column for the
New Yorker, which ran from 1931 to 1963, quickly established him as
one of the nation's top critics of architecture and urban planning. It
would be difficult to think of anyone, before or since, who has displayed
a comparable grasp of Mumford's numerous fields of expertise: architecture, planning, literature, philosophy, art history, politics, sociology,
and the history of science and technology.

   As I suggested earlier, historians and philosophers have typically
ignored Mumford's place in the development of American conservation
and environmental thought in the interwar period, even though, as we
will see later, he repeatedly called attention to the waste and degradation of natural resources in his writing on regionalism and regional planning during the 1920s and 1930s. Mumford also played an important
role in resurrecting the conservation and landscape visions of George
Perkins Marsh—author of Man and Nature[26] and considered today to
be the founder of the national conservation impulse—and Olmsted, both
of whom had been largely forgotten by the time Mumford wrote about

them in his 1931 book *The Brown Decades*.[27] In the polymath geographer Marsh, Mumford saw a philosophical fellow-traveler:

Geography, for Marsh, embraced organic life. Man, during the nineteenth century, had played the part of an irresponsible, destructive being—as he had, to his own misfortune, in classic times. It was time for him to become a moral agent: to build where he had destroyed, to replace where he had stolen—in short, to stop befouling and bedeviling the earth.[28]

In Olmsted's work, Mumford recognized the roots of the idea of using landscape in an active and creative fashion to serve social, political, and aesthetic ends, as well as the more specific notion of expanding the function of the public park (in the form of parkways and promenades) to naturalize the city and connect the natural world to the pulses of contemporary urban life.[29]

In addition to Marsh and Olmsted, Mumford was also enthralled with the efforts of conservationists like Liberty Hyde Bailey, whom he saw as attempting to advance a more balanced cultural and environmental worldview, one that celebrated organic life and recognized its value to industrial civilization. As Mumford wrote in *The Culture of Cities*:

Bailey was one of the great leaders in that revitalizing, and, as it were, re-ruralizing of thought that took place under the surface of the mechanical exploitation of the nineteenth century. The work of the state colleges, with their rising schools of agriculture, carried on in detailed surveys and in practical experiments tasks that were being undertaken on a wider scale by the United States Department of Agriculture. Indeed, the county soil surveys of the latter department, though highly specialized reports on geological data, had in them also the germs of those broader land utilization surveys which are one of the characteristic instruments of regional planning. The unit-area was an arbitrary one; but the method itself was capable of being pushed further.[30]

Mumford was indeed deeply impressed by Bailey's work. As he wrote in his autobiographical account, *Sketches from Life*, Bailey's vision of nature "in some degree offset the depredations of the reckless land-skinners and timber-miners and subdivision-exploiters who had scarred the land, neglecting or obliterating many of its organic potentialities."[31] Mumford shared the rural philosopher's concern for the continuing decline of rural culture and the devaluation of provincial life by the dominant metropolitan order. Echoing Bailey, for example, Mumford wrote that rural residents were taught by the metropolis to "despise their local history, to avoid their local language and their regional accents, in favor of the colorless language of metropolitan journalism."[32] The net effect of this influence, according to Mumford, was exactly what Bailey had feared years before: "Not merely is the exodus to the city hastened, but the domination of the surviving countryside is assured."[33] Mumford's respect for Bailey's contribution, in fact, led him to propose writing an article on the importance of Bailey as a rural philosopher for the *New Republic*. It was not to be, however. "The progressive minds of the twenties were so remote from such rural interests," Mumford would later recall, that the magazine's editors turned down his suggestion.[34]

As I have suggested, Mumford's involvement with conservation issues would come through most powerfully in his writing on regional planning in the 1920s and 1930s. Mumford encountered the work of Patrick Geddes while a student at City College in the Fall of 1914.[35] This early fascination with Geddes's ideas led to an active and philosophically intimate correspondence between the two men, and Geddes would become Mumford's most significant intellectual mentor. Their relationship would soon become strained, however, as the perpetually scattered Geddes tried (unsuccessfully) to make Mumford his literary editor and to press him into what for Mumford was the uncomfortable dual role of co-collaborator and disciple.[36] Still, Geddes's philosophical and personal imprint on Mumford was profound. As Edward K. Spann writes, the Scotsman "encouraged the development of what was central to Mumford's regionalism, the habit of viewing humankind in ecological perspective, emphasizing the dynamic relationship between human beings and their natural environment."[37] Mumford also adopted a modified version of Geddes's historical methodology and was heavily influenced by the latter's organicism and its role in a regional outlook. Together, this ecological-organic holism would set Mumford's (and, through his and MacKaye's influence, the RPAA's) approach to regional planning apart from other contemporaneous enterprises that operated under the same name, such as the approach of Thomas Adams and the "metropolitan" regional planners who produced the Regional Plan of New York in 1931.[38]

As Mumford worked through the substance and import of Geddes's regionalism and later became involved in the RPAA in the 1920s, his writing often made explicit links between the approach he was forming with his planning colleagues and the natural resource conservationism of the interwar period. In doing so, he also significantly expanded the conservation agenda and strengthened its underlying philosophical justification. Mumford was, in effect, fashioning a completely new way of thinking about human influence and dependence on natural and built landscapes. Specifically, what I believe he was developing during this period (again, in tandem with Benton MacKaye) is a more philosophically and socially ambitious conservationism—and a potentially more comprehensive policy framework—than the era's prevailing utilitarian model of resource development. He was certainly building a more holistic planning model, one that took its point of departure from the significance of the natural region and the limitations it imposed on development, rather than from the assumed inevitability of metropolitan expansion.

This integrative approach was therefore sympathetic to many of the commitments of the more conventional conservation movement, but Mumford pushed beyond the latter's often narrow utilitarianism and technocratic ethos by openly embracing the broader social and cultural values of the community within the context of the natural region. As he put it in 1925:

Regional planning is the *New Conservation*—the conservation of human values hand in hand with natural resources. Regional planning sees that the depopulated countryside and the congested city are intimately related; it sees that we waste vast quantities of time and energy by ignoring the potential resources of a region, that is, by forgetting all that lies between the terminal points and junctions of our great railroads. Permanent agriculture instead of land skinning, permanent forestry instead of timber mining, permanent human communities, dedicated to life, liberty, and the pursuit of happiness, instead of camps and squatter-settlements, and to stable building, instead of the scantling and falsework of our "go-ahead" communities—all this is embodied in regional planning.[39]

For Mumford, "conservation" implied much more than a Pinchot-style "sustained yield" of natural resources for economic development, at least economic development narrowly understood. Instead, it was the practice of sustaining genuine communal values, social organization, and environmental health in the face of invasive and destructive industrial and metropolitan forces. It was clear, too, that his proposals were not simply an attempt to reform current metropolitan planning by nibbling at the edges. "Regional planning asks not how wide an area can be brought under the aegis of the metropolis," Mumford wrote, "but how the population and civic facilities can be distributed so as to promote and stimulate a vivid, *creative life* throughout the whole region."[40] In the end, this required a new orientation to industrial and political institutions, one supported by a broad life-affirming worldview:

Our industrialism has been other-worldly: it has blackened and defaced our human environment, in the hope of achieving the abstract felicities of profits and dividends in the industrial hereafter. It is time that we came to terms with the earth, and worked in partnership with the forces that promote life and the traditions which enhance it. Regionalism suggests a cure for many current ills. Focussed in the region, sharpened for the more definite enhancement of life, every activity, cultural or practical, menial or liberal, becomes necessary and significant; divorced from this context, and dedicated to archaic or abstract schemes of salvation and happiness, even the finest activities seem futile and meaningless; they are lost and swallowed up in a vast indefiniteness. In this sense regionalism is a return to life.[41]

The task of regional planning, according to Mumford, was thus more culturally and ecologically grounded than the approach taken by conservationists, which in his view merely attempted to protect wilderness areas from intrusion and sought to avoid the wasteful development of natural resources. While he thought such a strategy was to be praised for protecting the rare and spectacular environments of the continent and for its injection of efficiency measures into the exploitation of resources, he feared it was too limited in scope to serve as a guide for a true environmental ethic. "If the culture of the environment had yet entered deeply into our consciousness," Mumford wrote, "our esthetic appreciations would not stop short with stupendous geological formations like the Grand Canyon of Arizona: we should have an equal regard for every nook and corner of the earth, and we should not be indifferent to the fate of less romantic areas.[42] Here Mumford anticipates the arguments of contemporary scholars, such as William Cronon, who have criticized the persistent "wilderness bias" in modern environmentalism. Mumford's conclusion is also Cronon's; that is, we must adopt a broader and more humanized environmentalism, one capable of instilling solicitude for human communities as well as natural ones, and one that recognizes the value of the rural and the urban along with the wild.[43]

Mumford's moral orientation to nature during this period may be seen to contain anthropocentric and nonanthropocentric elements, including a Geddesian organicist and quasi-biocentric concern for the web of life on earth (including human life) and an equal, if not even more powerful, regard for "authentic" tightly knit human communities held together by a sense of shared cultural values and regional traditions. The organic sense, defined by its holistic view of life, environment, and culture, was to serve as a guide for the built landscape (e.g., architectural forms), and also a norm for the reorganization of human communities within a new, planned regional framework. For Mumford it provided an antidote to the ideology of the machine, which was defined by a philosophy of quantitative expansion, mechanical control, and the exercise of brute power on the landscape and in culture.[44] As he wrote in *The Culture of Cities*:

Every living creature is part of the general web of life: only as life exists in all its processes and realities, from the action of bacteria upward, can any particular unit of it continue to exist. As our knowledge of the organism has grown, the importance of the environment as a co-operative factor in its development has become clearer; and its bearing upon the development of human societies has become plainer, too. If there are favorable habitats and favorable forms of association for animals and plants, as ecology demonstrates, why not for men? If each particular natural environment has its own balance, is there not perhaps an equivalent of this in culture?[45]

Modern metropolitan development not only led to the continued waste and exhaustion of natural resources (to which the conservation movement was a response), Mumford believed, it also drove the organic realm away from human experience. "As the pavement spreads, nature is pushed farther away: the whole routine divorces itself more completely from the soil, from the visible presence of life and growth and decay, birth and death."[46]

Mumford's reconstruction of conservation to embrace the context of the larger region over the single resource, his attention to the built environment as well as the natural world, his life-promoting environmentalism, and his commitment to securing the long-term sustainability of community values through regional planning, was thus a profound expansion of early twentieth-century conservation philosophy. "If the conservation of a single resource is important," Mumford wrote, "the conservation of the region, as an economic and social whole, is even more important."[47] Like Geddes, Mumford viewed the regional survey as a key tool in advancing the regionalist approach. And, like Geddes, Mumford believed that the act of regional planning possessed a great civic potential; it was not simply a narrow technical activity to be undertaken by experts. Yet Mumford also brought an additional justification and methodological underpinning to the planning discussion, especially in his fuller reflections in the 1930s. These contributions were, I believe, a pragmatist-inspired logic of inquiry and an explicit theory of social learning, commitments I will suggest owe much to Mumford's contact with the work of the pragmatist philosopher John Dewey. If I am correct in these claims, by the 1930s Mumford's approach to regional planning had developed into an overtly pragmatic endeavor. So much so, in fact, that Mumford's reconstruction of conservation as regional planning and his Deweyan conceptualization of the planning method combined to form a new environmental philosophical program: a holistic, pragmatic variant of conservationism in the interwar period.

Mumford and Pragmatism: For and Against

Mumford recognized and openly acknowledged the influence of John Dewey's pragmatism on regional planning, although I believe he underestimated the significance of this intellectual debt. Looking back on the RPAA's philosophical outlook in 1957, for example, Mumford described the group's agenda as an amalgam of several sources, including "the civic ideas of Geddes and Howard, the economic analyses of Thorstein Veblen, the sociology of Charles Horton Cooley, and the educational philosophy of John Dewey, to say nothing of the new ideas in conservation [and] ecology."[48] While a Deweyan educational ethos certainly can be read in Mumford's emphasis on the transformative potential of regional surveys and the planning process itself, it is clear that Dewey's pragmatism—especially his theory of inquiry—was embedded in the very method of Mumford's approach to regional planning.

As a student at City College before World War I, Mumford had been exposed to an early form of pragmatism through the teachings of John Pickett Turner, a "self-professed pragmatist," who Mumford credited with turning him into a "loyal" devotee of the philosophy for a time.[49] Soon, however, Mumford's immersion in the work of Geddes and his budding Neoplatonism would find him moving in a different direction. This shift was perhaps most pronounced in Mumford's cultural criticism of the 1920s, which suggested a growing preoccupation with an aesthetic transcendentalism and a greater emphasis on the symbolic elements of cultural life than the American pragmatists had demonstrated to that point.[50] Yet I believe the evidence supports the view that Mumford would never completely jettison the pragmatic elements in his thinking, even if his hostility toward these strains tended to come across more in print in the 1920s.

Indeed, Mumford's ambivalence toward pragmatism would be put on full display in an exchange he had with Dewey in the pages of the *New Republic* in the late 1920s. In his influential study of antebellum literary culture, *The Golden Day*, Mumford had criticized Dewey and the pragmatists (notably, William James) for their "acquiescence" to the crass utilitarianism of American life.[51] The attempt to tar pragmatism with the brush of commercialism was far from novel. The philosopher Bertrand Russell, for example, had said similar things about pragmatism some years before, remarks that drew a forceful rebuke from Dewey in which he asserted the "anti-pragmatic" character of the reigning commercialism and defended pragmatism's critical ability to reform these inherited American ideologies and practices.[52] In *The Golden Day*, however, Mumford also assailed pragmatism on broader cultural and aesthetic grounds. He blasted what he saw as pragmatism's unreflective capitulation to science and instrumental logic over the imaginative arts and values, a submission to a mundane practicality and a retreat from fuller aesthetic experience and symbolic forms of expression.

This line of argument, too, was a rehearsal of earlier criticisms of Dewey and pragmatism, most notably those advanced by Randolph Bourne and the other young American radicals who tangled with Dewey during World War I.[53] Still, because of Mumford's forceful prose and the cultural heft provided by grounding his claims in the American literary renaissance, the critique had a fresh bite:

Mr. Dewey speaks of the "intrinsic worth of invention"; but the point is, of course, that except for the inventor, who is *ipso facto* an artist, the invention is good for what it leads to, whereas a scene in nature, a picture, a poem, a dance, a beautiful conception of the universe, are good for what they are. A well-designed machine may also have the same kind of esthetic value: but the independent joy it gives to the keen mechanic or engineer is not the purpose of its design: whereas art has no other purpose. . . . Esthetic enjoyment will often lead to other things, and it is all the happier for doing this: the scene in nature may lead to the planting of a park, the dance may promote physical health: but the essential criterion of art is that it is good without these specific instrumental results, good as a *mode of life*, good as a beatitude. An intelligent life, without these beatitudes, would still be a poor one: the fact that Bentham could mention pushpins in the same breath as poetry shows the deeply anesthetic and life-denying quality of the utilitarian philosophy.[54]

The larger problem, Mumford wrote, began with the disintegration of a much earlier medieval organic culture, one governed by shared symbols and living in balance with the natural environment. The ensuing subjugation of the imagination to practical affairs, as well as to science and technology, led to the subordination of nature under the boot of the pioneer and produced a situation in which it became nearly impossible "to recognize the part that vision must play" in organizing practical activities within a common cultural worldview.[55]

To counter the forces of utilitarianism and the atomistic philosophy of the machine, Mumford appealed to the aesthetic and imaginative qualities he believed were extolled by the nineteenth-century writers of the "golden day," a time of great hope and spiritual-aesthetic unity that he believed existed before the fragmentation of American culture and the loss of poetic vision following the Civil War. Mumford had in mind the work of the American Romantics, especially Emerson, Thoreau, Whitman, and Melville. Their writing, he believed, displayed an organic character and cultural vitality that had been crushed under the mechanical and commercial weight of the Gilded Age. "In their imagination, a new world began to form out of the distracting chaos; wealth was in its place, and science was in its place, and the deeper life of man began again to emerge, no longer stunted or frustrated by the instrumentalities it had conceived and set to work. For us who share their vision, a revival of the moribund, or a relapse into the pragmatic acquiescence is equally impossible; and we begin again to dream Thoreau's dreams—of what it means to live a whole human life."[56] Indeed, Mumford believed that without a prior articulation of such symbolic and transcendent values, pragmatism was simply "all dressed up, with no place to go."[57]

Dewey's reply took Mumford to task for misunderstanding the pragmatist emphasis on instrumentalism and for his claim that in embracing the potential of science and technology, Dewey and the pragmatists were celebrating an undernourished philosophy of mechanical technique and method over a richer kind of aesthetic value and a fuller realm of cultural experience:

> It would require a mind unusually devoid both of sense of logic and a sense of humor—if there be any difference between them—to try to universalize instrumentalism, to set up a doctrine of tools which are not tools for anything except for more tools. The counterpart of "instrumentalism" is precisely that the values by which Mr. Mumford sets such store are the ends for the attainment of which natural science and all technologies and industries and industriousnesses are intrinsically, not externally and transcendentally, or by way of exhortation, contributory. . . . The implied idealization of science and technology is not by way of acquiescence. It is by way of appreciation that the ideal values which dignify and give meaning to human life have themselves in the past been precarious in possession, arbitrary, accidental and monopolized in distribution, because of lack of means of control; by lack, in other words, of those agencies and instrumentalities with which natural science through technologies equips mankind. Not all who say Ideals, Ideals, shall enter the kingdom of the ideal, but those who know and who respect the roads that conduct to the kingdom.[58]

Without taking control of the instrumentalities that led to Mumford's valued ends, Dewey believed, their realization in culture could at best be only partial, fleeting, and arbitrary.

The conversation continued. In a rejoinder, Mumford wrote that contrary to Dewey's characterization, he was no woolly idealist detached from the realms of science and technology. Rather, Mumford claimed that he merely sought a more balanced approach to cultural experience, one in which science and technique were not elevated high above value and aesthetic life. He even trumpeted his own practical credentials by noting his close alignment with architects, a group that had "the professional distinction of thinking both scientifically, in terms of means, and imaginatively, in terms of the humanly desirable ends for which these means exist."[59] Finally, in what Dewey must have taken as an attempt to damn him with faint praise, Mumford tried a higher road. "It is not that we reject Mr. Dewey," he wrote, suggesting that doing so would be ingratitude. At the same time, Mumford noted that he and his fellow culturally occupied critics sought "a broader field and a less provincial interpretation of Life and Nature than he has given us."[60]

As intellectual historian and Dewey scholar Robert Westbrook has observed, the Mumford–Dewey debate was in many respects an unfortunate misreading on the part of both men.[61] Mumford's criticism of Dewey as a technocentric utilitarian, for example, fell wide of the mark. Among other things, it completely obscured Dewey's interest in and sustained attention to aesthetic concerns that is evident in such works as *Experience in Nature*[62] (which Mumford had read but did not fully appreciate, essentially ignoring Dewey's articulation of the role of art as a consummatory experience in his philosophical system). Dewey would even go on to devote an entire book to aesthetic questions, an effort that was perhaps in part motivated by Mumford's criticisms.[63] Furthermore, in 1934, Dewey would publish *A Common Faith*, in which he set forth (in his own naturalistic way), his thoughts on piety and religious faith.[64]

I think it is also true that Mumford missed the more creative and aesthetic aspects of Dewey's idiosyncratic understanding of "intelligence," especially its role in making the imaginative conceptual leaps required in ethical deliberation.[65] Mumford's misreading of Dewey during this period is all the more frustrating because it appears that he may have recognized, at least to some degree, the philosopher's mounting attempts to address such questions, even if he was reluctant to acknowledge it in print. For example, in 1926 (the same year he published *The Golden Day*), Mumford wrote in a letter to Patrick Geddes that "Dewey is only now beginning to be conscious of the lack of a place for religion and art in his philosophy; and he is making a brave effort to redeem this."[66]

Dewey, however, shares some of the blame for the misinterpretation that drove much of the debate between the two men. As Casey Blake notes, Dewey ignored the pragmatic potential of Mumford's cultural analysis in works like *The Golden Day*, particularly its promise for informing a wider social criticism.[67] And, as we will see shortly, I also think Dewey did not recognize the pragmatic underpinnings of Mumford's approach to regional planning, nor did he fully appreciate Mumford's hopes that science—albeit science of a more holistic and organicist variety—could help to transform modern industrial civilization into a more culturally balanced and ecologically harmonious order (a valorization of science that I believe Dewey would have found most appealing). In any event, the sympathies between their ideas leads one to wonder why they could not get past their differences (of which, it is important to note, there were undoubtedly many) and focus on the significant commitments they held in common. Perhaps Blake is correct when he suggests that Mumford may have failed to acknowledge just how much he agreed with Dewey because he "had come to depend on Dewey as a foil in his cultural criticism."[68] Yet it is probably also the case that Dewey, with all his talk of "intelligence" and "tools" and his general sunny progressivism made a large target, especially for Mumford's searing, though ultimately misdirected criticisms of "the utilitarian personality" and the technocratic philosophical outlook he thought accurately described Dewey's vision of a pragmatic America.

In sum, I agree with those "compatibilist" observers of the Dewey–Mumford debate such as Westbrook and Blake, who think that there was less intellectual distance between Mumford and Dewey than their public dust-up in the *New Republic* suggested (and than Mumford and Dewey may have recognized at the time). As I've said, I think this sympathy between their two approaches is nowhere more evident than in Mumford's philosophy of regional planning. Indeed, I believe that Mumford's pragmatic commitments would clearly show through in his later writing on regional planning in the 1930s.

In his 1938 book, *The Culture of Cities*, for example, Mumford took what I would argue is a strong Deweyan line on the necessity of bringing the scientific outlook into human experience through regional planning. In particular, Mumford believed that the instrument of the regional survey held great potential for advancing individual and collective moral development:

The scientific approach, the method of intellectual co-operation, embodied in the regional survey, are moralizing forces, and it is only when science becomes an integral part of daily experience, not a mere coating of superficial habit over a deep layer of uncriticized authority, that the foundations for a common collective discipline can be laid.[69]

This sentence could easily have been written by Dewey (had he taken an interest in regional planning). Indeed, this and other textual evidence suggests that by the late 1930s, Mumford had adopted an explicit pragmatic justification for the practice of regional planning. Before we move any further, however, it is helpful to briefly outline Dewey's instrumentalist views, since my claim is that Mumford employed a strikingly similar logic in his discussion of the method of regional planning.

Dewey's instrumentalism was advanced through his unified method of inquiry into the problems of human experience. This method applied to ends as well as means. Beliefs and articulated values and ends were to be viewed as experimental tools—instruments—for solving the myriad and thorny social, moral, and technological dilemmas confronting the public. This argument for a continuum of means and ends within an instrumentalist framework was perhaps one of the philosopher's most radical proposals. According to Dewey, moral principles were not fixed, absolute, or transcendental beliefs floating above the fray of human experience. They were instead "ends-in-view": action-guiding hypotheses that by means of intelligent social inquiry could be appraised in terms of their ability to transform disrupted, unsettled, "problematic" social situations into more secure and stable conditions.[70]

To tackle these problematic situations, Dewey proposed a method of inquiry that was directly modeled after the logic of problem solving in the natural and technical sciences. This method began with the initial recognition that a situation as experienced was indeed "problematic," and thus inquiry was required, owing to the real deficiencies of the situation. The second step involved an analysis of the problem's context and the creative generation of hypothetical solutions that might resolve the situation. This was followed by an appraisal, in the imagination, of the ability of each proposed solution to effectively and efficiently repair the vexing situation at hand. The final stage was the act of judgment: selecting a course of action from among a set of alternatives and carrying it out in practice (including subsequent reflection and monitoring of performance).[71]

I believe Mumford would come to embrace this Deweyan instrumentalist approach in his mature conceptualization of regional planning. As mentioned earlier, it is in his landmark book in urban studies, *The Culture of Cities*, that Mumford provided his clearest and most sustained discussion of the regional planning method. It is revealing to consider in some detail just how he infused his discussion with pragmatic elements and arguments. In *The Culture of Cities*, Mumford described the activity of regional planning as following a general four-stage pattern:

> The first stage is that of survey. This means disclosing, by first-hand visual exploration and by systematic fact-gathering, all the relevant data on the regional complex. . . . The second stage in planning is the critical outline of needs and activities in terms of social ideals and purposes. . . . The third stage in planning is that of imaginative reconstruction and projection. On the basis of known facts, observed trends, estimated needs, critically formulated purposes, a new picture of regional life is now developed. . . . Now these three main aspects of planning—survey, evaluation, and the plan proper—are only preliminary: a final stage must follow, which involves the intelligent absorption of the plan by the community and its translation into action through the appropriate political and economic agencies.[72]

This description of the regional planning method was essentially a Deweyan pattern of inquiry, right down to the "imaginative reconstruction and projection" of a desired future state of affairs (what Dewey referred to as "dramatic rehearsal"). And, like Dewey, who suggested that the values of prior experience must "become the servants and instruments of new desires and aims" through the method of social intelligence,[73] Mumford argued for the judicious union of tradition and invention in the planning process:

> Such plans, however, are instrumental, not final: what is planned is not simply a location or area: what is planned is an activity-in-an-area, or an area-through-an-activity. . . . new combinations of old elements, and fresh additions from new sources, make their appearance.[74]

This organic character of regional plans would, according to Mumford, allow communities to respond to changing social and biophysical conditions, altering and revising their planning goals to meet new demands and novel circumstances. Here, Mumford's commitment to experimentalism and his adaptive view of the regional plan call to mind Dewey's theory of knowing and the iterative design of the philosopher's logic of inquiry. Consider the following:

Regional plans must provide in their very constitution the means of future adjustments. The plan that does not leave the way open to change is scarcely less disorderly than the aimless empiricism that rejects plan. *Renewal: flexibility: adjustment: these are essential attributes of all organic plans.*[75]

Mumford's remarks regarding the fallible and contingent character of regional planning are solidly pragmatist epistemic commitments. Even more interesting, perhaps, is the degree to which they anticipate the late twentieth-century development of "adaptive management" models within ecosystem ecology and the resource sciences, approaches that also share a strong foundation in pragmatist thought.[76]

Mumford's observations about the experimental, dynamic quality of the regional plan were directly tied to his conviction that regional planning should be a robustly democratic activity. It was not only the purview of professional planners and designers, it was a critical public enterprise that required active and widespread participation by nonexperts. Through this opening of the planning process to the broader democratic community, the self-corrective, intelligent character of public deliberation could come out:

It is naïve to think that geographers, sociologists, or engineers can by themselves formulate the social needs and purposes that underlie a good regional plan: the work of the philosopher, the educator, the artist, the common man, is no less essential; and unless they are actively brought into the process of planning, as both critics and creators, the values that will be imported into the plan, when it is finally made, will be merely those that have been carried over from past situations and past needs, without critical revision: old dominants, not fresh emergents.[77]

Mumford's conclusion here repeats Dewey's well-known warning about the democratic and epistemological costs of social reliance on experts ("The man who wears the shoe knows best that it pinches and where it pinches").[78] It also affirms Dewey's epistemological justification for democracy, which suggested that "intelligence" could most effectively operate, and social problems could be most effectively addressed, through deliberative democratic institutions in which all citizens participated.[79] According to Dewey, this kind of broad-based public participation in a reflective dialogue on social goals would work to root out error and counterproductive bias in an individual's beliefs and values, a view of public discourse that Dewey shared with one of liberalism's founding fathers, John Stuart Mill.[80] Dewey summarized this argument in his 1935 book, *Liberalism and Social Action*: "The method of democracy—inasfar as it is that of organized intelligence—is to bring [social] conflicts out into the open where their special claims can be seen and appraised, where they can be discussed and judged in light of more inclusive interests."[81]

In addition to the methodological and epistemological similarities between Dewey's pragmatism and Mumford's view of regional planning, there is also the educational correspondence between the two conceptualizations mentioned earlier. Since Dewey's theory of knowledge hinged on his claim that all knowing flows from direct experience, it follows that by acting in (and on) the world, we learn about our environments, both natural and social. The knowledge gained in this activity then allows us to more effectively transform the outer world to meet our constantly changing social needs and interests. It also allows us to intelligently revise and adapt these needs and interests in ways that are more suitable (and therefore more sustainable) for our supporting environment. For Dewey, such educational transformation was also the key to creating democratic citizens, democracy being in his view, "the idea of community life itself."[82] As he wrote in 1927:

We are born organic beings associated with others, but we are not born members of a community. The young have to be brought within the traditions, outlook and interests which characterize a community by means of education: by unremitting instruction and by learning in connection with the phenomena of overt association."[83]

Like Dewey (and also Bailey), Mumford stressed the importance of experiential education for building an awareness of one's membership in the democratic community, and he believed that hands-on participation in regional planning activities could play an important role in this educative process. "Regional plans are instruments of communal education," he wrote, adding that without such education, "they can look forward only to partial achievement."[84] The regional survey would be a particularly important tool for bringing the younger generations into public affairs and political experience:

Such surveys, if made by specialist investigators alone, would be politically inert: made through the active participation of school children, at an appropriate point in adolescent development, they become a central core in a functional education for a political life. It is in the local community and the immediate region, small enough to be grasped from a tower, a hilltop, or an airplane, to be explored in every part before youth has arrived at the period of political responsibility, that a beginning can be made toward the detailed resorption of government—an alternative to that half-world of vague wishes, idle dreams, empty slogans, pretentious mythologies in which the power politics of the past has flourished.[85]

Following Geddes, Mumford wrote that one of the primary roles of the regional survey was to educate citizens.[86] By taking part in the survey process (i.e., by cooperatively gathering soil, climate, geological, industrial, and historic data relevant to their community and its surrounding natural region), individuals would become involved, morally invested members of a community and would develop a sympathetic regard for their local environment and culture:

These people will know in detail where they live and how they live: they will be united by a common feeling for their landscape, their literature and language, their local ways, and out of their own self-respect they will have a sympathetic understanding with other regions and different local peculiarities. They will be actively interested in the form and culture of their locality, which means their community and their own personalities. . . . Without them, planning is a barren externalism.[87]

For Mumford, meaningful public participation in the planning process thus promised to enlighten and transform individuals on a number of levels: social, political, and environmental. It could teach individuals to see themselves as having a shared, common interest in the health and sustainability of their own community and its biophysical context. Viewed in this manner, citizen involvement in regional planning had the potential to deliver what Dewey was so urgently calling for in his landmark work in political theory, *The Public and Its Problems*—the retrieval of enduring community self-awareness. Dewey saw this civic awareness as providing a critical foundation for future democratic social action. "Unless local communal life can be restored," he concluded, "the public cannot adequately resolve its most urgent problem: to find and identify itself."[88] Therefore, the involvement of the public in the practice of regional planning, whether by means of regional surveys or through participation in open deliberation about community goals and values, could stimulate civic self-organization and consequently lead to better and more intelligent social problem solving. Mumford was, in effect, providing Dewey with a necessary political technology—regional planning—

by which the philosopher's cherished democratic publics might be effectively realized.

To summarize: I have suggested that Mumford's mature work on regional planning reflects a Deweyan influence in several respects. First, Dewey's views may be seen in the instrumental logic of Mumford's planning methodology and the adaptive character of intelligent inquiry. Second, Mumford's justification of regional planning placed a Deweyan-style emphasis on social learning and the educative potential of public participation in the survey and planning process. Finally, there is Mumford's belief that the regional survey would create fully engaged democratic citizens with the ability to recognize their common membership in an interlocking political and geographic community, what Dewey identified as a vital goal in solving the "problem of the public." Despite the cultural and aesthetic criticisms he leveled against pragmatism in the 1920s, I would argue that many of the roots of Mumford's approach to regional planning were planted deep within a Deweyan soil.[89]

Mumford's Deweyan-influenced approach to regional planning, combined with his expansion of the conservation agenda to embrace urban and rural landscapes and communal ends beyond maximization of utility, represents an intriguing, pragmatic form of conservation philosophy in the period between the two world wars. For Mumford, the regional planning method had great potential to help citizens and planners make progressive, pragmatic adjustments and improvements in a community's relationship to its surrounding environment, and to revivify and bolster its civic life in the process. A retrieval of this important third way approach not only brings Mumford and regional planning into discussions of the intellectual history of conservation and environmentalism, which is significant enough, it also raises several questions about the assumptions and practices of contemporary environmental thought and practice, as I mentioned at the beginning of my discussion. I would therefore like to end this chapter by briefly considering these questions.

Conclusion

I believe that the preceding analysis of Mumford's interwar work in regional planning has several implications for current thinking about the historical development and commitments of American environmentalism. One conclusion I hope will be drawn from my discussion of Mumford (and this book as a whole) is that the moral foundations of modern environmentalism are more diverse than they are typically thought to be. Our environmentalist inheritance is not monolithic; rather, it is "multifoundational." There are significant alternatives to the nonanthropocentric accounts of environmental ethics, such as Mumford's pragmatic conservationism discussed in this chapter. While clearly enamored of an organicist view of nature and society, Mumford's humanism and concern for the revitalization of cultural life through regional planning is not consumed with the question of establishing the independent "moral standing" of nonhuman nature, nor does it ask citizens to look askance at the values flowing out of human experience, activities that seem to have become defining features of contemporary nonanthropocentric environmentalism. Mumford thus offers us a broader and more integrated environmentalist agenda, one encompassing human moral, cultural, and political values as well as certain strains of holistic nonanthropocentrism (i.e., organicism). His philosophical approach, moreover, like Bailey's, was a profound departure from the traditional utilitarianism and atomism that tended to dominate the professional conservation movement at the time.

A second point is that Mumford's philosophy reveals the roots of "environmental pragmatism" to be historically deep, and to spread out more widely in the soil of American intellectual thought than previously thought. It is important to realize that recognizably pragmatic elements in environmentalism were in place long before the emergence of professional environmental ethics and self-styled "environmental pragmatists" in the 1980s and 1990s. As I have suggested here, early forms of a pragmatic environmentalism were articulated in the 1920s and 1930s by Mumford. We have also seen the pragmatic elements in Liberty Hyde Bailey's work in the first two decades of the twentieth century. There may be even deeper roots to the pragmatist approach in environmental thought. For example, Donald Worster, in his appropriately epic biography of John Wesley Powell, writes that the great nineteenth-century explorer and conservationist adopted an experimental, fallibilistic theory of truth in his later writings, a view Worster describes as thoroughly

pragmatic, even if Powell did not explicitly discuss the work of the pragmatists at the turn of the century.[90] Pragmatism in environmental thought
is thus not something developed by environmental philosophers in the
late twentieth century; rather, it is found in the very roots of the
American conservation impulse.

Third, I think Mumford reminds us that a socially and culturally
anchored environmentalism needs to address the complex whole of
human experience in the landscape, including the urban, the rural, and
the wild (and the places where they intersect). Toward this end, environmentalists would do well to explore potential alliances with the
planning and design professions, in addition to their advocacy and
contributions within the realms of environmental policy and management. Influential developments and movements within the former, such
as New Urbanism (to be discussed in chapter 6), industrial ecology,
ecological planning, and sustainable architecture, to name but a few,
promise to direct human communities, development, and productive
efforts into more ecologically hospitable channels (and often in ways that
Mumford and his colleagues anticipated many decades before). I think
these efforts are environmental pragmatism at work, and both environmental theorists and practitioners interested in making contributions to
"intelligent practice" could do so by interacting with these fields more
systematically. As the prominent historian of technology Thomas P.
Hughes has written, we need to understand the values and choices that
we embody in our "ecotechnological" systems—i.e., our intersecting and
intermingling built and natural environments—if we are to learn how to
use technology to adapt and interact with nature rather than overwhelm
and destroy it.[91] Mumford, I believe, understood this better than anyone,
either before or since.

Fourth, I hope my discussion of Mumford (and the other third way
thinkers examined in this book) demonstrates that American environmental thought did not develop in isolation from broader intellectual
commitments. Reflective environmental thinking has not matured independently from American social and philosophical thought more generally. Indeed, environmental thought is not, and has never been a free-
standing "ideology of nature," nor does it represent a fundamental break
with the Western philosophical and political tradition. Rather, it is itself

suspended by these deeper moral, political, and social currents. It follows from this that instead of breaking away from these foundations in search of a "new environmental ethic" that is celebrated for its degree of independence of the tradition, we should be probing this philosophical bequest in our efforts to understand our place and obligations within our various surrounding environments: cultural, built, technological, and natural.

Last, I think Mumford's example reminds us that environmentalists need to think more critically about the intellectual history of their tradition. The received nonanthropocentric account, as interesting as it might be in certain places, is simply too indiscriminate. The intellectual historical record is much messier and more conceptually pluralistic than this account would suggest. When we relax the constrained semantic domains of "conservation," "planning," and "environmentalism," for example, a new intellectual landscape comes into relief, and the ideas of thinkers such as Bailey and Mumford can be seen to form part of a line of interconnected pragmatist-inspired environmental thought, one that has until now mostly escaped the notice of scholars and environmental activists.

In the next chapter we will see how this tradition is further extended by the work of Mumford's good friend and RPAA colleague Benton MacKaye, including how MacKaye also reached down into the loam of the American philosophical and political tradition in his extraordinary proposal for the Appalachian Trail, his (and the RPAA's) most lasting contribution to the American landscape.

4

Wilderness and the "Wise Province": Benton MacKaye's Appalachian Trail

Liberty Hyde Bailey and Lewis Mumford remind us that the American environmentalist narrative is more intellectually diverse, more grounded in civic and political life, than the conventional account has suggested. Their work also reveals the existence of a pragmatist-inspired tradition in American environmentalism, an ethical and general philosophical orientation that cuts across the conservation and planning communities in the first decades of the twentieth century. This tradition, as I said earlier, has been all but invisible on the historical landscape of environmental thought. Many environmental theorists (and not a few practitioners) have assumed that the "classic" conservation tradition has little to offer beyond an unsatisfactory utilitarianism, and they have sought instead moral inspiration in the later (and more ecologically informed) work of Aldo Leopold, as well as in the more radical ecological ideologies that emerged in the late 1960s and 1970s. I think that Bailey, however, shows the conservation inheritance to be much more philosophically fertile and vital; indeed, his work even carries an early formulation of intrinsic value—by most accounts the hallmark of a truly "environmental" ethic—within a rich pragmatic and civic outlook.

If there is a tendency today within certain academic and popular environmentalist quarters to dismiss early conservation thought (and its agrarian variant) as morally barren, the American planning tradition has not fared much better in discussions of the development of environmental ethics (in fact, it is usually ignored altogether). This reception probably owes much to planners' preoccupation with aspects of the built landscape, as well as their traditional and often unabashed ethical humanism. Yet as we saw in chapter 3, Mumford's approach to regional planning directly addressed conservationists' concerns about the over-exploitation of natural resources, while at the same time it expanded to include a broader cultural orientation and a participatory method of civic and regional survey. By moving the American planning tradition into the discussion of the foundations of modern environmentalism, I thus hope to broaden the latter's intellectual pedigree and also highlight the strength of the civic pragmatist strand in environmental thought in the first half of the twentieth century.

In this chapter I would like to continue to advance this third way tradition, i.e., the alternative environmentalism running between the pure anthropocentric and nonanthropocentric camps, by examining the work of Benton MacKaye, a thinker cut from both conservationist and regional planning cloth. A forester by training and a conservationist by practice and disposition, MacKaye was, as we have seen, also Mumford's good friend and philosophical ally in the regional planning movement between the wars. MacKaye is responsible for a number of significant although still underappreciated contributions to the conservation and planning fields during the 1920s and 1930s (and beyond). Like Bailey, however, he is a little-known figure in American environmentalism, vastly overshadowed in the intellectual history of the movement by his fellow Wilderness Society colleague, Aldo Leopold. My goal in the discussion that follows, as with the previous discussion, is therefore to reclaim MacKaye's work and insights for the contemporary scene and to add another unique and compelling voice to the civic pragmatist tradition in American environmentalism.

Unlike Mumford—the "child of the city"—the place to begin with MacKaye, at least as far as his signature contribution to environmental thought and practice is concerned, is the wilderness.

A Lost Voice in the "Wilderness Debate"

In their 1998 anthology *The Great New Wilderness Debate*, editors J. Baird Callicott and Michael Nelson devoted the first part of their voluminous text to a selection of "historically influential" writings on the American wilderness idea.[1] Most of the names appearing there are indeed of the household variety (at least in environmentalist circles), including

Romantic precursors like Emerson and Thoreau, as well as twentieth-century wilderness advocates like Bob Marshall, Aldo Leopold, and Sigurd Olsen. The editors certainly are not guilty of any sins of commission in compiling this lineup of "received" wilderness luminaries; surely any narrative on the subject worth its salt would be incomplete without them. Sins of omission, however, are another matter. On this count, the neglect of the contribution of MacKaye, who was a co-founder of the Wilderness Society with Marshall, Leopold, and others in the mid-1930s, is hard to defend. While MacKaye's absence in the anthology is unfortunate, especially given the overall thematic thrust of the volume, it would be unfair to place all the blame for this slight on Callicott's and Nelson's shoulders. This is because many, if not most of their philosophical and historical colleagues have, as I have suggested, also tended to look past MacKaye's contributions to American wilderness thought and environmental philosophy more generally. Perhaps this situation will change, especially considering the publication of Larry Anderson's fine full-length biographical study, which has at last given MacKaye the serious historical treatment he deserves.[2] Still, as it stands now, I would wager that most environmental ethicists know very little about MacKaye and his work. This is a shame, because MacKaye was an intriguing and often prescient practical environmental thinker, one from whom I believe we may still learn a great deal.

In particular, we would do well to reflect upon his innovative vision for one of the most culturally valued and successful wilderness projects of the twentieth century: the Appalachian Trail. The conceptual underpinnings of the Trail's original charter are really quite remarkable, especially when we consider, in hindsight, the novelty of his attempt to weave together the traditionally separate threads of wilderness preservation and community life. In terms of its socially progressive character, MacKaye's thinking in this early paper—and much of his work over the next two decades—was a step ahead of Aldo Leopold's own pioneering wilderness thought during the same period (even if, as we will see in the next chapter, Leopold's work reflects a fairly expansive political dimension that has largely gone unnoticed by environmental philosophers).

MacKaye was downright precocious in his grasp of the importance of integrating the institutional and cultural features of the human community with the natural landscape. This conclusion is by no means meant to detract from Leopold's contribution to American environmental ethics and policy (including that relating to the wilderness), for it is surely profound and irreplaceable. Nevertheless, an examination of MacKaye's work reveals an important cultural and political strand in the wilderness idea that has not received a fair hearing. Fortunately, there are encouraging signs that this lacuna is beginning to be filled by several scholars adopting a more contextual and socially minded approach toward environmental history, a development that holds much promise for revealing the complexity of the narrative of American conservation.[3] In addition, the emergence of overtly pragmatic approaches in sister disciplines like environmental philosophy suggests a complementary critical stance, especially in those studies seeking to revise the moral foundations of environmental thought to fit a more pluralistic reading.[4] One of the important messages of "environmental pragmatism" is the idea that environmental philosophy (including that relating to wilderness) cannot and should not be forced into predetermined evolutionary paths. That is to say, ideological accounts asserting the progressive (and philosophically necessary) rise of nonanthropocentrism are beginning to be seen as descriptively and normatively inadequate as more complex and subtle methods of historical and moral inquiry have made their way into the conversation.

I think that there are compelling reasons for placing MacKaye alongside Bailey and Mumford in the third way tradition in environmental thought. While MacKaye's justification for the protection of nature through the development of the Appalachian Trail was a clear ethical project, he significantly avoided an appeal to a set of moral ideals removed from cultural experience. Instead, MacKaye sought to ground regard for wild landscapes within the ongoing reconstruction of the values and commitments of the human community. And, like Mumford's encounters with Dewey, MacKaye's educational experience found him in direct contact with the American philosophical tradition through the teachings of one of its celebrated figures: Josiah Royce. Known today primarily for his (unpragmatic) absolutist metaphysics, Royce nevertheless shared several intellectual sensibilities with William James and John Dewey, his more squarely pragmatic colleagues. I believe that MacKaye's wilderness thought owes much to the social philosophy of Royce, specifically Royce's understanding of the "higher" or "wise" province as a defense against metropolitan threats to regional culture and community life. Furthermore, there are significant vestiges of the critical environmentalism of Henry David Thoreau in MacKaye's writing, as well as echoes of perhaps an even older form of American political provincialism that goes back to the founding impulses of the American Republic.

With these sorts of concerns in mind, in this chapter I proceed in the following manner: First, I discuss the main elements of Royce's writing on provincialism, highlighting those features I feel are of greatest relevance to MacKaye's work. Next I consider the extent to which these Roycean ideas, as well as older environmental and political commitments, found their way into MacKaye's designs for the Appalachian Trail, and see how he envisioned the Trail to be a pragmatic and political instrument for the broader social reform of the Appalachian region. MacKaye's regionalist view of wilderness preservation never really caught fire in conservationist circles, even though one of its leading voices, Leopold, strongly endorsed MacKaye's ideas on this count. I conclude by reflecting upon the relationship of MacKaye's environmental work to the lingering debate over the meaning and significance of wilderness in the environmentalist agenda.

Royce's "Wise Provincialism"

While his reputation has not yet experienced a full-scale resurgence in philosophical circles like that of his pragmatist contemporaries, Josiah Royce (1855–1916) nevertheless is considered to be one of the towering figures of the American philosophic tradition, part of an intellectual cohort that includes Charles Sanders Peirce, William James, George Santayana, John Dewey, and Alfred North Whitehead. Many of these men would converge at Harvard University: James and Royce were colleagues and friends in Cambridge (and often intellectual sparring partners); Santayana was Royce's student and later joined his former teacher and James on the faculty. An important figure in American post-Kantian idealism and a trail-blazing thinker in metaphysics, logic, and ethics, Royce's most significant and historically influential works are generally considered to be *The Religious Aspect of Philosophy*,[5] *The World and the Individual*,[6] *The Philosophy of Loyalty*,[7] and *The Problem of Christianity*.[8]

As mentioned earlier, while Royce's absolutist and idealist metaphysical commitments, especially in his early writing, were mostly at odds with the pluralism and naturalism of thinkers like James and Dewey, in places his work is quite compatible with his pragmatic brethren, especially that written in his later years.[9] The Absolute having diminished in his philosophical system, and his thought taking on a somewhat more practical cast during the last part of his life, Royce began to address more earthbound issues of social and moral philosophy (even though these frequently retained an idealist and universal character). For example, Royce's concern about achieving and maintaining the "beloved community," a metaphysical, but also ethical and social vision unites him with Dewey, whose own intertwining moral and political ideas were driven by a similar regard for the development of shared experience, albeit one with a less transcendent and more naturalistic grounding.[10]

In 1902 Royce delivered a talk, "Provincialism," as the Phi Beta Kappa address at the University of Iowa. His remarks were later incorporated into the collection *Race Questions, Provincialism, and Other American Problems*, a work Royce intended to be a practical application of his moral ideal of "loyalty," and his most explicit attempt to address a range of social issues of the day.[11] Through his notion of the province, Royce was able to expound a semantically rich concept that he hoped would empirically realize his metaphysics of community. By "provincialism" Royce not only sought to evoke the "peculiarities of a local dialect," as he put it, but also the more expansive "fashions, manners, and customs of a given restricted region of a country."[12] Moreover, in his mind the term suggested a clear fondness for and pride in such cultural forms, a loyalty to the ideal of the province that he celebrated as a fundamental moral virtue. Recognizing that the geographical referent of the concept necessarily must admit of degrees, Royce offered the following general definition:

For my present purpose a county, a state, or even a large section of the country, such as New England, might constitute a province. For me, then, a province shall mean any one part of a national domain, which is geographically and socially, sufficiently unified to have a true consciousness of its own unity, to feel a pride in its own ideas and customs, and to possess a sense of its distinction from other parts of the country. And by the term "provincialism" I shall mean, first, the tendency of such a province to possess its own customs and ideals; secondly, the totality of these customs and ideals themselves; and thirdly, the love and pride which lead the inhabitants of a province to cherish as their own these traditions, beliefs, and aspirations.[13]

Royce was, however, quick to distinguish this version of provincial spirit from the bitter or "false" sectionalism that had produced the American Civil War. "Our national unity" he wrote, "will always require of us a devotion that will transcend in some directions the limits of all our provincial ideas. A common sympathy between the different sections of our country will, in future, need a constantly fresh cultivation."[14] It is this recognition of the critical importance of balancing moral and political universalism with the "local independence of spirit" of the province that keeps Royce's ideas from descending into any sort of defensive and embattled parochialism. "No provincialism will become dangerously narrow," he predicted, "so long as it is constantly accompanied by a willingness to sacrifice much in order to put in the form of great institutions, of noble architecture, and of beautiful surroundings an expression of the worth that the community attaches to its own ideals."[15] Sensitivity to the interdependent relationship between local and more cosmopolitan or global loyalties remains one of our most challenging public philosophical tasks nearly a century later.[16] Royce's intriguing expression of the material manifestation of provincial goods also suggests an understanding of the close connections between community life and environmental quality, a view shared, as we will see, by Benton MacKaye.

Royce's celebration of the virtues of the "wise" province was at heart a response to what he took to be the principal evils afflicting the modern world of the early twentieth century. The first of these was the problem of social alienation, specifically the need to assimilate outsiders (both foreign immigrants and domestic "wanderers") into the tight-knit fabric of the local community. "The stranger, the sojourner, the newcomer"— all must be made integrated into the life of the province if the social danger of disunity is to be avoided.[17] According to Royce, it was only through the cultivation of regional "spirit"—the participation in the cultural affairs of the province—that these newcomers would be brought into the shared experience of the community. Somewhat prophetically, he seemed especially concerned about the increasing mobility of individuals and the effect that frequent changes in dwelling places would have on communal values, a subject we might now commonly discuss under the rubric of "sense of place." A transplanted Californian himself, Royce had first-hand experience with the difficulty of this integration of outsiders into new settings. While pitched at too great a level of abstraction and generality to offer any sort of incisive analysis, Royce's recognition of the problem of the roaming, lost individual in modern industrial America is indeed telling, and it is a theme that persevered as a major concern in late twentieth-century American life.[18]

The second disturbing trend that Royce believed the wise province would be able to counter was what he referred to as the "leveling tendency" in modern American life. By this he meant

that aspect of modern civilization which is most obviously suggested by the fact that, because of the ease of communication amongst distant places, because of the spread of popular education, and because of the coordination and of the centralization of industry and of social authorities, we tend all over the nation, and, in some degree, even throughout the civilized world, to read the same daily news, to share the same general ideas, to submit to the same overmastering social forces, to live in the same external fashions, to discourage individuality, and to approach a dead level of harassed mediocrity.[19]

Social and cultural uniformity were, according to Royce, the disastrous products of early twentieth-century technological and political evolution; provincial ways of talking, thinking, and living were being run through the homogenizing meat grinder of modern civilization. Dewey would later express a similar concern about the threats such forces posed to shared experience in his *The Public and Its Problems*: "The Great Society created by steam and electricity may be a society," he wrote, "but it is no community."[20] Closely related to this leveling tendency was a third malady: the explosion of the "mob spirit" and its pernicious effects on popular democratic governance. Greatly influenced by his reading of the book *The Crowd*, written by French psychologist Gustave Le Bon,[21] Royce argued that however highly trained individuals may be as individuals, "their mental processes, as a mob, are degraded." As a consequence, they cannot be safe rulers. Only the "men who take counsel together in small groups, who respect one another's individuality, who meanwhile criticise one another constantly, and earnestly, and who suspect whatever the crowd teaches" could be trusted with the responsibilities of popular government.[22] The province was not only the salvation of the individual from the steam-roller advance of the mob spirit, it was also the last stronghold of authentic American democracy.

Royce's plea for the cultivation of a wise provincialism, then, was in essence a pragmatic response to a growing litany of social, moral, and political problems he sensed around him in early twentieth-century cultural life. As John J. McDermott has observed, while some of Royce's more topical social reflections have faded into the sunset, his notion of provincialism still possesses a compelling normative force. Royce, McDermott writes, "put his finger on a serious dilemma in the pedagogy of culture. Surely we cannot be closed off from other cultures, persuasions, and ideas, if we are to achieve a human community in the fullest sense, as, for example, in Royce's vision of the 'beloved' or 'great' community. . . . For Royce, community is a flowering of deeply and integrally held commitments to one's local environment."[23]

These personalized aspects of community definitely seem to have engaged Royce more in the last years of his life because his writing took on a more social (and even quasi-political) character.[24] In one of his last essays, *The Hope of the Great Community*,[25] Royce wrote of the promise of a global, international community, one that transcended nationalities and geographic borders, a gentle plea for fraternity that was shaped by the raging conflicts of World War I. In many ways, it was an extension of his earlier thoughts on provincialism, complete with Royce's attempt to balance his provincial "golden mean", i.e., diversity within a larger unity, at the international scale:

While the great community of the future will unquestionably be international by virtue of the ties which will bind its various nationalities together, it will find no place for that sort of internationalism which despises the individual variety of nations, and which tries to substitute for the vices of those who at present seek merely to conquer mankind, the equally worthless desire of those who hope to see us in future as "men without a country." . . . The citizens of the world of the future will not lose their distinct countries. What will pass away will be that insistent mutual hostility which gives the nations of to-day, even in times of peace, so many of the hateful and distracting characters of a detached individual man. . . . What saves us on any level of human social life is union.[26]

Despite this increasing attention to more social and political (rather than purely metaphysical) aspects of human community, however, Royce never came close to offering anything programmatic with respect to the planning and maintenance of such social orders (at any scale), a neglect of political technology he was even more guilty of than Dewey.[27] Nevertheless, it would be difficult to deny that Royce had identified a real set of threats to what we might think of as the communal virtues and forms of the American province. To be truly persuasive, however, his insistence that the properly nourished sphere of community practices and traditions could effectively neutralize such dangers obviously required more concrete proposals than the philosopher was able to provide. I think that many of Royce's ideas would soon find tangible expression through the conservation work of Benton MacKaye, especially in his early charter for the Appalachian Trail. While MacKaye was more of a conceptual planner and grand visualizer than a nuts-and-bolts strategist, I believe that his work nevertheless provided the sort of practical vehicle that could deliver the Roycean values of the province.

Conservation and Community

Benton MacKaye was born in Connecticut in 1879, the son of Steele MacKaye, a well-known painter, actor, theater manager, and playwright in late nineteenth-century Boston. Talent was generously distributed among the MacKaye siblings. His brother Percy would most closely follow in his father's footsteps, becoming a respected poet and playwright himself, while his sister Hazel would go on to be a successful stage actress and an influential suffragist. Benton's older brother, James Medbury, would have a impressive dual career as an industrial chemist and professor of philosophy at Dartmouth. At the turn of the century he would make a few small ripples in leftist circles in New York City with his writings on "Americanized socialism," an amalgam of social democratic thought and a strongly positivistic reading of utilitarian theory.

Benton's first 8 years were spent mostly in New York City, with the family making a propitious move to Shirley Center, Massachusetts, in

1888. Life in this quintessential New England village quickly naturalized young Benton into the "archetypical Yankee," as his friend Lewis Mumford put it, and its communal ethos and rural environs would stoke the fires of his philosophical imagination up until his death there in 1975 at age 96. While he would live elsewhere in the intervening decades— including Cambridge, New York City, and Washington, D.C.—Shirley Center was the one place to which he would always return.[28]

MacKaye entered Harvard in 1896, taking a liberal curriculum that immersed him in the natural sciences and humanities. Shepherding MacKaye through the natural sciences were geographers and geologists William Morris Davis and Nathaniel Southgate Shaler, under whose tutelage MacKaye began to learn about and appreciate the intricate workings and aesthetic wonders of the physical landscape. Paul Bryant, whose 1965 dissertation on MacKaye was until recently the only comprehensive biography of its subject, writes that these distinguished scholars had a great impact on the young man's developing interest in the environment, with MacKaye struck in particular by Davis's opening words delivered to his introductory geography class. "Gentlemen," the professor began, holding a globe up in front of his students. "Here is the subject of our study—this planet, its lands, waters, atmosphere, and life; the abode of plant, animal, and man—*the earth as a habitable globe*."[29] The view of nature captured in the geographer's statement—the natural environment as home place—would be a sentiment running through the full sweep of MacKaye's conservation philosophy, including, most significantly, his thoughts on wilderness.

Shaler, by then the dean of the Lawrence Scientific School, taught "Elementary Geology," a 300-student course that was the most popular at the college.[30] A former student of Louis Agassiz, Shaler was a distinguished figure in American geological and geographical circles, and a renowned scientific generalist and popularizer. He was also a great champion of early conservation efforts, even though, like MacKaye, he is rarely discussed in the histories of American conservation and environmentalism.[31] A follower of George Perkins Marsh, but also heavily influenced by a Romantic philosophy of nature, Shaler's environmentalism reflected both conservationist and preservationist traditions. His scientific survey work, moreover, brought him into close contact with the U.S.

Geological Survey's John Wesley Powell (a conservation pioneer), as well as Charles Sanders Peirce, the mercurial founder of American pragmatic philosophy whose work for the U.S. Coast and Geodetic Survey (from 1859 to 1891) was the only steady employment the philosopher ever enjoyed.[32] These associations and influences clearly left their marks on Shaler's thinking, and it is interesting that we can see a similarly eclectic blend of pragmatism, utilitarianism, and Romantic transcendentalism in MacKaye's later conservation philosophy.[33]

Also among MacKaye's teachers at Harvard was Josiah Royce. In his brief mention of the influence of Royce on MacKaye's intellectual development, Bryant observes that while the latter never became a technically consistent philosopher as the result of his classroom study, there is nevertheless a strong element in MacKaye's thinking that parallels Royce's. Bryant sees this influence to be primarily a metaphysical one, particularly MacKaye's sympathy with Royce's view of nature as a "social production."[34] While this is certainly true, I do not believe that it fully captures the most significant relationship between Royce's philosophy and MacKaye's subsequent environmentalism. Surely speculative arguments about intellectual debts must proceed with caution. I think there is evidence to support the view, however, that Royce's notion of provincialism resounded in MacKaye's later environmental philosophy.

While MacKaye completed his undergraduate degree at Harvard in 1900, 2 years before Royce's talk on the subject at Iowa and 8 years before it saw publication, it is not unlikely that the major elements of Royce's views would have been in place during MacKaye's time in the professor's classroom. Moreover, MacKaye returned to Harvard in 1903 to pursue a master's degree in forestry, which he received in 1905. He also remained closely associated with the university until 1910, splitting his time between teaching forestry courses there and working for the U.S. Forest Service. Given this, as well as MacKaye's intellectual curiosity and his penchant for philosophical discussion, it seems quite reasonable to suspect that during this time he would have been aware of his former teacher's thoughts regarding provincialism.[35] In any event, and as I hope will become clear, we can certainly see a number of close similarities in their philosophical stances.

After receiving what was then a conventional training in the utilitarian tradition of forest management, MacKaye joined the U.S. Forest Service in 1905, the year of its official organization under Chief Gifford Pinchot. True to the times, MacKaye's early duties involved advising New England farmers and foresters on the proper techniques of woodlot management. In 1912 he took a job mapping watersheds in the White Mountains of New Hampshire for the U.S. Geological Survey, a project that was instrumental in the establishment of the White Mountain National Forest. During the war years, MacKaye surveyed the cutover forest lands of the upper Midwest and devised a plan to resettle this abandoned "stump country" with forestry and agricultural cooperatives. This project in "rural recolonization," as he put it, merged MacKaye's evolving and intertwining interests in community planning and conservation. Shortly thereafter, and as a result of this earlier work, MacKaye transferred to the U.S. Department of Labor, where he published his report *Employment and Natural Resources* in 1919.[36] In this report, which MacKaye considered his first book, he called for the federal creation of new employment opportunities on unsettled lands as well as organized community building; resource conservation; and the economic restructuring of agricultural, timber, and mining industries to be more compatible with the goals of social stability.

The new farm, forest, and mining communities described by MacKaye would be committed to the ideal of economic cooperation, thereby providing a more permanent and well-formed cultural and physical environment for community life to flourish. MacKaye hoped that with such intelligent planning an end could be put to the socially and ecologically pernicious "cut-and-run" patterns that had characterized earlier rural resource relationships in regions like the midwestern lake states. This plan for the promotion of stable community settlements was thus linked to the development of a more responsible, sustained-yield approach toward resource conservation. While the latter was not an unusual sentiment in conservation circles during this time, MacKaye's close attention to a range of social and more expansive economic issues certainly distinguishes his work from that of his forestry contemporaries and was a clear departure from his narrow forestry training at Harvard. The upshot is that by 1920 MacKaye had built an impressive, if not unique, resume as a conservationist and community planner, although the political radicalism attributed to most of his proposals during this period ensured that they met with little real government support.[37]

Already, then, in his early career we can see MacKaye searching for ways to build stronger communities through the tools of conservation and economic planning. Like Royce, MacKaye's concern about the problem of rootless individuals—in this case the quasi-anarchic and short-sighted forestry, farming, and mining activities of American migrants as they swept across the continent—led him to endorse the provincial values of stable community life as a practical and constructive response. As mentioned earlier, however, his most compelling proposal in this vein would appear in 1921 with his plan for the Appalachian Trail. Here MacKaye was able to visualize and outline a powerful tool for enhancing shared experience in concert with wilderness protection, thus laying the groundwork for an innovative and pragmatic philosophy of the environment.

The Appalachian Trail: Defending "Indigenous" America

MacKaye's historic proposal for the Appalachian Trail was precipitated by a tragic personal loss. His wife Betty, a dedicated feminist and social activist, committed suicide in the spring of 1921, following a severe bout of depression. Devastated, MacKaye accepted the offer of his friend Charles Harris Whitaker, editor of the *Journal of the American Institute of Architects* (AIA), to spend some time at Whitaker's farmstead in North Olive, New Jersey (MacKaye and his wife had been living in New York at the time). Shortly after his arrival at the farm in June, MacKaye began working on what he first referred to as a "memo" on regional planning. The memo quickly expanded into a sweeping and ambitious proposal for a new recreation trail running along the crest line of the Appalachian Mountains. Whitaker was intrigued, and informed his friend Clarence S. Stein, a like-minded social progressive and architect, of MacKaye's project. On July 10, 1921, MacKaye, Whitaker, and Stein met at the nearby Hudson Guild Farm, which served as a cooperative camp for urban youth and a meeting place for social reformers. At this meeting

Whitaker expressed his desire to publish MacKaye's Appalachian Trail proposal in the AIA journal, and Stein told MacKaye that he would further publicize the trail idea through his AIA Committee on Community Planning.[38] The meeting turned out to be a landmark event in American conservation and planning history because it set in motion, not only the development of the Appalachian Trail, but also the ideas and personal alliances that would soon coalesce into the Regional Planning Association of America.

Billing his plan for a wilderness footpath running from Maine to Georgia as a "new approach to the problem of living," MacKaye's prospectus for the Appalachian Trail that appeared in the AIA journal began with a plea for an improved recreation aesthetic: "The customary approach to the problem of living relates to work rather than play. Can we increase the efficiency of our *working* time? Can we solve the problem of labor? If so we can widen the opportunities for leisure."[39] His intention, however, was to "reverse this mental process." In other words, MacKaye thought the real concerns were on the other side of the equation, for instance, in questions like: "Can we increase the efficiency of our *spare* time?"; and "Can we develop opportunities for leisure as an aid in solving the problem of labor?"[40] He quickly moved past such utilitarian talk about the efficiency of recreation by making it clear that he had more on his mind than simply advocating the "utopia of escape" in the wilderness. In presenting leisure as a problem, MacKaye opened the door for a much more profound and complex reexamination of the values of the American social and political community and its relationship with the natural environment.

According to MacKaye, in addition to its obvious therapeutic and physical benefits, a trek along the ridges of the Appalachian range would allow individuals to place their harried yet lifeless metropolitan existence in a larger philosophical context. More to the point, he suggested that the "reposeful study" of natural processes along the Trail would encourage individuals to evaluate the crass commercialism and industrialism of American life, and that the experience of wild nature would revitalize our productive relations:

Industry would come to be seen in its true perspective—as a means in life and not as an end in itself. The actual partaking of the recreative and non-industrial life—systematically by the people and not spasmodically by a few—should emphasize the distinction between it and the industrial life. It should stimulate the quest for enlarging the one and reducing the other. It should put new zest in the labor movement. Life and study of this kind should emphasize the need of going to the roots of industrial questions and of avoiding superficial thinking and rash action. The problems of the farmer, the coal miner, and the lumberjack could be studied intimately and with minimum partiality. Such an approach would bring the poise that goes with understanding.[41]

I think MacKaye's claims here accord well with what environmental philosopher Bryan Norton calls the "transformative value" of experiences in the natural world, the recognition of the many ways in which the "experience of nature can promote questioning and rejection of overly materialistic and consumptive felt preferences."[42] These "felt preferences" refer to the unquestioned "givens" that an individual desires without reflection or appraisal of the appropriateness of the goods in question (e.g., the demand for resource-based commodities without regard for the ecological impact of their procurement and use). Instead, according to Norton, reflective experience in nature leads individuals to transform their attitudes and values toward the environment into more ecologically benign commitments.

This sort of thinking certainly has an impressive pedigree in environmental thought. A similar position may be found, for example, in the writings of many of the American Transcendentalists, especially MacKaye's philosophical idol, Henry David Thoreau, who saw in nature a moral weapon that could be employed in a critique of mid-nineteenth-century political and social life. As Bob Pepperman Taylor has observed:

The role of nature in *Walden* is essentially political: it is the means by which Thoreau proposes to break the chain of conventional wisdom that prevents us, in his view, from seriously doubting the necessity or the desirability of the status quo, or imagining an alternative. It is a tool for social criticism but a tool with a difference: it is universally available and must be reckoned as a necessary resource for all citizens of a democratic society.[43]

MacKaye's predictions about the recreational and nonindustrial life experienced "by the people" on the Trail, and the clear-eyed view of twentieth-century political economy it provides clearly echoes this critical turn to nature by Thoreau. Consider the following passage from "Spring" in *Walden*:

Our village life would stagnate if it were not for the unexplored forests and meadows which surround it. We need the tonic of wilderness. . . . We can never have enough of Nature. We must be refreshed by the sight of inexhaustible vigor, vast and Titanic features, the sea-coast with its wrecks, the wilderness with its living and decaying trees, the thunder cloud, and the rain which lasts three weeks and produces freshets. We need to witness our own limits transgressed, and some life pasturing freely where we never wander.[44]

Although Thoreau was unnerved by the raw wilderness he encountered in places like Mount Katahdin in Maine, he nevertheless understood its political and social importance; the wild was a check on human arrogance and excess, a reminder of our moral and material limits. Unspoiled nature, for both Thoreau and MacKaye, thus offered the necessary distance from American industrial and commercial values so that the latter could be seen in their true perspective, i.e., as means, not as final ends.[45]

The reformist hopes that MacKaye held for the Appalachian Trail— that it would be an instrument for going to the "roots" of industrial questions and for imagining a countervailing social and moral order— also evokes Thoreau's near obsession with finding hard "foundations" in *Walden*. In "The Pond in Winter," for example, he ventures out onto the ice to survey the depths of Walden Pond, which, he tells us, local rumor held to be bottomless. While Thoreau finds the pond to be reassuringly deep, thus suggesting its purity and uniqueness, he also confirms that it does indeed have a solid bottom. The empiricist in Thoreau is satisfied by this discovery, but the Transcendentalist in him still requires something more: "I am thankful that this pond was made deep and pure for a symbol. While men believe in the infinite some ponds will be thought to be bottomless."[46] The hard bottom of the pond was important to Thoreau because it offered a metaphysical and moral foundation in nature, i.e., a point outside of the conventions and institutions of society, from which he could objectively appraise the culture and economy of mid-nineteenth-century America.

At the same time, however, Thoreau's nature could not be the truly separate realm that he wanted it to be; its "foundation" was to no small degree also a human creation. As Walter Benn Michaels has suggested, for Thoreau, the act of looking into the pond (and the appeal to nature generally) was in a significant sense also a sounding of one's own nature; the natural world reflected the very cultural and social values it was supposed to be defined against.[47] Even so, a belief in extrahuman foundations and a sense of infinite in nature—a belief in bottomless ponds—were necessary for Thoreau, since such beliefs had the effect of encouraging a deeper sense of mystery and humility about humans' place in the world. Faith in the vastness of nature and its inscrutable character ultimately has a kind of pragmatic quality in Thoreau's writing. Even if Walden was simply an especially deep pond, its symbolic bottomlessness was useful as a foundation for moral criticism, and nature generally could serve to elevate our cultural and political aspirations.

Although Thoreau is clearly one of his intellectual ancestors, MacKaye departs from his fellow Yankee naturalist by bracketing such deeper metaphysical speculations (MacKaye seems to have simply assumed that nature was thoroughly embedded with human values and will). Nevertheless, MacKaye shares with Thoreau this notion of a pragmatic foundation in nature in which the unique human experiences and cultural values produced by intimate contact with the wilderness are the justification for its protection, as well as the means to criticize the economic and social loyalties of industrial America. MacKaye's Appalachian project therefore draws from this older critical tradition in American environmental thought, one in which the idea of nature becomes a tool for diagnosing social ills and a rhetorical device for staking out the proper course of American moral and political reform.[48]

In addition, although related to its use as a source for criticism of a stifling industrialism, MacKaye's Appalachian plan was offered as a practical solution to an alarming trend he saw in the growth of modern urbanism: the encroachment of socially and environmentally destructive metropolitan forces into authentic rural communities. "This invasion of an over-wrought mechanized civilization," he wrote in 1927, "is as foreign . . . to our innate indigenous country, and to its promised culture, as the invasion of a foreign army. '*Metropolitan* America' is a contradiction; it is no real part of America; it is an exotic influence with which the inherent country and its promise must contend."[49] It is important to note, however, that MacKaye was not getting at some sort of radical antiurbanism. Like Mumford, he believed that the "true" urban form was part of a balanced regional landscape, one that also included village and hinterland. As he wrote in 1928, the smaller and more organic "regional city," conceived and planned in a larger geographic context, represented the "giant orchestration of varied life (urban, communal, and even primeval) as against the dull cacophony of standardized existence presented by the modern metropolis."[50] The community of the regional city was therefore, as Royce might have put it, a bulwark against the leveling effects of modern civilization that afflicted the false metropolitan form.

MacKaye's almost Manichaean opposition of the "indigenous" to the "metropolitan" was the centerpiece of his environmental philosophy. Remarking on the purpose of the Trail to the Blue Mountain Club in 1927, he observed that "it is the love of country, the love of primal nature and of human nature, the lure of crestline and comradeship, which we like to think of as being indigenous to our own homeland." "In short," he concluded, "the object of the Appalachian Trail is to develop indigenous America."[51] Such a reconstructive social project for American life suggested that the Trail was not an end in itself, but rather was, as MacKaye put it, "A base for more fundamental needs." Specifically, it was "The equipment required for a certain line of badly needed social education, the power within a people's mind to see their common ends, not as a tangle of antagonistic parts but as a single, integrated whole."[52] The marshaling of the indigenous social and biophysical resources of the Trail against the invading influence of metropolitanism was, as MacKaye put it, a way of developing our common mind, our shared cultural experience within a balanced natural environment. "The development of a common mind and real environment is something deeper . . . in the community and countryside than architecture and the platting of roadways."[53] We therefore needed to take advantage of all available tangible ways and means—like the planning of the Appalachian Trail—to develop this common culture in order to make both the community and countryside truly live.

I think that the parallels between MacKaye's organic ideal of indigenous America and Royce's concept of the wise province are striking, if not unmistakable. Most obvious is the concern for the shared life of the region and its protection from the forces of metropolitan alienation and mechanization that runs through both of their thinking. "The mould most conducive to cultural life seems to be the *community*," MacKaye wrote, concluding that regardless of its size, a true community, like a province, is "something essentially different from the *mass*. It is a body of population having some vital, common geographic interest."[54] MacKaye's idea of a common mind fostered by the real or indigenous environment and Royce's remarks on the essential consciousness of unity shared by a province are surely two ways of saying the same thing. Moreover, as we will see in the next chapter, the association of nature with the common good or greater public interest also figures prominently in Aldo Leopold's environmental thought.

In addition to its Roycean and Thoreauvian elements, MacKaye's vision for the Appalachian Trail also may be seen to reach down into the farthest depths of the American political experience. In his recent book, *To Begin the World Anew*, the noted American historian Bernard Bailyn has discussed the significance of the provincial character as it shaped the political imagination of the Founders. The revolutionary generation (i.e., Jefferson, Adams, Franklin) was, Bailyn writes, "one of the most creative groups in modern history,"[55] a creativity he believes owed much to their location in what was at the time the North Atlantic hinterland of the great metropolitan centers of Europe. Bailyn argues that the Founders drew from their local traditions and native values a powerful sense of moral integrity, one that in turn shaped the political context for their resistance to European metropolitan forces. This native American provincialism also allowed them to make a great leap of imagination to envision a new kind of constitutional democratic order:

Their provincialism, and the sense they derived from it of their own moral stature, had nourished their political imaginations. Uncertain of their place in the established, metropolitan world, they did not think themselves bound by it; they were prepared to challenge it. . . . In the most general sense, what conditioned and stimulated the Founders' imagination and hence their capacity to begin the world anew was the fact that they came from outside the metropolitan establishment, with all its age-old, deeply buried, arcane entanglements and commitments. From their distant vantage point they viewed what they could see of the dominant order with a cool, critical, challenging eye, and what they saw was something atrophied, weighted down by its own complacent, self-indulgent elaboration, and vulnerable to the force of fresh energies and imaginative designs. Refusing to be intimidated by the received traditions and confident of their own integrity and creative capacities, they demanded to know why things must be the way they are; and they had the imagination and energy to conceive of something closer to the grain of everyday reality and more likely to lead to human happiness.[56]

MacKaye's promotion of indigenous culture against metropolitanism, and his vision for the Appalachian Trail as a native force working against the "wilderness" of industrial and economic encroachment into the countryside, is, I believe, part of this rich democratic and American provincial dialectic of resistance and creation. In his 1928 book *The New Exploration*, MacKaye presented his broader philosophy of regional planning and its role in marshaling oppositional cultural and political forces against the metropolis with the rhetorical flair one might expect from the son of a great dramatist. The Appalachian region was poised to be a contested battleground, he wrote. On the one side was the spiritually deadening and environmentally ruinous "iron civilization" flowing out of the eastern megacity into the Appalachian countryside. Squaring off against the allied "foreign" forces of industrialism and metropolitanism was MacKaye's nature-based provincialism, whose

tiny evidences are seen in the tame little movements to establish National Parks and Forests, to restore the realm of nature as Thoreau glimpsed it for us, to develop the realm of art through local drama, and otherwise to invoke the "spiritual form," in our society. . . . There is a dormant barbarian thrill for freedom beating beneath the waistcoat of the average citizen, and it is beginning to awaken. The immediate job of the regional planner is to prepare for this awakening—not through unconstructive and chimerical efforts on the metropolitan "Bottle-Neck," but through a synthetic creative effort back on the crestline sources where an indigenous world of intrinsic human values (and specifically an Indigenous America), awaits its restoration and development as a *land in which to live*.[57]

In a real sense, MacKaye's designs for the Trail were an attempt at a new kind of political founding. The culture and values of MacKaye's indigenous America were being advanced as an alternative social order, one to be realized through the deliberate and controlled planning of the regional landscape.

In addition to its political and social commitments, MacKaye's Appalachian project was also an expression of a strong environmental ethic, although one that was ultimately more humanistic than non-anthropocentric in character. On this count, and as discussed earlier, there are similarities between Royce's and MacKaye's environmental ontologies; both subscribe to a view of nature shot through with human values. "Our job is to make an American sanctuary," MacKaye wrote, "for the birds and the trees yes, and through them for ourselves."[58] The "intrinsic human values" of indigenous America, i.e., the organic and communal culture of the province, formed the core of MacKaye's normative project. Such values, however, were the product of the transaction between provincial culture (e.g., Appalachian America) and the primeval or wild landscape, which offered a field of experience to citizens that was in sharp contrast to the metropolitan environment. While his position is fairly anthropocentric, MacKaye by no means exhibits an arrogant humanism in his views toward nonhuman nature. Rather, the care for and betterment of the natural environment is always fundamentally connected to the improvement of the human moral and social condition.[59]

Although it would be a stretch to claim Royce as a conservation philosopher or environmental thinker, the Harvard professor does seem to have expressed similar sentiments. Like MacKaye, Royce viewed appreciation and regard for the natural (and built) environment in terms of the civic affairs and general good of the human community. A wise provincialism, he wrote, was most tangibly represented by the "spirit which shows itself in the multiplying of public libraries, in the laying out of public parks, in the work of local historical associations, in the enterprises of village improvement societies."[60] Royce was also concerned, as was MacKaye, about the impacts of modern industrialism on the beauty and physical integrity of the natural world. As he wrote in 1908:

Let the province more and more seek its own adornment. Here I speak of a matter that in all our American communities has been until recently far too much neglected. Local pride ought above all to centre, so far as its material objects are concerned, about the determination to give the surroundings of the community nobility, dignity, beauty. We Americans spend far too much of our early strength and time in our newer communities upon injuring our landscapes, and far too little upon endeavoring to beautify our towns and cities. We have begun to change all that, and while I have no right to speak as an aesthetic judge concerning the growth of the love of the beautiful in our country, I can strongly insist that no community can think any creation of genuine beauty and dignity in its public buildings or in the surroundings of its towns and cities too good a thing for its own deserts.[61]

Environmental quality was thus an expression of the values of the province, one that provided the training for the higher moral principle of loyalty that Royce held so dear.[62]

If MacKaye presumably found much of the philosophical guidance for his Appalachian plan in Royce's provincialism and in earlier environmental and political traditions in American thought, he drew practical inspiration from the trail conservation projects familiar to him in the Northeast, as well as from his past professional experiences. With respect to the former, MacKaye took special note of the planning initiatives carried out by the Appalachian Mountain Club in New Hampshire's White Mountains and the Green Mountain Club's "Long Trail" in Vermont. Indeed, MacKaye saw his Appalachian plan as a logical extension of these projects, especially the latter, remarking that he was essentially proposing the creation of a "'long trail' over the full length of the Appalachian skyline."[63] The operational form of the Trail, however, was most powerfully inspired by his earlier conservation and settlement work in the U.S. Department of Labor.

In his 1921 article, MacKaye proposed the development of an evolving series of community settlements along the Trail's length, beginning with basic shelter camps and followed by more fixed, planned recreation communities that would also become places for scientific study and physical recuperation. Eventually these would be supplemented by larger food and farm camps, which, "in the spirit of cooperation" would provide the agricultural base for the new outdoor living establishments. These in turn were to be joined by sustainable forest communities lining the Trail, which, like the farm cooperatives, would provide both employment and a healthy living environment for a new rural population. MacKaye hoped that this positive development of a secure Appalachian "domain" would reverse the flow of rural populations into the crowded cities of the East Coast. Claiming that the purpose of the Trail was to establish a base for a more extensive and systematic development of outdoor community life, MacKaye clearly sought to firmly link the recreational and therapeutic values of the Appalachian region with deeper social democratic and economic reforms. As he wrote, the Trail was to be a "project in housing and community architecture," an ambitious task of social and environmental reconstruction that went beyond the creation of an eastern wilderness footpath for leisure and recreational benefit.[64]

These specific goals clearly suggested an expansive and, at the time, unprecedented planning project, a point not lost on MacKaye. As he wrote in 1931, "A realm and not a trail marks the full aim of our effort. The trail is but the entrance to the final thing we seek—that thing eternal which we have called primeval influence."[65] The development of this "primeval" influence (a term he preferred over "wilderness") entailed an interlocking geographical and cultural task, one larger and more ambitious than a narrowly circumscribed objective of wilderness protection. As his original proposal's subtitle makes clear, the Appalachian Trail was intended to be an advance in the philosophy of regional planning, an intellectual and practical movement that reached its peak in America in the 1920s and early 1930s. As discussed in chapter 3, the Regional Planning Association of America was devoted to bringing the British "garden city" ideal to the United States—a decentralized, green vision for an aesthetically, politically, and ecologically reconstructed urban and rural environment. Mark Luccarelli observes that group members like MacKaye and Mumford essentially sought to translate a naturalized and expanded version of the garden city into the more complex regional city concept, with the broad goal of changing the context of modern industrial life. As he puts it, "Urban life would not cease to exist but would simply have a different context. . . . The natural world would be felt: the garden city would provide rural landscapes, agricultural products, and electric power; it would nurture architecture and literature as well as particular kinds of industry."[66]

MacKaye and Mumford provided the RPAA with the strongest philosophical leadership, exerting a great influence over the group's direction in the 1920s. Specifically, they were responsible for pushing the group toward a more environmentally inclusive vision of the region and its cultural potential, a direction not immediately embraced by many of the group's housing specialists and community planners.[67] MacKaye's Appalachian Trail proposal was particularly important to this broader emphasis within the group. As Edward Spann writes, the Appalachian project "dramatically expanded the boundaries and potential of regional planning, promising to break it free from its preoccupation with big cities and their contiguous areas."[68] Mumford himself, in his introduction to *The New Exploration*, wrote that MacKaye's vision "played a decisive part in all our work, modifying our city-minded approach, enlarging our horizons, and bringing into our lives the voice and touch of an older America, the America of the Eastern wilderness and the Western frontier: a heritage we ignore at our peril."[69]

Regionalism and Conservation

If the primeval and rural orientation of MacKaye's Appalachian project enlarged the vision of the architects and planners in the RPAA, his influence on the conservation community, especially that branch pertaining to wilderness thinking and policy making during the early and mid-1920s, is another story. Aldo Leopold's first major articulation of the need for wilderness protection, "The Wilderness and Its Place in Forest Recreational Policy," appeared in the *Journal of Forestry* in 1921.[70] Arguing that Gifford Pinchot's doctrine of "highest use" should be stretched to accommodate the protection of wilderness from both industrial and intrusive recreational and tourism development, Leopold suggested that the recreational use of forest lands was equivalent to a "minority right," one that the young Forest Service was neglecting on a daily basis. As Paul Sutter has rightly pointed out, this early argument for wilderness preservation, contrary to the opinion held by most observers, was not an attempt by Leopold to seek a "romantic escape from the politics of resource use."[71] Rather, Leopold's argument was a practical response to specific technological and consumer trends in interwar America, including the advance of the automobile, increased road building, and rising recreational demands on the public lands.

While Sutter's insightful analysis restores an important social and materialist element to Leopold's early wilderness thought and rescues the conservationist from the morass of some bad intellectual history, I think it is still the case that Leopold's motives for preserving wilderness in the public domain at the time MacKaye proposed the Appalachian Trail were based upon a rather modest social philosophy, one that, at least in 1921, had little to say beyond the call for the protection and provision of primitive recreational values for the American public. As the decade wore on, however, it is clear that Leopold would augment these arguments for wilderness protection with broader cultural and civic justifications, including classic Progressive claims about the contribution of wild lands and sentiments to the American character and a greater public interest in the wilderness. By the 1940s, he was regularly employing ecological rationales for protecting wilderness, although a certain amount of tendentiousness surrounds discussions about the continuity of his philosophical commitments over this period (we will discuss Leopold's contributions in the next chapter).[72]

MacKaye was certainly sympathetic to Leopold's early arguments; they were quite similar to his own. Still, MacKaye went a bit further than Leopold during the early 1920s with respect to the integration of community values and the cultural aspect of regionalism into wilderness planning and preservation. Leopold, for his part, applauded MacKaye's regional philosophy, reacting positively in 1930 to an article MacKaye had recently published on the subject in the *Journal of Forestry* with a wry dig at their shared profession. "This kind of thing [regionalism] is what foresters need," Leopold wrote in a personal letter to MacKaye, "even though the majority of them will be incapable of understanding it."[73] Reciprocating, MacKaye observed that Leopold's 1920s writings about wilderness provided "one of the very few contributions thus far to the psychology of regional planning."[74] It was also clear that MacKaye saw the regional mission as part of the professional management of natural resources at the time, observing that the RPAA "seems to be a development of the conservation movement of the Roosevelt–Pinchot days."[75]

Despite this conclusion, however, MacKaye's regionalist Appalachian project never really caught on in conservation or wilderness preservationist circles. While the hiking trail would become a reality in the ensuing decades, it would not develop into the instrument of social reform that MacKaye outlined in his original proposal, a political verdict that MacKaye had certainly faced before during his stint in the Labor Department. Ronald Foresta traces the Trail's eventual status as an "alternative to nonconstructive urban leisure" to the usurpation of the Trail's communitarian goals by professional planners and land managers interested chiefly in protecting a recreation facility, and to the virtual abandonment of the Trail by radicals and the working class, the constituency on which MacKaye had pinned his early hopes.[76] The Trail's failure to become a Roycean wise province and the relative invisibility of MacKaye's thought in conservation history suggest a schism between the regional planning and conservation movements during this time. Indeed, despite the philosophical compatibility and even collaborative efforts between MacKaye and Leopold (e.g., the founding of the Wilderness Society), the relationship seems best characterized as one of missed opportunities. Robert Gottlieb puts it well when he notes that "The connection between conservationists and community planners never did extend beyond these initial ties [between MacKaye and Leopold], particularly as conservationist groups such as the Wilderness Society and the Sierra Club divorced themselves from the issues and concerns of radical urban and industrial movements during the Depression years."[77] The ironic consequence of this split, what Robert Dorman refers to as a "single-focus environmental politics," was that wilderness actually became more endangered than ever before:

Quite simply, if the successful advocacy of a Bernard DeVoto or the lobbying of Leopold and MacKaye's Wilderness Society might arouse public pressure to prevent the despoliation of a wilderness patch out in the hinterland (like Dinosaur National Monument), it little affected or referred to conditions, lifestyles, and attitudes back in the urban cores. Because this setting (where most Americans lived fifty weeks a year) was omitted, that wilderness patch remained vulnerable to all manner of urbanoid "glaciation," no matter how benevolently intended—it might begin with a mere few access roads to allow the public to see the sights the preservationists had promoted as worth seeing. Thus the ill-prepared cultural foundation of environmentalism."[78]

This is not to suggest that MacKaye dropped his regional philosophy after the original support for his Appalachian project waned and the RPAA drifted apart in the mid-1930s, or that Leopold was unaware of the need to adopt a broader perspective on wilderness planning that included a range of urban and rural land uses. Nevertheless, the more progressive and innovative elements of MacKaye's Trail proposal, having never taken hold in the conservation movement and so closely tied to the fate of the RPAA, have all but disappeared from the annals of American conservation history. I believe that this is regrettable, because it seems to me that MacKaye presents us with an intriguing environmental philosophy, particularly with respect to our thinking about the relationship between the values of the human community and public justification for conserving and protecting wilderness.

Conclusion: MacKaye's Place in the Wilderness Debate

Earlier in this chapter I complained that MacKaye has been neglected in the contemporary debate over the meaning of wilderness in American culture and society. This contest, in a general sense, is between what we might label environmental "historicists" or "constructivists" like William Cronon, and environmental "essentialists," such as the poet and essayist Gary Snyder and the philosopher Holmes Rolston. Cronon has done the most to advance the historicist line on wilderness, especially in his provocative and well-known essay, "The Trouble with Wilderness; or, Getting Back to the Wrong Nature," which appeared in his edited volume of revisionist papers on the human–nature relationship, *Uncommon Ground*.[79] In his opinion, the inherited wilderness idea is deeply flawed and needs to be "rethought":

The trouble with wilderness is that it quietly expresses and reproduces the very values that its devotees seek to reject. The flight from history that is very nearly the core of wilderness represents the false hope of an escape from responsibility. . . . The dream of an unworked natural landscape is very much the fantasy of people who have never themselves had to work to make a living—urban folk for whom food comes from a supermarket or a restaurant instead of a field. . . . Wilderness embodies a dualistic vision in which the human is entirely outside the natural. . . . In its flight from history, in its siren song of escape, in its reproduction of the dangerous dualism that sets humans outside of nature—in all of these ways, wilderness poses a serious threat to responsible environmentalism at the end of the twentieth century.[80]

Instead, Cronon writes, we should accept the fact that wilderness is a profoundly human creation, an evolving social product that has been variously conflated with the myth of the garden, the Romantic sublime, and nostalgia for the vanishing or lost frontier. According to Cronon, many of these images still persist in modern wilderness thinking, hopelessly entrancing environmentalists with "the illusion that we can escape the cares and troubles of the world in which our past has ensnared us."[81] Cronon argues that the negative consequences flowing out of these faulty myths of wilderness held by modern environmentalists are numerous, including the churlish devaluation of human labor on the land, the neglect of the more prosaic landscapes of the town and city in favor of the pristine, "big outside," and an elitist disregard of the plight of the urban and rural poor, who live in places far removed from the million-acre roadless areas of environmentalists' fancy.

In response, essentialist critics like Gary Snyder have suggested that such historicist analyses of the wilderness concept are little more than "dumb arguments being put forth by high-paid intellectual types in which they are trying to knock Nature, knock the people who value Nature, and still come out smelling smart and progressive."[82] Snyder's blunt phrasing aside, his employment of an upper-case "N" when referring to nature speaks to essentialists' reverence for the metaphysical realism of the wilderness concept, a commitment shared by the environmental philosopher Holmes Rolston. Contrary to Cronon's assertion of the cultural dependence of the wilderness idea, Rolston argues for a moral universalism based on a strongly nonanthropocentric view of value in wild nature:

Wilderness is not a state of mind; it is what existed before there were states of mind. We may not have noumenal access to absolutes; we do have access to some remarkable phenomena that have taken place and continue to take place outside our minds, outside our cultures. Some of such nature ought to continue to exist, wild ecosystems, over and beyond whatever of nature (what "wildness") we humans embody within ourselves or need for ourselves.[83]

Rolston derives an ethical imperative for conserving wilderness from a more general philosophical claim about "remarkable phenomena" of an autonomous nature. There are objective natural values "out there" in the world that we do not totally command or exhaust with our cultural images and preferences regarding wildness, whatever they may be at any one time and place. The recognition of these culturally independent natural values immediately gives rise to a series of ethical duties and obligations that we must abide by if we are to have a principled relationship with the environment.

It is, however, a mistake to view Cronon's and others' historicist orientation toward the meaning and significance of wilderness within a changing culture and society as supporting the more radical claim that wild landscapes themselves are purely inventions of human thought; i.e., that they do not exist except as mythical representations in our shifting cultural self-images. Critics like Rolston seem to think that arguments for the cultural and historical roots of the wilderness idea and our environmental values imply an idealist position in which physical nature is thought to be only a projection of the human mind (or perhaps many human minds working in cultural concert). Of course, Cronon and other like-minded historicists would not agree with such a position; their constructivism is epistemological and ethical (that is, having more to do with how we come to know and value wilderness) rather than metaphysical. In this particular fight, Rolston and other "nature essentialists" would seem to be wrestling with a man of straw.

In light of the struggle over the meaning and utility of the wilderness idea in contemporary American environmentalism, we might ask how Benton MacKaye's earlier wilderness philosophy would fit within the contemporary debate. It should be clear from the preceding discussion that MacKaye's culturally driven views of wilderness conservation—his linkage of the protection of primeval environments with social reform, his integrated concern for the urban and wild landscapes of the region, and his desire to develop the enriching "influence" of wild nature on modern American society—would mark him as one of the key progenitors of wilderness constructivism. Consider, for example, one of the major recommendations Cronon makes near the end of his essay: "We need to embrace the full continuum of a natural landscape that is also cultural, in which the city, the suburb, the pastoral, and the wild each has its proper place, which we permit ourselves to celebrate without needlessly denigrating the others."[84] MacKaye (and Mumford for that matter) would have wholeheartedly agreed.

I believe that MacKaye's justification for wilderness protection was at its core a pragmatic claim about the role this kind of planned regional conservation project could play in the revitalization of communal values and civic life, including the reform and reconstruction of economic, industrial, and demographic trends along the eastern portion of the country. MacKaye did not seek to ground his arguments for wilderness conservation in the Appalachian region in any sort of foundational metaphysical position about the value of wild nature, i.e., those ahistorical, mythic images of the natural world that so rightly trouble historicists like Cronon. Rather, his justification for preserving wilderness was drawn primarily from a desire to expand the "primeval influence" in American society, and consequently to nourish the growth of the communal spirit and the democratic culture of the common mind. These social and moral ends—the goals of MacKaye's environmentalism—certainly mirrored Royce's call for a "wise" provincialism, even if the conservationist never explicitly articulated his intellectual debts to his former philosophy professor at Harvard.

Moreover, far from subscribing to the ideal of the unworked landscape, MacKaye sought a balanced regional environment that included urban, agrarian, and primeval elements in a reconfigured relationship, one that encouraged a more cooperative and democratic economic order and a socially authentic form of human labor on the earth. All this supports the judgment that for MacKaye, wilderness preservation was part of a larger vision that saw in conservation, not just a means for protecting the natural environment from metropolitan insults, but a Progressive tool for reforming the moral and political community and a means to pursue the founding of an alternative indigenous social and cultural order within a metropolitan age.

In his recent book *Rewilding North America*, wilderness activist and former Earth First! figure Dave Foreman claims MacKaye's Appalachian Trail idea as a philosophical and practical predecessor to the Wildlands Project, an attempt to "reconnect, restore, and rewild" North America that takes its marching orders from certain elements within the fields of conservation biology and landscape ecology.[85] In a nutshell, the Wildlands Project embraces a bold and large-scale conservation vision. Among its many goals are the restoration and protection of wide-ranging carnivores in their native ecosystems, the elimination of barriers to movement of wildlife across the landscape, the removal of invasive species and livestock from most of the public lands, and a host of strategies for returning and protecting big-scale wilderness over large swaths of the continent.

Although MacKaye's wilderness philosophy is compatible with isolated parts of the rewilding agenda (for example, I think MacKaye would have applauded some of the Wildlands planning efforts on behalf of

greater connectivity of the landscape and increased attention to the protection of roadless areas), I think Foreman and many of his Wildlands
Project colleagues have assumed a much more rigid and dogmatic
posture toward wilderness restoration and preservation than MacKaye
would have been comfortable with. Consider, for example, the following statement by rewilding boosters Michael Soulé and Reed Noss, taken
from an essay in the journal *Wild Earth,* the official publication of the
Wildlands Project. Here, Soulé and Noss, the scientific leaders of the
movement, address advocates' concerns about potential public resistance
to the Wildlands agenda.

Some activists are excessively anxious about the attitudes of certain stakeholders, particularly those with negative perceptions of wolves or other carnivores.
There is a danger in granting too much weight during the design phase to such
considerations, and letting politics interfere prematurely with reserve planning.
A conservation plan cannot give equal weight to biocentric and socioeconomic
goals, or the former will never be realized. Biology has to be the "bottom line."
. . . Timidity in conservation planning and implementation is a betrayal of the
land.[86]

For Soulé and Noss, the business of rewilding demands that we place
biocentric values front and center in the conservation enterprise.
"Politics," however, which presumably includes public debate about and
criticism of the merits and overall goals of the rewilding effort, should
be kept from "prematurely" interfering with the planning and design of
biological reserves. The conservation planning process, in other words,
is purely scientific (biological) in character. More moderate approaches
are summarily rejected; indeed, failure to advance the unswerving biocentric rewilding agenda in a conservation project is a "betrayal" of the
natural world.

Foreman's remarks notwithstanding, it is difficult to see how this way
of thinking has any real claim to the MacKaye inheritance. The deeper
civic and cultural currents of MacKaye's wilderness philosophy seem to
have been completely lost. Unlike MacKaye's effort to build a philosophy that promoted wilderness values while respecting (and revivifying)
rural traditions and sustaining working landscapes, rewilding advocates
appear to view many of these very same stakeholders (e.g., rural producers) as little more than obstacles to the wilderness preservation
agenda. Even citizen conservationists are marginalized in the Wildlands

vision. Their role seems mostly limited to helping Wildlands Project scientists and advocates implement a biologically predetermined conservation plan rather than, for example, taking an active part in the formulation of the values and objectives of a broad-based wilderness recovery strategy.[87] The philosophical headwaters of the Wildlands Project are therefore not to be found in the third way environmentalism of MacKaye's interwar environmental thought, but rather in the biocentric environmentalism of the deep ecologists.

Given these current debates over the conceptual and practical implications of the wilderness idea and its significance for contemporary environmentalism, I believe that MacKaye's work demands more of our attention today. This is especially true if American environmentalism is, as the political theorist Leslie Thiele has suggested, gravitating toward more "co-evolutionary" approaches, those that seek the integration of our social and ecological commitments rather than the adoption of an uncompromising environmental preservationism based on the presumed incompatibility of environmental values with the human political economy.[88] In the end, I think that MacKaye's Appalachian vision is a reminder that our solicitude toward wilderness, despite its historical tendency to draw environmentalists' attention elsewhere, need not compete with a concern for the social, moral, and economic health of the community. Proper conservation of the wilderness may in fact be the key to the development of good community life, the missing vehicle for the delivery of Royce's quaint, yet still compelling ideal of the wise province.

5

Aldo Leopold, Land Health, and the Public Interest

The Father of Environmental Ethics

Unlike Benton MacKaye (and, for that matter, Bailey and Mumford), Aldo Leopold enjoys a commanding position in the history of American environmental thought. Much of this eminence may be attributed to Leopold's powerful literary legacy, which for most readers centers on one small book. *A Sand County Almanac,*[1] Leopold's beautiful collection of nature sketches, conservationist elegies, and philosophical reflections, is widely recognized as a masterpiece in the environmentalist literature. Along with *Walden* and *Silent Spring*[2] it stands as one of the few books in the canon widely acknowledged to have shaped our modern environmental consciousness. It is also the work that more than any other is identified as the founding document of contemporary environmental ethics. Perhaps because of the weight he carries in the intellectual origins and development of the field, and because his life experiences and writings are so rich and full of philosophical import, the exact nature of Leopold's legacy for environmental ethics has not gone uncontested. For example, many observers, probably most, view Leopold's mature position as expressed in the land ethic as displaying a form of nonanthropocentrism, emphasizing the human-independent moral status (variously understood) of ecological systems and processes. A smaller number of others, however, see instead a more humble, more ecologically chastened humanism in his work. To complicate matters, there seems to be textual evidence supporting both readings, not only in *Sand County*, but also in Leopold's earlier essays, many of which have only seen publication in the past two decades.

In the following pages I propose an alternative approach to Leopold's thought that I think avoids taking sides in the nonanthropocentrist–anthropocentrist debate, at least as this debate has unfolded in the literature. In line with the interpretive tack I have followed with Bailey, MacKaye, and Mumford, here I want to consider Leopold's views in broader conceptual terms than are typically used in environmentalist discussions. More exactly, I would like to read Leopold not as a provincial "nature philosopher" focused on philosophical questions of "moral considerability," but rather as a more public-minded thinker, one attentive to the problems created by materialistic ideals of American progress and to the proper constitution of "the public interest." These ideas were, I believe, a significant part of Leopold's conservation vision, yet I don't think that this broader critique of the technological and commercial drift of American society and Leopold's positive articulation of the public interest have been sufficiently appreciated in environmental ethics discussions.

As we will see, this reading does not demand that we ignore or underplay Leopold's specific environmental ethical views so much as it shifts attention to their place within his attempt, as the most prominent third way thinker, to articulate a notion of the public interest that ran counter to narrow, mainstream utilitarian and technocratic visions. I will suggest that the key to Leopold's strategy was his employment of "land health" as a substantive notion of the public interest in his later work. If my discussion is on the mark in the following pages, then Leopold deserves to be viewed as much a "public philosopher"—that is, a thinker who spoke plainly to issues of great social and political significance—as an environmental philosopher, in the narrower sense of one primarily concerned with questions surrounding the value of nonhuman nature.

From Forester to Land Ethicist

As I have mentioned, Leopold is fortunate to have received a great amount of scholarly scrutiny in the past three decades. His biography is therefore relatively well known in environmental studies circles. Still, I think it is helpful to spend some time reviewing the high points of his life and work because they provide context for our later discussion.

A midwesterner like Liberty Hyde Bailey, Aldo Leopold was born in Burlington, Iowa, in 1887. Growing up along the Mississippi River, the young Leopold had no shortage of opportunities to explore the dramas of the natural world, and he soon developed a sharp eye for the intricacies of environmental phenomena, as well as the seeds of an aesthetic and ethical appreciation of flora and fauna that would come into full bloom in his later writing. In 1904, Leopold went east to spend a year at the Lawrenceville School in New Jersey, where his zeal for all things out-of-doors and his fondness for long hikes in the New Jersey countryside earned him the nickname "the naturalist" among his classmates.[3] Leopold's growing interest in natural history and conservation soon led him to the Sheffield Scientific School at Yale University, which he entered in 1905. The following year, he began his studies at the Yale Forest School, the nation's first graduate school of forestry. Established only a few years before Leopold's arrival with a gift from the Gifford Pinchot family, the Forest School reflected the philosophical and administrative bent of the Roosevelt–Pinchot conservation agenda. Its mission was to train a new breed of professional foresters to manage the fledgling national forest reserves in an efficient and scientific manner, one that ensured the sustained production of timber and forage and the protection of forest watersheds from overcutting and degradation of critical water supplies.[4] In 1908, the university awarded Leopold a master's degree in forestry.

Like his future colleague and conservation ally Benton MacKaye, Leopold was one of the nation's first professionally trained foresters, spending all but one of the next 15 years of his life working for the U.S. Forest Service in Arizona and New Mexico, which comprised the Service's new Southwest District (District 3). Leopold's early years on the Apache National Forest in the Arizona territory were spent on a variety of tasks, from timber reconnaissance to predator control. The latter task resulted in the infamous shooting of the wolf memorialized decades later in his essay "Thinking Like a Mountain," which appears in *A Sand County Almanac*. In step with other conservation professionals (and most citizens) of the time, in his early years Leopold viewed wolves, mountain lions, coyotes, foxes, and other predatory animals as worthless "varmints" that preyed on valuable livestock and game animals. It was an attitude that he would later look back upon as woefully misinformed and morally juvenile.

Leopold quickly moved up the Forest Service ranks, from assistant on the Apache to supervisor of New Mexico's Carson National Forest. A prolonged illness in 1913 took him away from his supervisor duties for more than a year; when he returned to work, it was as an administrator of the district's Office of Grazing in Albuquerque, New Mexico. In this new position, Leopold focused primarily on issues relating to game conservation, promoting the cause around the state and working to help establish several game protective associations.[5] In 1918, with wartime support for game conservation efforts nearly all dried up, Leopold left the Forest Service to take a position as secretary of the Albuquerque Chamber of Commerce, where he hoped to continue to advance his game conservation agenda in the region. A year later, however, he was back with the Forest Service, this time as chief of operations for the district, a position which carried with it a demanding set of responsibilities, from personnel and finance matters to fire fighting and road and trail construction on the district's twenty million acres of national forest lands.[6]

Over the course of the next 5 years, Leopold would become engaged in a group of conservation and management issues in the Southwest that would take him well beyond the traditional forestry concerns of the period, including landmark early efforts at wilderness protection. For example, his 1921 article in the *Journal of Forestry*, "The Wilderness and Its Place in Forest Recreation Policy," argued that, at least in some cases, the principle of "highest use" as articulated within the reigning Pinchot model of resource conservation required setting aside wilderness areas so that they could provide "primitive" recreation experiences.[7] As Curt Meine observes, Leopold's early argument had its desired impact, opening the subject of wilderness preservation within the forestry community.[8] Three years later, as a result of Leopold's efforts to promote wilderness preservation in national forests (as well as those of Forest Service colleagues such as landscape architect Arthur Carhart), the Gila Wilderness Area was established in New Mexico. Leopold continued to write on the wilderness issue into the mid-1920s, enlarging his arguments along the way to incorporate the cultural and historical values carried by wilderness landscapes, further underscoring their public importance and social value.[9]

During this same period, he also began to develop a sophisticated view of the functional ecology of southwestern watersheds, knowledge that grew directly out of his field inspections. He observed at first hand the damage caused by overgrazing in the mountain valleys and its threat to what he depicted as the "hair-trigger" biological equilibrium of the arid southwestern landscape.[10] Erosion, siltation of rivers, mineral exhaustion, loss of farmland, and the lack of irrigation all suggested that human settlement in the region was on an unsustainable path, one that was posted with a growing number of ecological warning signs. Leopold documented these conditions in a series of addresses and articles in the early and mid-1920s. One of the most penetrating essays he wrote on the subject was a 1923 paper titled "Some Fundamentals of Conservation in the Southwest," which would not see publication until 1979, when it appeared in the journal *Environmental Ethics*.[11] This essay captures what is perhaps Leopold's first real attempt in print to wrestle with deeper philosophical aspects of the human–nature relationship and its implications for cultural practices in the southwestern landscape. Leopold's remarks in "Some Fundamentals" have generated great interest among environmental philosophers, mostly because of his open flirtation with organicism and a nonanthropocentric worldview in what would prove to be a rare indulgence in metaphysical speculation.

In 1924 Leopold took a position with the U.S. Forest Products Laboratory in Madison, Wisconsin. By all accounts, he was out of place amidst the lab's engineers and scientists. His prodigious writing talents and organizational skills, however, proved to be a great asset for the lab's work.[12] In Madison, Leopold oversaw the lab's program to reduce industrial wood waste, writing articles such as "The Home Builder Conserves," which sought to link conservation to individual consumer behavior as well as the practice of good citizenship.[13] By 1928, however, he was ready to move on. At the end of June in that year, he left the Forest Service to conduct a major game survey for the Sporting Arms and Ammunitions Manufacturers' Institute. For 18 months, Leopold toured the game fields of the upper Midwest, investigating habitat conditions, talking with farmers and other citizens, haunting local libraries, and consulting public officials.[14] In 1931, he would compile all this information in his *Report on a Game Survey of the North Central States*. The document instantly established him as a leading national authority on game management.[15] Leopold's reputation would be further cemented 2 years later with the appearance of his book *Game Management*, which would exert an enormous influence over wildlife management and conservation efforts for decades.[16] By that time, Leopold had also been hired by the University of Wisconsin in Madison as professor of game management in the Department of Agricultural Economics, placing him in a key professional and institutional position to shape a generation of wildlife managers.

Also in 1933, Leopold published "The Conservation Ethic," a milestone in the historical development of American environmental ethics, and an essay that signaled a return to the more philosophical questions he had probed 10 years earlier in "Some Fundamentals."[17] In "Conservation Ethic," he drew from his earlier observations and experiences in the southwestern watersheds as well as his more recent study of wildlife conditions in the north central states. "A harmonious relation to land is more intricate, and of more consequence to civilization, than the historians of its progress seem to realize," he wrote, adding that true civilization was not to be found in the subjugation of a dead earth, but rather was to be defined as "a state of *mutual and interdependent coöperation* between human animals, other animals, plants, and soils, which may be disrupted at any moment by the failure of any of them."[18]

In an interesting analogue to his approach to game management, Leopold discussed three alternative "controls" that might govern the human–nature relationship: legislation, self-interest, and ethics. Concluding that the first two approaches were ultimately insufficient (among other problems, both legislative compulsion and the appeal to the self-interest of the private landowner seemed hopeless in areas already severely degraded and devalued), Leopold argued for the extension of ethical concern to the natural world. "The land-relation is still strictly economic, entailing privileges but not obligations," he wrote, in language that would 15 years later form an indelible part of his essay "The Land Ethic."[19] Leopold's ambivalence toward New Deal conservation—he did not believe the federal approach was sufficiently coordinated or that it effectively addressed the problem of conservation on private land—was also partly tempered during this period as he became involved in the experiment at Coon Valley in southwestern Wisconsin, a New Deal demonstration project of the newly consolidated Soil Erosion Service (SES). Uniting local farmers in a voluntary effort to restore and conserve the land, the Coon Valley project adopted the kind of integrated approach to resource conservation that Leopold had advocated since his early days with the Forest Service.[20]

By any measure, 1935 was a significant year for Leopold's professional and philosophical development. It was then that he acquired the abandoned and eroded Sauk County, Wisconsin, farmland that he and his family would slowly and painstakingly begin to restore to ecological health. The old farm's chicken house, the only building left standing on the property, was cleaned out and eventually converted into a weekend residence.[21] "The shack," as it was affectionately known, would become a focal point in Leopold's mature writing and thinking; his poetic meditations on the natural world at the farm would significantly inform the descriptive essays that would later appear in the first section of *A Sand County Almanac*. That same year, Leopold also returned in earnest to the wilderness question that he had done so much to press within the Forest Service in the early and mid-1920s. He joined forces with the newly organized Wilderness Society, which was devoted to unyielding protection of wilderness lands and values from the road-building frenzy unleashed by industrial tourism in the interwar era.[22]

Finally, in August of 1935, Leopold traveled to Europe, where he and a small group of American foresters toured the German forests and observed the ecological consequences of centuries of intensive management. The decision by German foresters in the early 1800s to substitute fast-growing and high-yield spruce and pines for the region's naturally occurring mixed conifers and hardwoods had led to declining timber yields and extensive soil damage. While a more naturalistic forestry movement was starting to take hold in the country, the dire state of the German forests made a big impression on Leopold, providing a dramatic illustration of the consequences of unhealthy land-management practices.[23]

Leopold's conservation philosophy continued to develop and mature during the second half of the 1930s. His earlier eliminativist view of

wolves and other carnivores was replaced by recognition of the necessary role of predation in ecological systems, and he began to devote
increasing attention to nongame species. All the while, he was moving
toward a more holistic and ecological model of land management. These
hardening commitments were further reinforced by his experiences
during a hunting trip along the Rio Gavilan in the Sierra Madre Occi-
dental of Northern Mexico in September 1936. Physiographic and historical factors had protected the Sierra Madre from the kind of abuses
Leopold had seen in the Southwest and in the intensively managed forests
of Germany. The trip turned out to be a powerful experience for him.
"The Sierra Madre was an almost exact counterpart of my beloved
mountains of Arizona and New Mexico, but fear of Indians had kept
the Sierra free from ranches and livestock. It was here that I first clearly
realized that land is an organism, that all my life I had seen only sick
land, whereas here was a biota still in perfect aboriginal health."[24] The
relatively pristine conditions of the Sierra Madre provided Leopold
with a physical, tangible model of healthy and well-functioning land.
In the process, it also lent him a new kind of scientific justification
for preserving wilderness; we needed to understand the dynamics of
healthy land systems (the undeveloped wilderness) so that we could recognize unhealthy land and begin to reverse the course of land sickness.
Wilderness thus had great value for the emerging science of land ecology,
not to mention for all manner of land conservation and restoration
efforts.

Leopold's expanding scientific and philosophical perspective during
this period is reflected in a remarkable 1939 essay "A Biotic View of
Land," published in the *Journal of Forestry*.[25] He noted that the rise of
ecological science had put the traditional "economic biologist" in a
dilemma: "With one hand he points out the accumulated findings of his
search for utility, or lack of utility, in this or that species; with the other
he lifts the veil from a biota so complex, so conditioned by interwoven
cooperations and competitions, that no man can say where utility begins
or ends." The only valid conclusion, Leopold thought, was that "the
biota as a whole is useful, and the biota includes not only plants and
animals, but soils and waters as well."[26] It was in this groundbreaking
article that Leopold first described in detail his understanding of the

biotic pyramid concept, describing the land as a "fountain of energy" that flowed through "a circuit of soils, plants, and animals."[27] In his discussion, he made an explicit linkage between the structure and complexity of the biotic community (the composition of the layers of the land pyramid) and its healthy functioning, suggesting that the unnatural "violence" of human modifications of the biotic pyramid (e.g., the removal of predators, exhaustion of the soil, the pollution of watercourses) could, if sufficiently severe, produce conditions in which the successful readjustment of the community was no longer possible.[28]

In advancing the "mental idea" of the biotic pyramid and the ecological community model generally, Leopold was influenced by the work of the young British ecologist Charles Elton, whose 1927 book *Animal Ecology* established what have since become the core ecological concepts of "niche," "food chains," and the "pyramid of numbers" (the latter having to do with the size and relative abundance of animals at different trophic levels).[29] Leopold had met Elton in 1931 at the Matamek Conference in Quebec, and the two men had quickly struck up a friendship and correspondence.[30] Leopold was also presumably aware of the work of another British scientist during this period, the plant ecologist Arthur Tansley. In 1935, Tansley published a landmark paper in the journal *Ecology* that coined the term *ecosystem* and helped set the agenda for subsequent work in ecosystem ecology in the 1940s and 1950s.[31] Among the more significant insights in this paper—and one that surely had a major impact on Leopold's notion of the biotic community—was Tansley's integration of biotic and physical processes in a unified conception of the ecosystem. In "A Biotic View of Land," Leopold had thus in essence arrived at an early systemic view of the land and the dynamic interplay of its living and nonliving elements and processes.

Leopold would continue to develop his ecological understanding of the land throughout the 1940s. More and more, he would focus on the unifying notion of "land health" in his writing, a notion informed by his growing understanding of the structure and function of the biotic community. At the same time, he was also writing a number of more lyrical and quasi-biographical essays based on his accumulated managerial experiences and observations of nature, from his early days in the

Southwest to his current reflections at the shack on his Wisconsin farm. Along these lines, in April 1944 he wrote the aforementioned "Thinking Like a Mountain," one of his most well-known essays and a piece that offered a poetic and powerful statement about the evolution of his views on the value of predators and their important place in an ecologically oriented scheme of environmental management.[32]

It is not surprising that Leopold wrote this particular essay while in the midst of his most frustrating and protracted foray into conservation politics: the Wisconsin "deer debates" of the early and mid-1940s. The irruption of white-tailed deer in the state's northern forests, a situation produced by the cumulative effect of a series of management decisions over time, including eradication of predators (such as that lamented in "Thinking Like a Mountain"), closed hunting seasons, and fire protection efforts, was becoming an increasing concern to wildlife managers and foresters in the state. Damage to vegetation and large numbers of starving deer were signs that the herd was simply too large for the range to handle.

In September 1942, Leopold was appointed chairman of a nine-member "Citizens' Deer Committee," which was formed to investigate the situation and submit a report the state's conservation commission. The following winter was harsh, resulting in great dieoffs of deer from starvation and promoting the further denudation of the forage area. In May 1943, Leopold's committee recommended to the conservation commission that an antlerless hunting season be opened that fall. They also recommended closing the buck season to regulate the sex ratio of the deer herd and to emphasize to the public that their plan was not an attempt to cater to sport hunters. Ultimately, the conservation commission decided that a split season (open to both antlerless and buck hunting) should be held that fall, a decision that indicated their reluctance to anger sportsmen, a traditional political power in the state. The resulting hunt in the fall of 1943 did not go as well as the commission and Leopold had hoped. Although more than 100,000 deer were taken over 4 days, the kill was not well distributed geographically, and reports of illegal kills and abuses quickly made the rounds.[33]

Public outcry followed. The Save Wisconsin's Deer Committee, a citizens' organization, was formed and began churning out a newspaper in which the editor pummeled Leopold relentlessly for his support of the herd reduction. Many of the state's northern residents either refused to recognize or simply did not understand the deer population problem. The area's resort owners and recreation and tourism interests in particular did not wish to see one of their region's totemic animals—and one of vacationers' favorites—"slaughtered" under the auspices of the conservation commission.[34] Leopold did not back down, although the tumultuous politics of the situation and public resistance to the very idea of reducing the herd to protect the health of the forests would continue to produce compromise and half-a-loaf solutions from the commission throughout the rest of the decade. He recorded some of his thoughts from this experience in the unpublished 1946 essay "Adventures of a Conservation Commissioner."[35]

During this period, Leopold would also continue to fine tune his broader conservation philosophy. In June 1947 he delivered an address, "The Ecological Conscience," to the conservation committee of the Garden Club of America at their annual meeting in Minneapolis.[36] It was a forceful plea for citizens to assume personal responsibility for conservation of the land, an act that would require cultivation of the "ecological conscience," of Leopold's title. Such responsibility entailed, he said, the recognition of an ethical obligation to promote the "integrity, beauty, and stability" of the community, including the soil, plants, wildlife, and people.[37] The essay was in many respects the culmination of Leopold's ethical evolution over the previous decades, and it stands as one of his most penetrating attempts to combine ethical reflection and argumentation with a scientific view of the land as a dynamic ecological community. His remarks in "Ecological Conscience" about the moral obligation of citizens to practice good land use would appear 2 years later in "The Land Ethic" in *A Sand County Almanac*. The land ethic essay would form part of the final and most philosophical section of the book ("The Upshot"). Other sections in *Sand County* contained more descriptive essays recounting Leopold's observations of the ecological "dramas" on and around the Sauk County shack, and reflective observations about the landscapes encountered in his travels across the midwestern and southwestern United States and northern Mexico.

Leopold struggled to get the manuscript published. Knopf and Macmillan both rejected it, the latter citing wartime paper shortages, the former complaining that the essays were too varied in tone and length to form a coherent volume. Largely through the efforts of Leopold's son Luna the manuscript was finally picked up by Oxford University Press, which published it in 1949.[38] The publication, however, was posthumous; Leopold had died the year before at age 61, suffering a heart attack while helping a neighbor fight a brush fire near the shack. Although *Sand County* was well received upon its publication, it would begin to find a much wider audience in the late 1960s, when an inexpensive paperback edition appeared and Leopold's voice began to resonate with a readership that was increasingly attuned to environmental issues. Today the book is viewed as a masterwork of environmental writing, one that, with Rachel Carson's *Silent Spring*, has also served as one of the few literary bellwethers of modern environmentalism.

Patrimony in Environmental Ethics

While *A Sand County Almanac* is all but worshipped among environmental ethicists today, it is of course the essay "The Land Ethic" that has received the most attention, for understandable reasons. Philosophers and others searching for the moral foundations for a new relationship between humans and the environment were struck in particular by Leopold's provocative statement near the end of his essay, what J. Baird Callicott has referred to as the "summary moral maxim" of the land ethic: "A thing is right when it tends to preserve the integrity, stability, and beauty of the biotic community. It is wrong when it tends otherwise."[39] Drawing directly from several of his earlier essays, in "The Land Ethic" Leopold seamlessly welded the philosophical discussion from "The Conservation Ethic" and "The Ecological Conscience" onto the ecological community or ecosystem concept advanced in "A Biotic View of Land." The result was an ecologically infused moral outlook promoting, among other ends, the obligation to maintain native diversity and soil fertility as key components of a self-renewing, "healthy" landscape.[40] Writing near the end of the essay that it was inconceivable that an appropriately ethical engagement with the land could exist "without love, respect and admiration" for it, and an accompanying high regard for its value, value understood not in dollars but "in the philosophical sense," Leopold seemed to suggest that the land ethic entailed assigning value directly to the biotic community (i.e., intrinsic value).[41] Such a reading would appear to be bolstered by the summary maxim, not to mention by other remarks in the essay where he refers to the "rights" of soils, waters, plants, and animals to "continued existence."[42]

This has indeed been the hegemonic interpretation of the land ethic among environmental philosophers. Leading the group of nonanthropocentric readers of Leopold in environmental ethics is J. Baird Callicott. Callicott has argued consistently for viewing Leopold as speaking to the direct moral status of the biotic community, suggesting that he attributed intrinsic value to natural systems through a Humean–Darwinian framework in which subjective moral sentiments (the ground of ethics, in Callicott's view) were extended from the human community to the biotic one (i.e., nature).[43] Leopold's land ethic, according to Callicott, is therefore both holistic, in that it countenances larger systems and their constituent dynamics and processes, and nonanthropocentric, since it accords these systems a dynamic intrinsic value rather than an instrumental one.

Callicott's reading has been joined by a number of related nonanthropocentric treatments of Leopold in environmental philosophy. George Devall and Bill Sessions, for example, have woven Leopold into the deep ecology tradition, suggesting that he contributed to one of the movement's "ultimate norms": the idea of "biocentric equality," or the intrinsic value held by all organisms and entities on the earth.[44] Similarly, Max Oelschlaeger has described Leopold's ecological philosophy as a "foundational or deep ecology," a "subversive science" that entails a cultural and scientific revolt against mechanism, atomism, and sundry other Cartesian hang-ups.[45] The philosopher Eric Katz has likewise written that Leopold's primary and lasting contribution to environmental ethics is to be found in his rejection of anthropocentrism and his extension of moral consideration from the realm of human persons to nonhumans and the ecological community as a whole.[46]

As I mentioned earlier, the nonanthropocentric claiming of Leopold and the land ethic, although a dominant practice in the field, has not gone unchallenged. One of the most sustained counterpoints to the nonanthropocentric Leopoldian melody in environmental ethics has come from the philosopher Bryan Norton. Norton's approach was first formulated in a 1988 paper, "The Constancy of Leopold's Land Ethic," published in *Conservation Biology*.[47] Arguing against the view that Leopold underwent a profound metaphysical or moral shift in his thinking (i.e., from a utilitarian forester to a nonanthropocentric land ethicist), Norton suggested in this paper that Leopold instead held fairly consistently to an attitude toward nature that was ultimately more anthropocentric than anything else. In particular, Norton claimed that Leopold tapped into philosophical pragmatism through the work of Arthur Twining Hadley, who was the president of Yale University during Leopold's years there as a student. In his 1988 paper, Norton made much of Leopold's acknowledgment of Hadley in his 1923 essay "Some Fundamentals of Conservation in the Southwest," an intriguing reference that took place in the context of one of Leopold's few written reflections on the relative merits of what we would refer to today as anthropocentrism and nonanthropocentrism. Norton wrote that Leopold broke the apparent philosophical logjam between the two positions by borrowing from Hadley a pragmatic definition of truth that effectively allowed the forester-philosopher to sidestep the question of the ultimate validity of nonanthropocentrism as a metaphysical position. Yet Norton also pointed out that Leopold, despite his equivocation on the nonanthropocentrism issue, was nevertheless still able to criticize cultural practices as unsustainable from the more anthropocentric perspective of long-term human survivability.

In summary, whereas philosophers like Callicott have and continue to read Leopold as a nonanthropocentric sage addressing the question of the direct moral considerability of the biotic community, Norton instead sees him as an enlightened environmental manager and pragmatic epistemologist, one concerned with achieving the goal of sustainable land use and judging to be "true" those values and cultural practices that survive the test of experience over time. This position, Norton believes, in effect made Leopold an agnostic on the question of direct moral obligations to nature.[48]

Another philosopher who has attempted to place Leopold within the pragmatist tradition is the John Dewey scholar Larry Hickman, who has argued for a compatibility between Leopold's land ethic and certain features of Dewey's pragmatic naturalism. Dewey's philosophy, according to Hickman, encourages "management" in the sense Leopold understood it: the "intelligent reworking of what is unsatisfactory in order to render it more satisfactory."[49] Beyond this logic of instrumentalism at the level of human action, Hickman also finds common ground between Dewey and Leopold in their shared notion of community, as well as in their views surrounding the embeddedness of culture (and human experience) in natural systems. While Hickman writes that Dewey was not as willing as Leopold to assert the existence of foundational "rights"—as when the latter speaks of the "right" of organisms to their continued existence—Hickman believes that Dewey's pragmatism is entirely capable of supporting the land ethic. The integrity, beauty, and stability of natural systems as expressed in the summary maxim, Hickman proposes, can be defended as "immediately *valued*" goods in the Deweyan sense. That is, they produce a kind of instant "aesthetic delight" in individuals. These goods are in turn *valuable* "as a source of continually emerging values, including those that are aesthetic, economic, scientific, technological, and religious."[50]

As I mentioned at the beginning of this chapter, both the nonanthropocentric and anthropocentric or pragmatic readings of Leopold enjoy considerable textual support in his writing. For every passage that evokes a humanistic tone, it seems that there is an equally resonant passage that suggests a nonanthropocentric stance (indeed, both orientations may be found in *Sand County*, as well as in many of Leopold's other essays). Each interpretation also fits, in various ways, with Leopold's professional experiences and personal biography.[51] In addition, I think it is important to note, and this seems to have gotten lost in the discussion, that both Callicott and Norton, the leading proponents of these alternative readings, have conceded that Leopold employed a combination of anthropocentric and nonanthropocentric arguments in his work, and that his ethical approach to nature was, in Callicott's words, both "deontological", i.e., emphasizing the duties humans owe directly to biotic communities, and "prudential," or oriented toward human welfare and well-being.[52] Whereas Callicott insists on a sharp, almost Kantian cleavage between these two outlooks, Norton deliberately muddies the waters by suggesting that Leopold, in places such as "Some Fundamentals," took a pragmatic line that held both orientations as potential components of a sustainable worldview, one that must be tested and judged in the arena of human cultural experience. In other words, despite his recognition of the prudential (or instrumentalist) aspects of the land ethic, it seems that Callicott has chosen to emphasize the moral standing discussion and the nonanthropocentric dimensions of Leopold's work. And Norton, although he acknowledges the nonanthropocentric aspects of Leopold's thought, has instead chosen to accent its pragmatic epistemological thrust and defends Leopold's work as providing a practical philosophy of environmental management.

While most philosophers and activists have quite naturally paid much attention to the overt environmental ethical dimensions of Leopold's writing, especially those passages that seem to speak to the philosophical status of natural values and the nature of human moral obligation to the land community, they have for the most part ignored the public and political dimension of Leopold's thought. This is, of course, not that surprising, given the relatively narrow focus adopted by most ethicists, especially nonanthropocentrists, on the question of "moral considerability" and their desire to fit Leopold's commitments into one or another ontological theory of environmental value. Bob Pepperman Taylor, however, has recently suggested that we reconsider Leopold's philosophy in terms of its normative political character. Taylor has argued, in fact, that Leopold is more properly seen as a democratic educator and political thinker rather than as a more circumscribed environmental ethicist. For Taylor, Leopold consciously evokes a vanishing American political tradition centered on the values of self-sufficiency, moderation, and restraint, and a corollary sense of civic obligation, in his writing. Leopold's work, Taylor believes, was aimed more at reinvigorating American political culture in a crass utilitarian age than it was focused on the comparatively more truncated philosophical task of establishing the moral value of nature independent from such considerations.[53] On his view, Leopold was articulating a kind of classical political vision fed by the recognition of nature's ability to teach citizens a sense of natural limits, as well as the virtues of humility and personal sacrifice. Taylor further claims that Leopold's attempts to ground his ethical outlook in science—an attempt most significantly advanced in "The Land Ethic"—represents the exception to his political strategy, rather than its grand consummation. Leopold only made such efforts, according to Taylor, in moments of great personal frustration with the moral traditions of democracy.[54]

The reading of Leopold as a civic thinker has also been advanced by historian and Leopold biographer Susan Flader. Specifically, Flader locates Leopold in the republican political tradition, with its orientation toward concerns of citizenship and the active participation in the shared life of the political community.[55] In support of her thesis, Flader notes Leopold's engagement in a number of public causes over the course of his career, from early efforts to organize game protective associations in the Southwest and his attempts to promote civic improvement during his chamber of commerce stint in Albuquerque, to his involvement with the Coon Valley project in the 1930s. Flader also suggests that Leopold's hands-on restoration work at the shack led him to view the husbandry of private land as an act of citizenship, one in which the active restoration and maintenance of land health contributed, not just to the interests of the individual landowner, but also to the good of the community. For Leopold, Flader writes, this community included humans as well as nonhuman flora and fauna.[56]

I sympathize with these efforts to expand the intellectual and activist terrain in which we locate Leopold. In the rest of this chapter, I would like to offer a further spin on this rereading, one that I believe can accommodate, at least to some degree, both the pragmatic and civic-oriented Leopold of Norton, Taylor, and Flader, and the intrinsic value-minded Leopold of Callicott and the nonanthropocentrists. In my view, Leopold is a kind of practical and public philosopher—one concerned with citizens' shared interest in a biologically diverse and fertile, or "healthy," natural environment. I believe that this interpretation is compatible with a pragmatist and civic reading, but that it can also accommodate, at least to some degree, the nonanthropocentrists' view of Leopold as a proponent of nature's intrinsic value. While I do not argue that Leopold should be considered as primarily a political or pragmatic policy theorist, I do believe that the public interest is a significant part of his philosophy, and that it nicely encapsulates his mature scientific and ethical views of the land.

First, however, let us return to Leopold's life and thought to examine just how the notions of public interest and land health developed in his writing, and see how he would eventually fuse them together in a unique third way environmentalist approach in his later work in the 1940s.

From Public Interest to Land Health

One of the earliest indications of Leopold's concern for the public interest may be found in an unpublished manuscript titled "The Civic Life of Albuquerque," which is the text of an address he delivered to the Albuquerque Woman's Club in 1918.[57] At that time he was serving as secretary for the Albuquerque Chamber of Commerce, and his address was clearly intended to be a rousing civic call to arms. Obviously influenced by the reformist impulse of the Progressives, Leopold talked of the need to cultivate the "public-spirit," which he defined as "intelligent unselfishness in practice." He further proposed that this view of the public spirit was nothing less than "the new morality of the Twentieth Century."[58] A deep sense of civic responsibility, Leopold said, was a core part of the American political tradition, one in which the "democratic community and its citizens have certain reciprocal rights and obligations, and for the efficient discharge of any or all of them the intelligent citizen is alternately and absolutely responsible."[59] He went on to share with his audience his wish that all of Albuquerque's social clubs and organizations—from the chamber of commerce and the Rotary and Kiwanis clubs, to the merchants association and various public health and welfare groups—could be organized and "made to work toward a common end."[60] Leopold lamented in particular the lack of representation of trade, craft, and labor organizations in the chamber at that time. While he diplomatically noted the past resistance of "business men" to participation in collective enterprises, he made clear his hope that all groups would soon be able to see the value of "projects so obviously for the common good as to merit universal support."[61]

One such project, Leopold suggested, was the creation of a grand civic center plaza in the heart of the Albuquerque business district. Leopold justified this proposal by pointing out that whenever citizens sought to organize some sort of public interest group or hold an outdoor meeting, they had no choice but to depend on some other citizen, firm, corporation, or other private interest to provide resources, space, or services, often at a price. Instead, Leopold asked, why not construct a community building and public plaza that could provide the space for civic groups and citizens generally to gather and pursue common public programs and enterprises? Leopold's plea for a more functional and accessible civic architecture was certainly in keeping with other Progressive initiatives of the times. Indeed, the civic center proposal calls to mind a design element common to both the era's Social Centers and City Beautiful movements.[62] Leopold also proposed that Albuquerque adopt a Spanish or Pueblo Indian design for all new buildings, which he believed would not only enhance regional culture and identity, but would also instill civic pride and boost the overall commercial prospects of the city.

Leopold would explicitly invoke the normative force of the public interest in "Pioneers and Gullies," a 1924 essay in which he once again chronicled the problem of soil erosion in the valleys of Arizona and New Mexico. There he noted that the area's residents were facing a most critical question: Were they going to "skin" the region and move on, or were they instead going to "found a permanent civilized community with room to grow and improve"?[63] This essay is significant for a number of reasons, including its succinct statement of the erosion problem in the Southwest and its recognition that a sense of obligation to use land wisely on the part of the private landowner (in this case, ranchers and farmers) would ultimately be needed to reverse the problem, a core insight of Leopold's later land ethic. The essay is also notable for Leopold's direct connection between the biophysical conditions of the Southwest and the public interest threatened by private landowners' myopic overgrazing of cattle on an arid landscape. To "protect the public interest," Leopold wrote, key resources should be held in public ownership, and eventually all would need to be put under some form of public regulation.[64] He would soon grow quite pessimistic about the ability of public landownership to solve the conservation problem. Nevertheless, it is clear from this essay that he associated a productive and stable land community with the public interest, attaching in this case a normative weight to the phrase as justification for reforming the ownership of land and the regulation of its use. And, although he did not come out and explicitly define it, Leopold implied that the public interest in the southwestern rangelands referred primarily to the future economic outlook of the region, one that was being threatened by individual landowners motivated by a selfish interest in intensive exploitation of resources.

The following year, Leopold would again enlist the language of the public interest, this time as part of a defense of wilderness against the encroachment of roads. Unlike his usage in "Pioneers and Gullies," however, the public interest now took on a decidedly noneconomic character. In "Wilderness as a Form of Land Use," a key paper in the development of American wilderness philosophy and policy, Leopold argued that the intrusion of roads into wilderness landscapes typically not only made little economic sense, but in the few cases where road building did generate economic returns, "their construction is not necessarily in the public interest, any more than obtaining an economic return from the last vacant lot in a parkless city would be in the public interest." He proposed, on the contrary, that the public interest required "the careful planning of a system of wilderness areas and the permanent reversal of the ordinary economic process within their borders."[65] We can see that Leopold here employed the rhetoric of the public interest as an ethical and political lever against the destructive economic interests he thought were responsible for degrading or destroying public values tied to the land, in this case the cultural and recreational values served by the wilderness that offered Americans a taste of the independence and rugged beauty of the vanished frontier experience.

One of Leopold's most significant appeals to the notion of the public interest in conservation policy would appear in his 1934 essay, "Conservation Economics," in which he delivered a devastating critique of the fragmented and uncoordinated government approach to land conservation under New Deal programs.[66] Leopold was by now quite skeptical about the role of federal land purchases and the use of government subsidies to achieve conservation goals. While these policies certainly had their place, they did not, he believed, strike at the heart of the problem, i.e., the need to reform the land-use standards of the private landowner so that they met the principles of good land husbandry. "The thing to be prevented," he wrote "is destructive private land-use of any and all kinds. The thing to be encouraged is the use of private land in such a way as to combine the public and the private interest to the greatest possible degree."⁶⁷ Whether they knew it or not, private landowners were responsible for safeguarding the public interest in the land:

The landowner whose boundaries happen to include an eagle's nest, or a heron rookery, or a patch of ladyslippers, or a remnant of native prairie sod, or an historical oak, or a string of Indian mounds—such a landowner is the custodian of a public interest, to an equal or sometimes greater degree than one growing a forest, or one fighting a gully. We already have such a welter of single-track statutes that new and separate prohibitions or subsidies for each of these "minority interests" would be hard to enact, and still harder to enforce or administer. Perhaps this impasse offers a clue to the whole broad problem of conservation policy. It suggests the need for some comprehensive fusion of interests, some sweeping simplification of conservation law, which sets up for each parcel of land a single criterion of land-use: "Has the public interest in *all* its resources been protected?"⁶⁸

Leopold was obviously searching for a new approach to conservation policy, one that went beyond the New Deal's atomistic "single-track statues" that he felt were focusing too narrowly on individual pieces of the conservation puzzle (e.g., soils only, or forests only, or particular game or nongame species) rather than the entire land community. The public interest, as a standard for conservation policy and practice on both public and private land, offered the kind of "comprehensive fusion" Leopold was after. Indeed, he thought that conservation would "ultimately boil down to rewarding the private landowner who conserved the public interest,"⁶⁹ the public interest here standing for the aesthetic and historic values found in wildlife and natural elements, and perhaps even a regard for nature's own good.

Following his 3-month trip to Germany in 1935, Leopold once again sounded this theme in an unpublished essay titled "Wilderness." The intensive and heavily managed German forests had made an indelible impression on him, and the German experience was one he definitely did not want to see repeated in the United States. "I hope that we may begin to realize a truth already written bold and clear on the German landscape: that success in most over-artificialized land-uses is bought at the expense of the public interest. The game-keeper buys an unnatural abundance of pheasants at the expense of the public's hawks and owls. The fish-culturist buys an unnatural abundance of fish at the expense of the public's herons, mergansers, and terns. The forester buys an unnatural increment of wood at the expense of the soil."⁷⁰ Although he was not yet able to present his thoughts fully in the conceptual framework and language of ecology—this would come soon enough—it is clear that Leopold, as the year before in "Conservation Economics," was groping toward a definition of the public interest that revolved around the multiple public goods (including recreational and aesthetic values, and perhaps even intrinsic value) at stake in a biologically diverse and fertile land community.

After the mid-1930s, Leopold appears to have drifted away from references to the public interest in his writing. I think that this does not signal a conceptual shift in his thinking so much as it represents an evolving scientific understanding and a corollary shift in his rhetorical strategy. By the end of the 1930s, I believe that Leopold had latched on to what was in part an ecological understanding of the public interest, one informed by a more scientific model of the structure and function of a land system: the concept of a biotic community and the notion of "land health." This provided him with a powerful ecological-scientific and normative definition of the public interest, a definition that he had been toying with in his earlier work but had not yet been able to articulate. In 1939, however, Leopold delivered an address to a joint meeting of the Society of American Foresters and the Ecological Society of America in Milwaukee that revealed how completely he was now engaged with the biotic community concept. The talk, "A Biotic View of Land" (later published in the *Journal of Forestry*), would, as we saw earlier, form the scientific cornerstone of Leopold's land ethic as presented in *A Sand County Almanac*. Whereas several years earlier he had written of the need to achieve a fusion of interests in land for a new, comprehensive conservation policy, he now also saw such conceptual unification in scientific terms. "Ecology," he said, "is a new fusion point for all the natural sciences."[71] The idea of the biotic community, informed by the Eltonian model of the pyramid of numbers and the ecosystem concept of Tansley, among others, had provided Leopold with a coherent and elegant model—a clear mental image—of the workings of the ecosystem, and perhaps more significantly, a standard against which to judge land-use practices and human economic and technological development.

Leopold further expounded on his view of land health as an integrative conservation goal in a number of papers in the early and mid-

1940s, including "Wilderness as a Land Laboratory,"[72] "Conservation: In Whole or In Part?,"[73] and especially "The Land-Health Concept and Conservation,"[74] an essay that remained unpublished until 1999. Reaching back to the organicist ecological paradigm he tested more than a decade earlier in "Some Fundamentals," Leopold presented the notion of land health as analogous to the sense of well-being associated with the proper functioning of a living organism. While his characterization did not require thinking of the land community in a direct organismic sense (i.e., as a distinct living entity with literally defined "interests") and thus did not entail speculative metaphysical commitments to a "live earth" or a subscription to the outmoded Clementsian superorganism paradigm, Leopold did believe that the analogy held insofar as we could intuitively understand and intelligibly speak of the indicators of "land sickness." Trends such as uncontrollable loss of species, the spread of biological "pests," abnormal rates of erosion, accelerating infertility of the soil, and so on could, he thought, accurately be viewed as "symptoms" of poor or declining health in the larger land system.

Leopold would continue to refine the structural and functional criteria of land health throughout the 1940s. In "Biotic Land Use," an essay written in the early 1940s but one that would also not see publication until 1999, he wrote again of the failure of various uncoordinated stopgap measures to achieve conservation goals and suggested that the piecemeal technological approach represented by isolated erosion and flood control efforts, crop rotation, woodlot improvement, and so on, was woefully inadequate for achieving real progress. What these approaches lacked, Leopold thought, was a collective or common purpose. For this, he proposed the "stabilization of land as a whole," or land health.[75]

There were two basic "yardsticks" or criteria by which Leopold thought the stability and health of land might be evaluated and measured: the fertility of the soil and the diversity of flora and fauna.[76] The two indicators were connected through Leopold's appropriation of Elton's concept of food chains and the British zoologist's model of the pyramid of numbers. The land community was stable, Leopold wrote, "when its food chains are so organized as to be able to circulate the same food an indefinite number of times," a process that is essential in maintaining soil fertility.[77] The stability Leopold had in mind did not imply a single equilibrium point for ecological systems; as we discussed earlier, Leopold was reluctant to fully embrace a static view of ecological order. Instead, he apparently had in mind a more dynamic notion of stability, what ecologists today might refer to as the maintenance of ecological resilience and complexity, that is, the capacity of the land (ecosystem) to absorb change and retain a critical threshold of numbers and interactions of species over time.[78] Healthy land was land that held sufficient biotic complexity to maintain its self-organizing functions and remain resilient to perturbations over the long run.[79]

In 1944's "Conservation: In Whole or in Part?" Leopold delivered one of his clearest statements of the land health idea. Writing that conservation was "a state of health in the land," he again evoked the organism analogy. Land health was a "state of vigorous self-renewal" in the soil, water, plants, and animals. "In this sense," he concluded, "land is an organism, and conservation deals with its functional integrity, or health."[80] Again, it is obvious that Leopold was speaking more metaphorically about the organismic qualities of the land, as indicated by his important qualification (i.e., "In this sense . . .").[81] Still, it was a powerful metaphor, not to mention a strong normative standard, and he continued to argue for the adoption of land health as a core conservation goal. It was, he proclaimed, a "unity concept" for land ecology and management.[82] As such, it produced a rule of thumb for public and private conservation efforts. To the extent possible, we should attempt to protect the diversity and complexity of the land community. To his credit, Leopold was neither a naive utopian nor a conservation ideologue on this issue; he acknowledged that human modification of the land was unavoidable and a part of the human condition on the earth. He also wrote, however, that his proposed standard of land health directed that this be done "as gently and as little as possible."[83]

How could one be confident that land health would be achieved where it was most desperately needed, namely, on private land? Leopold reiterated his belief that appeals to profit and the self-interest of the landowner would prove insufficient for this task. Only a sense of community welfare, and a personal pride in the health or "unity" of the land would motivate the landowner and the wider public. Good land use practices, he suggested, must be presented "primarily as an obligation to the community."[84] The context of this remark implies that he was referring chiefly to the human community, that is, as a commitment to the common good or the wider public interest. This interpretation is further supported by his discussion at the end of this essay, where he wrote that a unified conservation must be put forward "as an obligation to the community, rather than an opportunity for profit."[85] Such a reading is also reinforced by Leopold's remarks in essays such as "Planning for Wildlife" written in 1941 (and another paper that has only recently seen publication). As he wrote there, "Stable (i.e., healthy) land is essential to human welfare. Therefore it is unwise to discard any part of the land-mechanism which can be kept in existence by care and forethought. These parts might later be found to contribute to the stability of the land."[86] In "Land Use and Democracy" Leopold again reiterated the connection between land health and human good, specifically, human cultural survival: "Culture is a state of awareness of the land's collective functioning. A culture premised on the destructive dominance of a single species can have but short duration."[87] We can see, then, that Leopold clearly conceived of land health as tied to human interests (in this case, human survival), a paradigm of an anthropocentric position on the value of nature. A culture could neither flourish nor persevere in the long run if it rested upon a "sick" land community.

In "The Land Health Concept and Conservation," written in 1944 but first published in 1999, Leopold restated the anthropocentric case for land health. He also appeared to open the door to include less material, perhaps even quasi-intrinsic values:

The biota is beautiful collectively and in all its parts, but only a few of its parts are useful in the sense of yielding a profit to the private landowner. Healthy land is the only permanently profitable land, but if the biota must be whole to be healthy, and if most of its parts yield no salable products, then we cannot justify ecological conservation on economic grounds alone.... The divorcement of things practical from things beautiful, and the relegation of either to specialized groups or institutions, has always been lethal to social progress, and now it threatens the land-base on which the social structure rests.[88]

While a healthy land system was ultimately critical for long-term productivity, economic arguments and the appeal to landowners' profit motive would, he believed, ultimately fail to support effective conservation on private land. Not only were there simply too many incentives for a landowner to exploit and degrade the land quickly, with little regard for any ecological and social toll, but Leopold pointed out that in many cases significant elements and processes of the land community were deemed to have little or no market value, even though they might be of great significance in maintaining land health over time.

The larger criticism, however, was the hopelessly dualistic approach to valuing nature. Leopold decried the segregation of "things practical from things beautiful," that is, the failure to see the interplay of means and ends in nature, and suggested that real social progress required recognizing the value of and achieving this integration in policy and practice. Otherwise, society would continue to take a dangerously lopsided approach to managing the land. A dominant economic orientation would drive individuals and institutions to undercut the health of the land by attaching only one kind of value, market value, to parts of the biotic community. Without a sense of the biotic community's aesthetic qualities and its greater cultural resonance, which could chasten and restrain the economic motive and prevent society from running roughshod over the land, Leopold thought that the prospects for effective conservation were not encouraging. Consequently, he wrote that the real challenge was to "achieve *both* utility and beauty, and thus permanence."[89] Permanent or long-term land health could not be achieved if it was justified by appeals to economic self-interest alone; it also required a widely shared sense of the aesthetic and cultural value of the land, or values in addition to utility. "In actual practice," Leopold wrote in 1938, "esthetics & utility are completely interwoven. To say we do a thing to land based on either alone is prima facie evidence that we do not understand what we are doing, or are doing it wrong."[90]

From Land Health to the Public Interest

Now although the aesthetic values Leopold had in mind could be construed as anthropocentric and instrumental (inasmuch as they delight, or otherwise satisfy the preferences of humans), I think there is also an increasingly articulate argument for the intrinsic value of nature present in his work in the 1940s. Not surprisingly, this rhetorical trend peaks in "The Land Ethic" essay in *A Sand County Almanac*. A good example is

Leopold's remark, referenced earlier, about the "right" of the land community to "continued existence."[91] Another is his observation that a land ethic reflects the existence of an "ecological conscience" embodying a sense of individual obligation and responsibility for the health of the land, a responsibility that Leopold implied also carried a direct ethical concern for the good of the land itself.[92] Consider, too, his statement, discussed earlier, that it was inconceivable that an ethical orientation toward the land could be adopted "without love, respect, and admiration for land, and a high regard for its value." This value, once again, was for him "far broader than mere economic value"; rather, it was value in "the philosophical sense."[93]

Nevertheless, an acknowledgment of this dimension of Leopold's thought would seem to leave us in something of a muddle. This is because, as we have seen, most environmental ethicists typically make much of the distinction between instrumental and intrinsic values and between wider anthropocentric and nonanthropocentric philosophical orientations. On these subjects, however, Leopold would appear to raise more questions than he answers. For instance, are we to think of land health as an anthropocentric goal? That is, does Leopold justify it by ultimately appealing to its contribution to human desires, values, and ends? If so, how do we square this with his apparent endorsement of the intrinsic value of nature in remarks such as those referenced earlier? Or should we view land health in Leopold's writing as more of a nonanthropocentric standard, that is, as a scientific and normative policy goal advanced to promote the good of the biotic community, independent of its value for humans? If we follow this route, though, what are we to make of his explicit and frequent linkages between the goals of land health and human well-being, including long-term economic stability, as well as other public values? Furthermore, how do we understand Leopold's defense of land health (which may include a notion of intrinsic value) in light of what I have claimed is an abiding concern with the public interest, a concern that, on its face, certainly appears to be an anthropocentric notion?

These are important questions. Before we address them, though, we must remember that Leopold was not consumed, as perhaps many of his philosophical interpreters are, with parsing these kinds of issues in his writing. He was not a professional philosopher, and at any rate his work suggests that he was less interested in all the analytical nuances in discussions of environmental value than he was in bringing his practical knowledge and experiences to bear on conservation questions, occasionally plumbing the philosophical depths to rationalize and make sense of these experiences. Still, it is certainly not a mistake to think of Leopold as a philosopher of sorts. We may consider him to be, like Benton MacKaye, a kind of practical philosopher, based on his involvement with the concrete affairs of human environmental experience and the overall method of his thinking and writing. More to the point, however, is that Leopold resisted, as did Bailey, MacKaye, and Mumford, the simplification and reduction of the diverse field of environmental values to either a one-note, rigid "intrinsicalism" (for lack of a better term) or a crude, narrow utilitarianism.

Accordingly, I would argue that the normative elements of Leopold's notion of land health can be combined in the following manner: First, Leopold's discussion of the "rights" of plants, animals, the land, etc., his notion of an "ecological conscience" that bestows love and respect on the land, and so on, should be seen as an invocation of what environmental ethicists today would refer to as nature's intrinsic value. I think it is undeniable that Leopold felt such emotional, aesthetic, and even spiritual stirrings on a deeply personal level. The intuitive sense of a live earth that he writes of in "Some Fundamentals," the "fierce green fire" he sees die in the wolf's eyes in "Thinking Like a Mountain," and the evolutionary and ecological wonder evoked by the soaring cranes in "Marshland Elegy" in *A Sand County Almanac* all express, to varying degrees, a sense of the intrinsic value of nonhuman nature. Even when this attitude is not floating on the surface of Leopold's prose, it is pulsing through it, especially in his later work. Any interpretation of Leopold as an anthropocentrist or "ethical humanist" must, I believe, come to grips with this aspect of his writing and experience.

On the other hand, and here is where things get a little interesting, I believe Leopold recognized that such attitudes, in addition to their expression of a profound direct ethical regard for the good of the land, could at the same time be instrumentally valuable. Specifically, these commitments could provide a compelling and necessary motivational force within the conscience of private landowners, moving them to promote land health out of a respect for the biotic community as such. Once achieved, land health would contribute many useful and otherwise desirable material and nonmaterial benefits to landowners and society, from nondeclining production of resources and the delight of natural beauty, to the challenge and thrill of wildland recreation and an enriched set of cultural and historical experiences. The public interest would thus be served by individual landowners' promotion of a healthy land system, a source of significant, and in many cases, irreplaceable public values.

It followed, then, that poor land use was against the public interest, just as it was in conflict with an ethical regard for the land and its non-human inhabitants. Leopold traced this logic for us in the foreword to *A Sand County Almanac*: "We abuse land because we regard it as a commodity belonging to us. When we see land as a community to which we belong, we may begin to use it with love and respect. There is no other way for land to survive the impact of mechanized man, nor for us to reap from it the esthetic harvest it is capable, under science, of contributing to culture."[94] Only by adopting a communal bond with the land defined by love and respect for the natural world, i.e., by a recognition of its intrinsic value, can we expect to establish and maintain over the long run a land base upon which our enjoyment of many public goods—economic, aesthetic, and cultural—depends.

To put this argument in a slightly different way, the "right to continued existence" extended by Leopold to the soil, plants, animals, and the land as a whole (as one of the more unequivocal statements of apparent nonuse value) confers something akin to intrinsic value on nonhuman nature. By establishing these elements as possessing a presumptive good or value, their worth is thus affirmed; they are no longer "useless" things to be discarded in the wake of development. Moreover, because land health, according to Leopold, depends on the maintenance of biotic diversity and complexity, these members of the biotic community contribute to that larger and most critical goal, even if, taken individually, they are deemed to possess little or no economic value.

Finally, since a fertile and biologically rich ecosystem is "the only permanently profitable land," and allows the fullest "harvest" of (human)
cultural values, the attribution of moral rights or intrinsic value to nature
is an important step in fulfilling the goal of achieving land health, upon
which a host of public values depend. This, to my mind, is Leopold's
most intriguing expression of pragmatism; his view that in some
cases what were properly seen as moral ends (e.g., the intrinsic value of
nature) could also be employed as critical means to realize further
goals, such as land health, that serve a range of human and nonhuman
needs.

Furthermore, even though Leopold did not employ the language of the
public interest as frequently in his later writing as he did in his work up
until the 1930s, he by no means abandoned his earlier concern with the
collective good of citizens and the protection and defense of the environment as a source of significant public values. Whereas "the public
interest" had once done significant rhetorical work for Leopold, holding
together his earlier arguments for conservation, in the last decade of his
life he turned much of his attention to a more ecologically informed
model that could effectively integrate and justify the conservation
agenda: the concept of land health. As we have seen, this notion, influenced by the work of scientists such as Elton and Tansley, and greatly
informed by Leopold's experiences as a forest and wildlife manager, his
observations in Germany and the Sierra Madre, and by his efforts to
restore the land at the shack, provided him with the "unity concept" he
needed to promote conservation across public and private land. In effect,
with the idea of land health, Leopold was advancing a descriptive definition of the public interest, a substantive standard for conservation
policy that would protect multiple public values in a healthy landscape,
long-term utility as well as beauty, from the abuses of narrow private
interests seeking to extract only short-term profits from the land. In the
long run, Leopold believed that such profits would be subject to the law
of diminishing returns, collected as they were at the expense of the
resilience of the biotic community.

It is here, then, in his effort to advance and defend the idea of land
health, where I think we find Leopold's most intriguing political ideas.
By attempting to redefine the public interest along ecological and broader

cultural lines (i.e., as land health), he was facing a formidable task, one that pitted him against the entrenched economic and political loyalties of mid-twentieth-century America. A relentless critic of commercial "boosterism" and the unbalanced culture of the marketplace, Leopold was confronted with a popular understanding of the public interest that was steeped in economic individualism and the gratuitous accumulation of material goods. Among other liabilities, this prevailing view held no regard for the beauty, diversity, and fertility of the land. "Is it too much to hope," he asked back in 1923, that the booster spirit, "harnessed to a finer ideal, may some day accomplish good as well as big things? That our future standard of civic values may even exclude quantity, obtained at the expense of quality, as not worth while?"[95]

Linked to this long-standing criticism of the growing commercialism and materialistic spirit of modern society was Leopold's disdain for the dizzy embrace of technology by his fellow citizens. He deplored the tendency to glorify tools and machines to the point that these instruments not only dominated cultural life, thus running roughshod over nonmaterial natural goods, but became viewed as ends in themselves, superior to nature's own products and processes. In "The Conservation Ethic" Leopold concluded that this uncritical acceptance of technology was common to the prevailing ideologies of the times; socialism, communism, fascism, and capitalism were all "apostles of a single creed: salvation by machinery."[96] He did not deny the many good things that technology had done to improve the lives of citizens. Although he could be a blistering critic of the American love affair with new gadgets and gizmos, Leopold was no Luddite. It was rather the "excess of tools," the lack of a sense of restraint, that he most regretted. This dynamic, he believed, had produced an unsustainable, out-of-balance relationship between society and the environment, an imbalance that threatened to undercut both over time. Again, however, he was a realist about the issue; he frankly acknowledged that the "tools cannot be dropped." At the same time, Leopold saw no relief in the ameliorative efforts of the technological cycle, in which new instruments were simply created to remedy some of the undesired effects of the old. Science, he knew, could continue to create more tools indefinitely, and some of these inventions might even allow citizens to eke out a minimal existence on what was in essence a ruined landscape. "Yet who wants to be a cell in that kind of body politic?" he asked. "I for one do not."[97]

Despite this gloomy assessment, Leopold believed that his fellow citizens could cast aside the "self-imposed doctrine of ruthless utilitarianism." Indeed, he wrote that it was the saving grace of democracy that society could free itself from the grip of doctrine, provided the collective will was properly exercised. Leopold saw the conservation impulse as one such attempt to achieve this "self-liberation."[98] One of his more significant rhetorical strategies to advance this political effort was his assault on the prevailing social philosophy of progress, which had no place for things "natural, wild, and free."[99] The maintenance of the fertility and diversity of the land over the long run, upon which the beauty and cultural worth of the landscape depended, were for Leopold the real measuring sticks of progress, not economic gain or various feats of technological mastery.[100] On this score, A Sand County Almanac can be read as a rejoinder to the dominant techno-economic notion of progress in Leopold's time. "We of the minority see a law of diminishing returns in progress; our opponents do not," he declared in the book's foreword.[101] The essays that follow provide numerous illustrations of this point, from the "floristic price" of progress lamented in "Prairie Birthday," to the "high priests" of progress responsible for draining the marshes and driving out the cranes in "Marshland Elegy."[102]

Sand County is, in a significant sense, Leopold's attempt to overhaul the philosophy of progress that propelled the earlier Pinchot–Roosevelt model of conservation and that formed the intellectual environment in which he was shaped into a natural resource professional, both at Yale and in the national forests of the American Southwest. Although it purported to be in the public interest, the dominant strain of Progressive conservationism was overwhelmingly skewed toward the goals of efficient production of commodities and a concern for the material well-being of the public. It is clear that Leopold, in Sand County and elsewhere, advanced a very different notion of "progress" and its place in the conservation agenda, and he proffered a conception of the public interest that went beyond satisfaction of individual preferences and the accumulation of consumer goods. Leopold's more qualitative notion of progress thus may be seen as an attempt to reform American social and political philosophy so that it would include the cultural and aesthetic values of the land and reflect the view that "the rocks and rills and templed hills of this America are something more than economic materials, and should not be dedicated exclusively to economic use."[103] His advocacy of these noneconomic environmental goods was thus an attempt to redefine and reaffirm what were for him the deepest commitments of American democracy.[104]

Leopold's long-standing effort to change both land-use practices and societal views of technology, utility, and progress—an effort that would be reinforced by his notion of land health in the late 1930s—underscores the tight links between his normative views of nature and broader concerns about the collective good of the democratic community. Like John Dewey and the other democratic theorists coming out of the Progressive Era, Leopold appealed to a larger sense of community and a widely shared set of public values—in his case, those requiring a healthy, sustainable land system—that tied citizens together and constituted the public interest. Just as Mumford's principles of regional planning may be viewed as offering a political technology for stimulating a Deweyan civic awareness among citizens, Leopold's notion of land health may be seen as providing a practical means for a diverse and diffuse public to recognize its common interest in land conservation in an industrial age. As Dewey wrote in *The Public and Its Problems*:

Indirect, extensive, enduring and serious consequences of conjoint and interacting behavior call a public into existence having a common interest in controlling these consequences. But the machine age has so enormously expanded, multiplied, intensified and complicated the scope of the indirect consequences, has formed such immense and consolidated unions in action, on an impersonal rather than a community basis, that the resultant public cannot identify and distinguish itself. And this discovery is obviously an antecedent condition of any effective organization on its part. Such is our thesis regarding the eclipse which the public idea and interest have undergone.[105]

Leopold's articulation of land health as a dual conservation and sociopolitical goal, one that attempted to define the public interest in citizens' common stake in the ecological, cultural, and aesthetic values of the landscape, called individuals' attention to their membership in a wider community, a Deweyan precondition for effective organization and political action. This suggests an additional and explicitly political value of his concept of land health. It held the potential to play a key role in constructing a common political identity, a shared civic consciousness in an individualistic age and a market-dominated culture. In its most ambitious formulation, Leopold's attempt to call citizens' attention to the issue of land health could help them to recognize that they were part of a larger democratic community, one in which all had a collective interest in a healthy landscape and its provision of multiple public values, now and in the future. With this "unity concept," Leopold also had a means of building diverse policy coalitions composed of sportsmen, preservationists, resource managers, and citizens to support important conservation goals, a political strategy that spoke both to his democratic temperament and to his desire to seek fruitful areas of common ground in public debates.

Despite Leopold's confidence in land health as a normative and scientific standard, however, his most significant attempt to persuade his fellow citizens to accept this as defining the public good in the public arena—the Wisconsin deer debates of the 1940s—was less than inspiring. It seems that despite the best intentions and a firm commitment to promoting the public interest in the management of the state's deer herd, Leopold was ultimately unable to cut through the din of interest group politics. As we saw earlier, his support for thinning the superabundant herd met with considerable public resistance, and he also struggled with his own deer committee members on the issue. Susan Flader suggests that even though Leopold's own understanding of and commitment to the public interest in a healthy landscape was apparent in the deer dilemma, he failed to articulate a truly constructive and unifying sense of this shared good to his fellow citizens. Instead, Flader writes, Leopold tended to frame the problem of land health in the narrower and more apolitical terms of deer population dynamics and herd reduction.[106] Flader's point reveals a possible disconnect between, on the one hand, Leopold's more expansive view of land health, which led him directly into the realm of public affairs and a normative standard of the public interest, and, on the other, his scientific orientation, which saw him focusing on more technical managerial problems and tactics.

While I think Flader is certainly correct to note this conflict, Leopold does seem to have tried, at least at times, to draw attention to the larger picture in his discussions within the conservation commission. As he put it in 1946, "I cannot escape the conviction that if we fail to reduce the deer herd now, we are taking the short view. . . . My plea is that we vote on this issue, not as delegates representing a County, but as statesmen representing the long view of Wisconsin as a community."[107] Perhaps Leopold's lack of effectiveness in the Wisconsin deer case might have been due as much to the resistance of entrenched recreational and commercial interests and the inherent conservatism of public opinion as it was his tendency to fall into a professional managerial approach. Still, it does seem to be the case that despite his own convictions on the matter, he failed to make a truly persuasive case for the links between land health and the public interest in the deer debate (and in his writing around this time). While the pieces of such connections appear in much of his work throughout the 1940s, they only rise to the surface with some reconstructive effort (of the sort I have undertaken in this chapter). Perhaps if Leopold had consciously employed more of the normative language of the public interest that he relied on in some of his earlier writing, this equation of land health and the public good would have been much clearer and easier to discern.

Conclusion: Environmentalism and the Public Interest

My main argument in this chapter has been that there are several philosophical strains in Leopold's work, that these commitments included a regard for social *and* intrinsic natural values, and that these were all tied together by his notion of land health as an integrative scientific and normative standard that defined the public interest in land conservation. The goal of land health therefore contained both nonanthropocentric elements (in its supporting intrinsic-value-of-nature justification) and anthropocentric commitments (in its yield of an array of public values, including aesthetic, cultural, and long-term economic goods). If Leopold were writing today, I think he would frame much of his discussion of land health in the language of "ecosystem services," those natural services, such as purification of water, cycling of nutrients, assimilation of wastes, and regulation of climate that human communities derive from healthy ecological systems. Not only are these services necessary for producing commodities and providing treasured recreational and cultural values, many of them are critical to ensuring our very survival on the planet.[108] Concern for the maintenance of ecological services obviously also supports the protection of the species and natural processes upon which these services depend.

I believe the preceding reading of Leopold's work clarifies the relationship between the many ethical claims and arguments he advances (either directly or indirectly) in his writing, especially work produced during the last decade of his life. I would argue, too, that it situates him somewhat differently in the founding narrative of American environmental thought. As we have discussed, the traditional approach in the field is to view Leopold's contribution through the narrow prism of the land ethic and to characterize his work and thought as mostly pitched at questions surrounding the "moral standing" of the biotic community, or, more simply, nature. Alternatively, I think we should see Leopold's philosophy as a broader and more integrated (if not always very explicit) public philosophy, one that incorporates a notion of the public interest premised on the goal of land health rather than on economic or technocratic foundations. The end of land health, in turn, is supported by multiple ethical claims, including a pragmatic appeal to the intrinsic value or good of the land and its flora and fauna.

To the extent that Leopold is viewed as the "father" of American environmental ethics, this interpretation has important implications for our understanding of the moral foundations of modern environmentalism. Of these, perhaps the most significant is that our environmental ethics, as well as the value we place on our environmental practices and policy goals, do not hinge solely on a theory of the intrinsic value of nature; rather, they form part of a larger philosophical, political, and practical tradition, one represented by Leopold, but also by intellectually sympathetic third way thinkers such as Bailey, MacKaye, and Mumford. In this narrative, environmentalist attitudes and commitments to the good of nature are bound up with the other moral and political aims of citizens: goals such as promoting civic vitality and renewal, strengthening rural culture and community identity, and, in Leopold's work, redirecting citizens' values toward a shared notion of the public interest in the health of the natural environment. The desire of many environmentalists to separate environmental values from human goods in their reform efforts therefore distorts (where it does not miss entirely) the legacy of these thinkers, pushing figures like Leopold into narrow philosophical categories and completely obscuring others, such as Bailey, Mumford, and MacKaye, who had much more on their mind.

I believe that we need to see Leopold as part of the civic pragmatist or third way movement within the conservation and planning community during the first half of the twentieth century. This strategy, in my opinion, provides a fuller view of Leopold's ideas than the conventional histories of environmental ethics and environmental thought that place him in more confined intellectual territory, i.e., as single-handedly negotiating the ethical divide between the conservationist Pinchot and the preservationist Muir. While the received account is not necessarily wrong (as far as it goes), I think it misses the pragmatic and civic nature of Leopold's work, and, more important, its continuity with that of other broad-thinking conservationists and planners during the first few decades of the twentieth century.

Finally, I think Leopold's classic progressivist concern for the public interest offers us a way to reimagine, in a historically powerful way, the relationship between American environmental values and political culture. I believe that environmentalists seeking to defend nature's intrinsic value, as well as those arguing from the more anthropocentric standpoint of securing options and goods for future generations of humans, would benefit from establishing linkages between these ends and a positive articulation of the public interest, given that the latter serves as one of the most politically resonant justifications for social policy and also draws attention to wider conceptions of the public good (over and above individual preferences).[109] Such a union of environmentalist discourse and the public interest not only would enhance the ability of environmentalists to contribute more effectively to environmental policy discussions, but it could also work explicit environmental commitments into substantive definitions of the public interest, just as Leopold did with his argument for land health in the 1930s and 1940s.

The articulation of environmental values as significant (if not essential) public values shared by citizens (rather than purely market goods or culturally independent claims for nature) would, I believe, also make for more expansive and compelling justifications of environmental policies than free-standing arguments that promote the intrinsic value of nature. I think this is a pragmatic and political point that Leopold understood. In the end, I believe it is this practical insight, and not any substantive nonanthropocentric or anthropocentric theory of environmental value, that should be seen as Leopold's most significant and enduring legacy for contemporary environmentalism.

6

The Third Way Today: Natural Systems Agriculture and New Urbanism

Liberty Hyde Bailey, Lewis Mumford, Benton MacKaye, and Aldo Leopold form a significant though previously unrecognized "third way" tradition in American environmental thought, one bonding together a broadly sympathetic group of reform-minded conservationists and regional planners during the first half of the twentieth century. From Bailey's conservation stewardship and Mumford's cultural and civic regionalism to MacKaye's communitarian wilderness philosophy and Leopold's vision of land health in the public interest, this civic pragmatist tradition offers a new way of thinking about the foundations of our environmental policies and practices. It is really an old way, but it appears new because it has been obscured by contemporary efforts in environmentalism to divorce environmental values from human goods; to argue for the "intrinsic value" of nature and assert its independence from our other moral and political ends.

I hope that the discussion in the foregoing chapters makes a persuasive case for reconsidering some of the historical justifications and moral commitments of contemporary environmentalism. In the tradition I have advanced here, a pluralism of values in nature is accepted and openly embraced; environmental values and civic ideals are taken as compatible, even mutually reinforcing commitments, each instrumental to the promotion of the other. Among other things, this account suggests that environmental ethical ideals are not culturally autonomous; they are not isolated from the rest of human experience.

In fact, I believe that a careful reading of this third way tradition leads to a view of the moral foundations of environmentalism in which claims made on behalf of nature are not viewed as what philosophers would call "first principles," but are understood as contingent (although often quite powerful) expressions of the diverse normative commitments of citizens within a moral and political community. In other words, environmental values in this pragmatist-inspired, civic-oriented tradition are in a very real sense social and political values, inasmuch as their expression embodies a substantive public good or interest, and because they also figure in the critical programs of environmental thinkers evaluating the culture and the material conditions of an industrial, urban, and commercial society.

I think this third way tradition offers a potentially transformative understanding of human relations with the environment. Perhaps most significantly, it avoids the excesses of, on the one hand, a purely economic anthropocentrism in which the environment is seen primarily as a fount of resources to be harvested for material benefit and, on the other, a moralistic ecocentrism in which human values and interests are rejected a priori as destructive forces that inevitably undermine nature's intrinsic value. The third way thinkers were not captives of the dualistic, humans-or-nature moral thinking that appears to grip many environmental theorists and advocates today. They advanced a more integrated approach, a novel combination of use and preservation, intrinsic and instrumental values, anthropocentrism and nonanthropocentrism, nature's good and the public interest.

I think it is important to note, too, that this is far from an abstract philosophical tradition in American environmentalism; indeed, the environmental thought of this pragmatic cohort of conservationists and planners grew out of their direct involvement in the land-use issues and problems of their day. These challenges ranged from the degraded (and disappearing) farm landscape and the congestion of the city, to metropolitan encroachment on the wilderness and the precipitous decline of in the health of the land. The thinkers in this third way tradition in environmental thought therefore did not simply reiterate the pragmatism of philosophers like Dewey and Royce. They created a new, environmentally grounded, highly concrete form of pragmatism that in many cases went well beyond the philosophical discussions of the originators of these ideas. They were often much more pragmatic than the pragmatists themselves!

In this chapter I want to bring the third way tradition into the present by examining two important and ongoing attempts to reform American land-use practices and values that I see as present-day, practical manifestations of the civic pragmatist approach in environmental thought. These two initiatives—the Natural Systems Agriculture of Wes Jackson and his colleagues at The Land Institute, and the growing planning and design movement referred to as New Urbanism—are, I believe, excellent embodiments of the ethically pluralistic, action-oriented, and civic-minded approach that is a hallmark of third way environmental thought. These iniatives also reflect the historical tradition of seeing the proper design and conservation of the landscape as promoting the ecological health and livability of these environments, as well as a stronger sense of community and the ends of good citizenship.

Environmentalism and the Problem of Human Agency

Given the great interest in Aldo Leopold's land ethic among environmental philosophers (and environmentalists generally), one might have expected them to have much to say about the ethical and political aspects of American land-use practices, i.e., issues of the sort encountered in such areas as sustainable agriculture, urban and regional planning, and allied fields in resource management. Yet this has generally not been the case. One reason for this neglect, mentioned before, is the enduring wilderness bias of many environmental philosophers and advocates, and the corollary attitude that "autonomous" nature (which of course is represented best by wilderness) should occupy the main policy stage in the field. This view goes along with many environmentalists' long-standing fascination with nonanthropocentrism (which again promises a philosophical outlook most in line with the values of wild nature), and the parallel repugnance for those practices—such as agricultural work and urban development—that are by definition motivated by human values and intentions.

A revealing academic example of this aversion to human activity and design in nature among environmentalists may be found in the lively debate in environmental ethics over the moral status of ecological restoration projects. For many years, environmental ethicists seemed to do little more than sneer at arguments defending ecological restoration as a way to recover lost environmental values by returning degraded landscapes to an approximation of their pre- (human) disturbance conditions. Philosophers such as Robert Elliot and Eric Katz, for example, both advocates of a sharply dualistic view of nature and culture, suggested that such restoration efforts were in effect "faking nature," or were premised on a "big lie," since the restored environments would lack the kind of natural value that previously resided in the landscape as a function of its unmolested evolutionary development.[1] In other words, ecological restoration efforts are fundamentally deceptive; we are led to think that what is being restored is the real thing (i.e., wild nature), when in fact restorations can only produce a lesser, counterfeit nature, one impregnated with "non-natural" human values and deformed by human intentionality.

These sorts of defeatist arguments about restoration have since been challenged (effectively in my view) by Andrew Light, who has distinguished between duplicitous and benevolent motives within restoration projects and drawn attention to the affirmative and pragmatic value of public restoration practices in encouraging an array of pro-environmental and pro-civic behaviors.[2] Light's supportive arguments on this score have been joined by those of other "anti-dualistic" restoration theorists, such as Eric Higgs and William Jordan, who find a similar store of social and cultural values residing in restoration activities.[3]

The two land-use reform movements I discuss in this chapter provide a way of conceptualizing the dynamic interplay of environmental and civic ideals in practice, one that I believe supports the third way view, illustrated throughout this book, that we should not separate human and natural goods, anthropocentric and nonanthropocentric principles, instrumental and intrinsic values. In short, the lessons of practice are fundamentally integrative, placing humans (and human moral and political experience) squarely within the natural and built environments. In the two cases featured later there is thus a recognition and acceptance of human agency in biophysical systems. At the same time, we will see that this agency is prevented from running environmentally amok by consciously imposed practical constraints and normative standards. While these controls probably do not offer the assurance of absolute moral principles of the sort desired by more doctrinaire nonanthropocentrists, they are the most that we can reasonably hope for, given that we need to dwell, produce, consume, and occasionally recreate on the land.

According to a recent report released by the Ecological Society of America, human-influenced ecosystems (including agricultural and urban land systems) will dominate the future of the planet, given projected trends of population growth, urbanization, and resource consumption. Among other things, this means that deliberate intervention in ecological systems to ensure critical ecosystem services, and the design of new "eco-technological" systems to provide desired natural products and services will play an increasingly significant scientific and policy role alongside more established conservation, preservation, and restoration efforts.[4] If the modification (and invention) of environmental systems is thus to some degree unavoidable, we can at the very least ensure that our environmental planning and policy decisions are informed by principles that respect contextual ecological limits, that they make a place for other species and their habitats (perhaps in line with what ecologist Michael Rosenzweig calls "reconciliation ecology"[5]), and that they incorporate strong and articulate notions of sustainability and a regard for community well-being.

I believe that the following two land-use reform movements reflect these sorts of third way commitments and that they provide useful illustrations of how the operation of responsible human agency on the land does not preclude sound environmental practices. They also offer important, tangible extensions and elaborations of the civic pragmatist tradition on the American landscape.

Harvesting an Environmental Ethic: Natural Systems Agriculture

Generally speaking, environmental philosophers and activists have not been very involved in agricultural issues and questions, at least compared with their focus on issues of protecting wild species and wilderness. For instance, on the scholarly side, while publications such as the *Journal of Agricultural and Environmental Ethics* routinely contain papers focused on the ethical aspects of farming, genetically modified food, animal biotechnology, and the like, *Environmental Ethics*, the primary journal within environmental philosophy, and the publication that largely defines the field to the academic community, seldom carries articles addressing agricultural topics. Paul Thompson, a philosopher who has done more than anyone else to bring agricultural issues to the attention of environmental ethicists (and, more important, philosophical attention to agricultural practices) noted this historical neglect of agriculture by environmental philosophers in his 1995 book, *The Spirit of the Soil*.[6] Thompson attributed this lack of interest to a number of factors, including, once again, the pro-wilderness ideology of modern environmentalism, as well as the nature of philosophy as a scholarly field that is entranced by its own in-house puzzles and problems. In the decade since Thompson's book was published, the situation has perhaps changed a little; for example, the latest edition of the large environmental ethics and policy anthology Thompson cites for its neglect of agricultural ethics now includes a section on food and agriculture (perhaps because of Thompson's criticisms).[7] In addition, several papers featuring agricultural issues have appeared in *Environmental Ethics* in the past decade, although probably not as many as one would have expected or hoped.[8]

Thompson is correct that the wilderness bias of academic environmentalists explains much of this continuing lack of attention to agriculture, as does ethicists' long-standing interest in more theoretical questions far removed from any particular geographies (rural or otherwise), historical traditions, and social practices. A further and related explanation, I would submit, is the enduring legacy of the philosophical and cultural founding (or more accurately, refounding) of environmentalism in the 1960s and 1970s, particularly the influence exerted by widely read and cited essays such as that written by the historian Lynn White, Jr. and published in *Science* in 1967, "The Historical Roots of our Ecologic Crisis."[9] White's argument, which many attribute with having set the course of environmental ethical discussions, emphasized the profound and negative historical impact of agriculture and agricultural technology on the natural environment, as well as on the Western worldview and psyche.

In "Historical Roots," White wrote how the development of the heavy plow in Europe in the seventh century, a new technology that "attacked the land" with such violence that cross-plowing was not needed, led to a fundamental metaphysical and moral transformation in the human–nature relationship. "Man's relation to the soil was profoundly changed. Formerly man had been part of nature; now he was the exploiter of nature," White concluded.[10] He argued that the development of modern science and technology took place in a cultural context shaped by Christian teachings that placed humans in a dominant position in the natural order, leading to a form of anthropocentrism in which humans had complete control over the earth and divine license to exploit it. White's thesis, which has cast a long shadow over a generation of environmental ethicists and activists, has a profound alienating effect. In this reading, humans and their agricultural practices are little more than a blight on the natural world. Productive work (including agriculture, but also forestry, ranching, and so on) is inherently destructive, defiling the earth. It is antithetical to a "true" environmental ethic.

While I think the White-ian view on this score has held sway over many environmentalists since the late 1960s, more nuanced writers like Thompson and James Montmarquet have painted a considerably more positive (though not uncritical) picture of the environmental credentials of agrarian thinking, one that is a good deal more textured and nuanced than the portrait sketched by White in his essay.[11] In various ways, this work has shown how in certain strands within the agrarian philosophical tradition, human work on the land is seen as positively transforming both individual character and community values, a process that creates and strengthens normative bonds of kinship between farmers and their environment. Indeed, Thompson notes that in this style of agrarian thinking, humans "shape and transform [nature] as surely as nature shapes and transforms them," and that communities evolved in this way "will see no tension between conservation of wild nature and the duties of the steward."[12] And as we saw in our discussion of Liberty Hyde Bailey, there are even traces of a biocentric environmental ethic in agrarian thought, a strain of thinking that challenges any sweeping thesis about the alienating effects of agricultural work on human–nature relations.

If a growing number of environmental thinkers are recognizing the potential of agriculture and the agrarian philosophical tradition, it is nevertheless true that the modern agricultural paradigm still leaves much to be desired from the standpoint of environmentalism and a moral concern for the health and sustainability of ecological systems. It is one thing to reject White's sweeping claims about the alienation of humans from nature produced by the development of agricultural tools and practices. Among other problems, this argument presents an oversimplified view of human technological development and a similarly undifferentiated and rigid understanding of cultural attitudes. It also completely dismisses the idea—defended by many agrarian environmental writers—that agricultural practices can provide a significant way of knowing and valuing nature, one that should be nurtured and protected in an increasingly urban and commercial society.[13] Still, it is another thing altogether to claim that the current industrial agricultural model—with its reliance on massive chemical inputs, heavy use of fossil fuels, intensive confinement of animals, and the production of crops in biotically simplified monocultures—offers an ethically appropriate model for human—environment relations. Environmentalist defenses of agriculture must have some other model in mind than this.

As indeed, they do. Emerging in the 1970s and 1980s, a wide range of approaches falling under the rubric of "sustainable agriculture" have provided the hope that a reformed agricultural approach, one driven by a concern for soil conservation, the recognition of ecological limits to production, and in some cases, an explicit moral regard for nonhuman species, the land, and/or the welfare of future generations of citizens, could supplant the industrial model and give rise to a new environmental ethic. The historical roots of contemporary efforts in sustainable agriculture reach down into a number of intellectual and scientific layers. These include the earlier views of adaptationist agrarian voices like those of Bailey, the "permanent agriculture" movement spearheaded by Rex Tugwell and Paul Sears in the 1930s and 1940s, the rise of ecological science and ecosystem ecology in the 1950s, and the counterculture communalism and organic farming movements of the 1960s and early 1970s.[14]

While they vary to a greater or lesser degree, contemporary principles and techniques of sustainable agriculture generally employ "softer" technologies, are less reliant on chemical fertilizers and pesticides (natural fertilizers and biological controls are commonly substituted), and are more occupied with maintaining fertility of the soil and overall ecological resilience than the conventional industrial model. Most approaches fitting this description also seek to conserve, to the extent possible in a production landscape, the native diversity of flora and fauna within the farm ecosystem.[15] Whether such approaches fall under the rubric of "ecoagriculture," or "permaculture," or "organic farming," all share a common general principle: Agricultural enterprises should attempt to follow natural systems (including native efficiencies, natural productive strategies, and ecological limits) much more closely than the standard industrial paradigm.[16]

One of the more ambitious and visible efforts to achieve an alternative agricultural regime may be found in the work of Wes Jackson and his allies at The Land Institute, a research and training center in Salina, Kansas, devoted to exploring and promoting the prospects of what Jackson and his colleagues now call Natural Systems Agriculture. For nearly three decades the institute has conducted research on the possibilities of a sustainable agricultural model based on the native prairie ecosystem. Jackson, a geneticist by training, left an academic post in California to found the institute with his wife Dana in 1976.[17] He had become convinced that the industrial agricultural system was leading us to the precipice of ecological disaster. It eroded soil through its reliance on constant tilling; it narrowed nature's genetic base through production-oriented plant breeding; it polluted the landscape with pesticides and chemical fertilizers; and it drew far too heavily on nonrenewable fossil fuel stocks for pesticides and fertilizers, and for running farm machinery. Jackson and his collaborators at The Land Institute began a series of experiments to determine whether an agriculture that used nature as a model could be both productive and ecologically sustainable, and whether it could offer a feasible alternative to the industrial system.

Their research focus is on the development of a "domestic prairie," an agricultural analogue of the native prairie ecosystem. The natural prairie is, Jackson suggests, admirably self-sustaining. It runs on sunlight (and rain); sponsors its own nitrogen fertility; keeps its precious soil covered year-round with perennial plants; and holds pathogens, weeds, and insect pests in check through a variety of natural mechanisms.[18] Perhaps most important, it builds rather than erodes soil. The traditional domestic wheat field, on the other hand, runs on fossil energy derived from oil and gas, is greatly dependent on chemical fertilizers, requires continual tilling, and is pretty much defenseless against pests and pathogens without the application of external controls (e.g., pesticides). It is also highly prone to erosion, owing to the intensive use of chemicals and machinery and the frequent tilling required by annual crops.[19] A primary goal at the institute has thus been to see if it is possible to construct a productive, high-yielding agricultural system based on the self-sustaining, solar-driven, perennial (unplowed) native prairie ecosystem. By modeling the structure of such a system on that of the native prairie, institute scientists hoped they could duplicate many of its natural ecological functions.

Jackson and his colleagues have been especially interested in the potential of a domesticated prairie system that features perennial herbaceous seed-bearing crops (the kind we eat). Such a system, composed of prairie-mimicking polycultural or multispecies mixes (e.g., grasses, legumes, and composites, especially sunflowers) would rely on the deep roots of the perennial plants to hold soil in place throughout the year and to fix nitrogen. This model is therefore a radical departure from the established agricultural regime, which relies on crops grown in annual monocultures (e.g., wheat, corn, and other grains). In addition to determining whether a perennial polyculture could produce high seed yields, Jackson and his team have sought to answer several other questions, including whether such a system could be made productive to the degree that it actually outproduced traditional monocultures. The Land Institute researchers have also been curious to discover the extent to which a perennial polyculture could, like the unplowed prairie, sponsor its own fertility (making large applications of chemicals unnecessary), as well as if it could effectively provide its own weed and pest control (thus being free from herbicides and pesticides).[20]

As their work moved forward in the 1980s and 1990s, Jackson and his colleagues began to get tentative but promising answers to these and other questions. Despite some caveats and qualifications, research at The Land Institute has revealed that high-producing perennials are indeed possible and that perennial polycultures in many cases have the potential to "overyield" (i.e., to outyield seed crops grown in monoculture).

Moreover, there are encouraging signs that mixed perennials can effectively manage weeds, pathogens, and pests, an ability that is largely a function of the greater genetic and species diversity of the mixed stands (which increases the likelihood of resistance among some species in the plot) and the increased amount of time the soil is shaded by the perennial crops. Finally, there are indications that crops grown in a perennial polyculture can create their own nitrogen fertility, at least to some degree, although the evidence is not yet conclusive.[21] While researchers at the institute acknowledge that much more work remains to be done and many more questions need to be answered (they admit that it will likely take several decades of additional research to fully resolve the core questions), Jackson and his team have nonetheless established scientific credibility for the natural systems model. They are making an increasingly compelling case for their approach as a potential supplement, and perhaps ultimately a viable alternative, to traditional industrial monoculture farming.

Although he has written that he did not fully appreciate it at the time, Jackson's founding of The Land Institute and his attempt to create an ecologically sound paradigm of sustainable agriculture draws from a deep scientific, cultural, and philosophical tradition, one that I would suggest includes the four third way thinkers discussed in the previous chapters, especially Liberty Hyde Bailey and Aldo Leopold. Jackson has, in fact, singled out both men in his work. He cites Bailey's *Outlook to Nature* and *The Holy Earth* as advancing key Natural Systems Agriculture tenets, such as the view that nature is the norm for civilization, and the notion that the farmer's task is to live in "right relation" with his natural conditions.[22] Jackson's praise of Leopold has been effusive. No other person in the twentieth century, he writes, was "more responsible for the intellectual underpinnings of our work at The Land Institute."[23] According to Jackson, Leopold's land ethic and overall conservation vision provided the necessary philosophical framework in which ecology could be married to agriculture, thus creating a more holistic agricultural model premised on eco-sustainability rather than production alone. Jackson's jeremiads against the "Baconian–Cartesian worldview," in which science is used as a tool to dissect nature into separate parts in order to manipulate and control it for human purposes, echo Leopold's ecological holism; Jackson also shares his forebear's epistemic modesty and sensitivity to the scope and limits of human knowledge of the natural world.[24]

Besides Bailey and Leopold, Jackson has acknowledged several other intellectual sources, including the poetry of Virgil and the evolutionary vision of Charles Darwin, as well as the work of Sir Albert Howard, the father of organic farming.[25] The contemporary novelist, poet, and neoagrarian thinker Wendell Berry also has clearly influenced Jackson's understanding of the literary and cultural tradition behind his efforts to achieve an alternative agricultural form.

In addition to these diverse influences, I think Jackson's effort also calls to mind the decentralist regionalism of Mumford and MacKaye. For example, Jackson closed his 1980 book *New Roots for Agriculture* with a description of an imaginary Kansas farm community in the year 2030.[26] This solar-powered agrarian utopia had completely accepted and internalized Jackson's sustainability paradigm. While a few large metropolitan centers remained, most urban areas were regional cities composed of no more than 40,000 people. The utopian farm was powered by renewable energy (solar, wind, and hydropower) and based on an agricultural blend of limited monoculture in appropriate areas and mixed herbaceous perennials. Land was no longer privately owned in the sense that it was in 1980 (or is today). In 2030 it was governed by a land trust that oversaw its proper use and that prevented it from being polluted or otherwise degraded. Yet a sense of ownership and the ability to pass on the land through the generations was maintained in Jackson's idealized community. A new land ethic was now being practiced, one that, unlike current methods in economic valuation, did not discount the future.

Culturally, much had also changed. "Most communities," Jackson wrote, "now emphasize the value of history, and history becomes more real when adults tell personal stories which link the past to the present."[27] One of the functions of these narratives was to educate the young about the mistakes of the past, which for Jackson included cautionary tales about "villainous corporations," nuclear power, the hopeless addiction to consumerism, and a litany of environmental abuses. The countercultural qualities of Jackson's idyllic farm community seem amusingly anachronistic 25 years later (in later work he seems to have cast aside some of his more utopian leanings, at least rhetorically). Still, it is a good illustration of some of his intellectual and moral commitments, including the agrarian and regionalist tradition of Bailey, Mumford, and MacKaye (not to mention Ebenezer Howard and Patrick Geddes—note Jackson's reference to a regional city), as well as Leopold's vision of ethical land use, which is manifest in Jackson's rehearsal of Leopold's standard of land health in his criticisms of a consumer lifestyle.

Jackson revealed more of the cultural, ethical, and political aspects of his work at The Land Institute in *Altars of Unhewn Stone*, a collection of essays that often took on a grand and provocative historical tone. "We live," he wrote, in "in a fallen world."[28] Sounding a theme popular among radical environmentalists (especially deep ecologists), Jackson argued that the development of agriculture 10,000 years ago had separated humans from nature, to disastrous spiritual and ecological effects. We had taken control of natural systems, and we were myopically abusing them with our machines, our chemicals, and our faulty ideas of human difference and superiority. All the while, Jackson wrote, we ignored natural limits and discounted the wisdom residing in natural processes. Despite the weight of this social and technological history, Jackson was not about to give up on agriculture; he was not going to go down the primitivist road and advocate a recovery of our hunter-gatherer ways. If agriculture marked the fall, Jackson believed, it could also help to repair the metaphysical and spiritual rift he discerned between humans and nature. To do so, it was clear to him that the agricultural system had to change, that it had to be radically reconfigured. By returning to nature's wisdom and working within the constraints of natural ecological systems (such as the prairie) rather than "hot-wiring" them and bypassing natural control mechanisms, we could bring ourselves back into our lost harmony with the natural world.[29]

While Jackson can at times sound like a deep ecologist in his quasi-religious evocation of "the fall" and his emphasis on repairing the foundational breach between humans and the natural world created by modern agriculture and technology, unlike many deep ecologists, he does not seek to remove human agency from the world, nor does he disparage productive human activity in the environment. Jackson is certainly not willing, as some radical environmentalists are, to sacrifice agricultural landscapes on the altar of wilderness:

> Would Earth First! Activists or Deep Ecologists be as interested in cleaning up East Saint Louis, for example, as they are in defending wilderness? Would Earth First! activists be as fervent about defending a farmer's soil conservation effort of chemical-free crop rotation as they are about spiking a tree or putting sugar in the fuel tank of a bulldozer?
>
> It is possible to love a small acreage in Kansas as much as John Muir loved the entire Sierra Nevada. That is fortunate, for the wilderness of the Sierra will disappear unless little pieces of nonwilderness become intensely loved by lots of people.[30]

Jackson thinks that any environmentalism that leaves agriculture behind is one that is doomed to failure. And even though he has spent his life thinking about, studying, and working on the farm landscape, Jackson recognizes that the city, too, must be included in any comprehensive environmental ethic. "Either all the earth is holy, or it is not. Either every square foot deserves our respect, or none of it does," he concludes.[31]

Jackson's environmental ethic, like the commitments of the historical thinkers in the third way environmental tradition discussed in the earlier chapters, is an interesting and idiosyncratic hodgepodge of normative principles and arguments. As we have seen, in some of his writing Jackson voices what sounds like a resolute nonanthropocentric position. He follows Bailey, for example, in trumpeting the value of the "holy earth," and in his suggestion that the entire landscape possesses a worth (perhaps divine) that goes beyond its usefulness to humans. Yet Jackson, like Bailey before him, also displays more classic anthropocentric commitments in his justifications of sustainability and natural systems agriculture. He has made a point, for instance, of emphasizing that conventional industrial agriculture is ultimately economically inefficient once the true cost of soil erosion and contamination is added into the equation. Specifically, Jackson has claimed that the standard agricultural model is wasteful in its use of materials, water, and energy, squandering precious resources and further adding to the costs of conventional operations. He has also noted that the heavy use of chemical pesticides on conventional farms has been linked to increased risks of human health problems among farmers, including Hodgkin's disease; leukemia; and skin, stomach, and prostate cancers.[32] The industrial agricultural system, therefore, is not only destructive of environmental goods (which may be valued intrinsically), Jackson believes it also fails on anthropocentric and instrumental grounds. It is, once all the accounts are settled, too costly, too inefficient, and too much of a threat to human health and welfare over the long run.

Alternatively, a more ecologically oriented and less fossil fuel- and chemical-dependent agricultural model, one patterned after natural ecosystems, would not only demonstrate a respect for the value or good of the earth (e.g., by being less polluting and more conserving of soil, water, and biological diversity), it would be much more energy and materials efficient and consequently less of a threat to the health of farmers (as well as consumers of agricultural products) and more in tune with our ideas about obligations to future generations. The upshot is that for Jackson, there are strong anthropocentric reasons to support Natural Systems Agriculture in addition to more nonanthropocentric ones. Considered as a whole, the philosophy of sustainability that underpins Jackson's work at The Land Institute is thus informed by a pragmatic suite of interlocking environmental and human value considerations. Both human interests and ecological health, Jackson believes, are ultimately served by the natural systems agricultural model over time.

Jackson's environmental philosophy possesses a further humanistic dimension: a concern for the cultural and civic vitality of the rural community and a desire to defend native democratic commitments against what he sees as the corrupting forces of consumerism and the marketplace. His criticism of the moral foundations of modern capitalism, which runs throughout much of his writing, takes no prisoners:

It is time that we seriously question our economic system, much of which is, after all, based on greed and envy. Now, lest you think I am unpatriotic, consider that there is a big difference between the economic system called capitalism and the political system called democracy. Because I believe in democracy, I have come to regard capitalism as un-American. Capitalism detracts from our democratic ideals partly because it destroys free enterprise. (By definition, capitalism depends on economic growth that must come from exploiting earth's resources and from forcing more and more people to provide services.) With finite resources, the accumulation of capital means that resources fall into the hands of fewer and fewer persons, and the freedom to be enterprising becomes restricted to those few.[33]

According to Jackson, one of the benefits of his model of sustainable agriculture is that it would ultimately produce more equitable distribution of land since the high capital investments required by the traditional corporate industrial farm (i.e., large sums of money tied up in machinery, energy, pesticides and fertilizers, irrigation, and seed) would be greatly reduced in his alternative agricultural system.[34] As a result, true "free enterprise" could operate, with greater opportunity for productive agricultural work now spread across all sectors of society. In addition, Jackson believes that tens of millions of acres of land that are considered to be marginal under the conventional regime (because of the land's potential to erode under current cropping practices) could be farmed using the "softer" natural systems model. More farmland would in turn decrease land prices, which would also make an agricultural living more affordable to a greater number of people.[35]

Jackson's views on the reform of rural land use are dependent upon what is essentially a civic republican vision because he places great stock in the ideal of local, tight-knit, highly participatory communities held together through the bonds of citizenship.

The establishment of a new economic order will require nothing less than the full citizenship that our founding fathers expected of us, which includes the obligation to speak and to participate in communities, in neighborhoods. To build a sustainable society will require nothing less than speaking our minds in wholesome, creative, and responsible ways, moving power from Washington and Topeka back closer to the land, to communities.[36]

Like Bailey, Jackson worries about the decline of the rural citizenry and the effects this will have on American cultural and social stability. While far from perfect, Jackson believes that the rural past yielded greater "cultural resilience"; urban residents who experienced economic hard times could fall back on their rural relatives, whose "cream and eggs economy" could prop everyone up when the bottom dropped out of the commercial markets. Jackson worries that the progressive loss of rural producers means that the older traditions, skills, and values of the small family farm—the very knowledge and commitments he feels are necessary to achieve a more sustainable, decentralized, agricultural life— run the risk of not being passed down to future generations.[37]

These and related concerns drove Jackson and his colleagues to purchase a number of houses, buildings, and land in the small Kansas town of Matfield Green (pop. 60) in the late 1980s and early 1990s. Their goal was to begin the process of community recovery, and at least implicitly, to see if The Land Institute's social and environmental ideals could be realized on a neighborhood scale. In this effort, Jackson and his allies have attempted to learn about the historical ecology and human cultural history of Matfield Green in the hopes of developing it into a model of sustainable living. As he writes,

I have imagined this as a place that could grow bison for meat, as a place where photovoltaic panels could be assembled at the old booster station, where the school could become a gathering place that would be a partial answer to the mall, a place that might attract a few retired people, including professor types, who could bring their pensions, their libraries, and their social security checks to help support themselves and take on the task of setting up the books for ecological community accounting. . . . Our task is to build cultural fortresses to protect our emerging nativeness. They must be strong enough to hold at bay the powers of consumerism, the powers of greed and envy and pride. One of the most effective ways for this to come about would be for our universities to assume the awesome responsibility for both validating and educating those who want to be homecomers—not that they necessarily want to go home, but rather to go someplace and dig in and begin the long search and experiment to become native.[38]

Jackson's project is a pragmatic mixture of the old and new. He wants to both preserve the cultural practices, traditions, and local wisdom required to live sustainably that reside in places like Matfield Green and bolster these well-worn ideas with advanced ecological accounting procedures to measure environmental performance. Furthermore, the project at Matfield Green is also political in nature. Jackson and his allies are seeking to create an alternative moral and economic order, one that resists the highly privatized, utilitarian culture of the market. Jackson's ideal community at Matfield Green is defined by a citizenry that takes a strong interest in the history, civic health, and proper material and ethical direction of its common life. In restoring a lost sense of "nativeness" to culture—in which local places such as Matfield Green and their shared traditions are valued rather than lampooned and seen as unflattering compared with the "official" extractive economic culture of the city and the suburban mall—Jackson thinks that we will be able to adopt the necessary attitudes and practices of an ecologically sustainable and good society. Among other things, Jackson's notion of "nativeness" evokes Benton MacKaye's defense of "indigenous" culture against metropolitan destruction. Indeed, like MacKaye, Jackson views a life lived close to nature as a moral and political defense against modern commercial and industrial corruption, an older provincialism fused to a Progressive ecological vision.

The attempts by Jackson and his partners at The Land Institute to construct an alternative agriculture, then, not only stimulate and draw support from a pluralistic and integrative land ethic, one in which good agricultural principles and practices follow (rather than dominate) nature and in the process benefit both ecological systems and humans, they also (in Jackson's hands) carry with them a civic pragmatism driven by the active participation of citizens in directing the shared environmental and cultural affairs of the community. In weaving environmental values together with such moral, civic, and political ends, Jackson's writing and The Land Institute's mission are another reminder that environmental and human social commitments need not be seen as mutually exclusive. Like the mix of wild and cultivated in the natural systems model, environmental and human values interpenetrate in daily experience.

The Environmental Humanism of New Urbanism

If the naked anthropocentric qualities of agriculture are beyond the pale for many environmentalists, the overwhelmingly human and artifactual nature of the built urban landscape is probably even more disturbing. The ecological degradation linked with urban and suburban land use and the pure artificiality attributed to these landscapes by environmentalist critics would seem to ensure that these landscapes are placed by ethicists in the realm of the "environmentally damned," those places where wilderness (and wildness), biodiversity, naturalness, and other value-laden concepts and qualities cherished by the environmental community are in the shortest of supply, if not, by some definitions, absent altogether. In their distaste for the urban environment, environmental thinkers are in some respects carrying forward the antiurbanism of much of the American intellectual tradition more generally, which, despite a few exceptions, has not developed the kind and degree of aesthetic and romantic attachments to the city that it has to the natural world.[39]

As with the case of agriculture, however, some environmental thinkers have attempted to correct what more than one observer has called a blind spot in American environmentalism when it comes to addressing the ethical questions raised by life in urban environments.[40] Philosopher Alastair Gunn is one theorist who has turned his attention to the urban realm, warning his fellow environmental ethicists of the social irrelevance they court if they continue to ignore cities and other developed areas in their work. "Unfortunately," Gunn writes, "the central concerns of environmental ethics have been and largely continue to be heavily slanted towards animals, plants, endangered species, wilderness, and traditional cultures and not towards the problems of life in industrial, urbanized society where most people now live."[41] Instead of lionizing Aldo Leopold, whom he views as having little to say about modern urban environmental problems and circumstances, Gunn suggests that environmental ethicists would instead be better off turning to the tradition of Ian McHarg, the famed ecological and land-use planner and author of the classic 1967 book, *Design with Nature*.[42]

While I think Leopold's philosophy, especially the concept of land health discussed in chapter 5, is more relevant to contemporary urban and suburban land-use issues than Gunn implies, he is nevertheless correct in his judgment that environmental ethics needs to pay more attention to the cities and to the built landscape if it is to be relevant to a wide audience, not to mention if it is serious about understanding the connections between dominant urban land uses and various environmental problems.

Independent of the question of whether the field should attempt to incorporate an ethics of the built environment itself,[43] there are still compelling reasons, based on environmentalists' traditional concerns for nonhuman nature, for those theorists and activists to address urban land-use issues. The physical design and layout of houses, buildings, parks, and streets; the planning and design of neighborhoods and local and regional transportation systems; and the control of metropolitan and regional growth patterns all have direct and significant implications for consumption of natural resources and the quality of the environment. Indeed, many of these issues bear directly on historically central environmentalist goals, such as sustainable use of resources, the preservation of wilderness and biodiversity, and the protection of wetlands and riparian areas. They also affect efforts to prevent agricultural lands from being converted to commercial and residential developments, as well as the preservation of open space for aesthetic enjoyment and public recreation.

One of the more intriguing and, for some, controversial efforts to reform urban design and land use that has emerged in the past two decades has been advanced by a group of architects and planners under the banner of New Urbanism. In general, New Urbanists are focused on reshaping urban and suburban landscape planning and design at several scales, from the individual building and the block, to the neighborhood and city, to the ecological region or watershed.[44] The more ecologically oriented practitioners of the movement have articulated a comprehensive agenda that attempts to incorporate a respect for natural and agricultural systems, parks, and open space within a proposed framework of traditional neighborhood planning.[45] Many of the New Urbanist ideas are not original to the movement, but are a creative repackaging of earlier planning and architectural traditions.

For example, we can see some of the social philosophy and design elements of the Garden City and City Beautiful movements, as well as the regionalism of Mumford, MacKaye, and their allies in the New Urbanist program. From the Garden City idea and the regionalists, New Urbanists have borrowed a dense design pattern and an emphasis on incorporating natural elements in the urban plan (e.g., parks and greenbelts), as well as many of the earlier movements' communitarian aims. From the City Beautiful movement, they have inherited a concern for civic architecture and public spaces, and an overarching desire for aesthetic improvements in the built environment. New Urbanism also demonstrates the affinity for diverse, mixed-use neighborhoods and compact community structure found in the work of the urban theorist and cultural critic Jane Jacobs, especially her classic 1961 book, *The Death and Life of Great American Cities*.[46]

Although the New Urbanists are a diverse lot, with some practitioners working more at the scale of the building and street, others on the neighborhood, the city, and/or the region, etc., they are of one mind in their hostility to the dominant post-World War II development pattern and its impact on built and natural environments. New Urbanists have thus emerged as some of the fiercest critics of the various manifestations of suburban sprawl: the rise of low-density settlements on the metropolitan fringe composed of single-family households in homogeneous subdivisions. Other illustrations of the sprawl phenomenon include the massive conglomerations of placeless office parks and large retail spaces—such as Atlanta's Perimeter Center area, Tyson's Corner, Virginia, and most of the greater Phoenix area—that form what journalist Joel Garreau has memorably termed the new "edge city."[47] New Urbanists are particularly concerned about how sprawl development has led to the loss of the traditional (compact) mixed-use neighborhood, and how it has promoted the blurring of spatial distinctions and physical boundaries at the center and edges of the city. They also lament how this process has promoted the physical and socioeconomic decay of the inner city and are greatly troubled by the erosion of a local sense of place as well the decline of community cohesion and civic spirit.

In *Crabgrass Frontier*, his classic account of the rise of the American suburb, Kenneth T. Jackson describes the historical forces and events that shaped the contemporary sprawl landscape.[48] Perhaps the most important of these was the federal subsidization of what eventually became the modern sprawl development pattern. The creation of the Federal Housing Authority (FHA) in the mid-1930s and the Veterans Administration (VA) a decade later ushered in an institutional insurance system that indemnified banks making long-term, low-interest loans for the construction and sale of new homes for millions of returning World War II veterans.[49] As Jackson writes, the FHA insurance was given largely to new low-density developments on the urban edge, which were generally seen as cheaper and less of a risk to lenders. This financial assistance, coupled with the high demand for new housing on the part of returning veterans, combined to fuel the legendary postwar housing boom. Also contributing to this surge in new home starts was the development of standardized mass-production construction techniques (which would produce the uniform "cookie-cutter" architectural styles that would later draw much scorn) and the rise of large entrepreneurial developers, such as William Levitt, the man behind the iconic development of the early suburban era, Long Island's Levittown.[50]

The result of all this was the abandonment of the inner cities by the (predominantly white) middle class, and the ensuing decline of the urban core. Public housing programs and private lenders exacerbated the class, ethnic, and racial divide between the new suburbs and the older inner city neighborhoods because banks were reluctant to grant mortgages to properties perceived to be in "blighted" urban areas.[51] The movement of jobs and people out of the inner cities and the building of homes and the setting up of shops on the urban fringe were also facilitated by the 1956 Interstate Highway Act, which, as a result of intense political pressure from a highway lobby made up of automakers, state and local officials, and bus and trucking interests (among others), created more than 40,000 miles of new highways that further promoted the flight of residents and industries out of the cities. In the process, it increased the role of the automobile and stunted the development of public transportation.[52]

Much of the New Urbanist critique of contemporary sprawl focuses on the negative environmental and social impacts that have resulted from these and related land-use and planning decisions over the past five-plus decades. On the environmental report card, New Urbanists, as well as most other critics, give the sprawl pattern a failing grade. They emphasize in particular how peripheral suburban development and long-standing single-use zoning practices (in which residential, commercial, and industrial land uses are spatially segregated, with residences often located far beyond walking distance to jobs, shopping, and other services) have forced citizens into an arrested state of dependence on the automobile. This dependence produces unsustainable and polluting use of fossil fuels, which in turn generates local and regional air pollution and contributes to greenhouse gas concentrations (exacerbating the problem of anthropogenic global warming). In addition, each new sprawl-type development built on former greenfield (undeveloped) sites either degrades and destroys natural communities and various types of open space or removes rural farmlands from production.

New Urbanists also argue that these modern suburban fringe settlements and their automobile-centered transportation systems are also socially corrosive. Among other problems, forced reliance on the automobile produces greater commuter stress, increases the risk of injury and death from traffic accidents, and is at least partly responsible for higher levels of obesity in the population (since we are driving to places where we might have walked if we lived within a traditional compact, mixed-use neighborhood). Furthermore, the burdens of dependence on the auto are not equitably distributed. The poor who cannot afford to buy and maintain cars are disproportionately affected, as are the elderly, who become "trapped" in suburbia if they become unable to drive.[53] For New Urbanists, all of these conditions, combined with a lack of adequate public transportation alternatives, paint an environmentally destructive and socially unjust picture of contemporary suburban and urban development.

New Urbanists have also, as mentioned earlier, made a point of lamenting the loss of a sense of "community" in the contemporary suburban neighborhood, and they have decried the shrinking amount of public space and the disappearance of inspiring civic architecture in American towns and cities. It is clear that many in the movement view the physical and social realms as closely connected, with physical design and planning seen as allowing, and in many cases strongly encouraging, forms of valued social interaction (e.g., pedestrians meeting on the street, sharing public transportation, or gathering in public places) seen as essential to building a vital and close-knit neighborhood life. As two of the movement's most influential founders, Andres Duany and Elizabeth Plater-Zyberk write in their New Urbanist manifesto, *Suburban Nation* (co-authored with Jeff Speck), "Community cannot form in the absence of communal space, without places for people to get together. . . . In the absence of walkable public places—streets, squares, and parks, the *public realm*—people of diverse ages, races, and beliefs are unlikely to meet and talk." [54] Civic life, as historian Christopher Lasch observed, rests upon conversation among citizens in public spaces where people meet as equals (e.g., the park, the coffeehouse, the street corner). With the decline of public space and civic institutions generally, Lasch believes, the opportunity to practice and develop this all-important civic art of conversation has been dramatically diminished.[55]

James Kunstler, popularizer of many of the New Urbanist ideas in books like the *Geography of Nowhere*[56] and *Home from Nowhere*,[57] has written with great moral fervor about the relationship between physical design and the creation of a strong community ethos. Kunstler believes that the incorporation of natural elements in urban designs is an important part of this civic revitalization and the fostering of a sense of the common good in public places:

Making our cities habitable again will take a rededication to forms of building that were largely abandoned in America after World War Two. It will call for devices of civic art that *never* really caught on here, but have always existed in older parts of the world—for instance, waterfronts that are integral with the rest of the city. The human scale will have to prevail over the needs of motor vehicles. There will have to be ample provision for green space of different kinds—neighborhood squares, wildlife corridors, parks—because people truly crave regular contact with nature, especially pockets of repose and tranquillity, and having many well cared-for parcels of it distributed equitably around town improves civic life tremendously.[58]

Kunstler concludes, however, that the shift to this sort of humanistic, environmentally sensitive, civic-minded order in our planning and design efforts won't be realized until "Americans recognize the benefits of a well-design public realm, and the civic life that comes with it, over the uncivil, politically toxic, socially impoverished, hyper-privatized realm of suburbia, however magnificent the kitchens and bathrooms may be there."[59]

These sorts of views about the relationship between a reformed notion of physical design, environmental protection, the revival of community, and an enhanced civic life—all supported by and supporting in turn the incorporation of nature and natural features (e.g., greens, parks, natural areas, even wilderness lands)—are set forth and ratified in the New Urbanist charter, which was formally adopted at the Fourth Congress of New Urbanism in 1996. "The Congress of the New Urbanism," the charter's preamble reads, "views disinvestment in central cities, the spread of placeless sprawl, increasing separation by race and income, environmental deterioration, loss of agricultural lands and wilderness, and the erosion of society's built heritage as one interrelated community-building challenge."[60] While admitting that physical design solutions by themselves will not solve these social and economic problems, the preamble states that "neither can economic vitality, community stability, and environmental health be sustained without a coherent and supportive physical framework."[61] New Urbanists thus hope to create what many observers have referred to as a "social architecture"; they seek to encourage social interchange and to renew civic bonds and public values through the implementation of neotraditional physical designs and features on the landscape.

The charter proceeds to enumerate a set of architectural and planning principles that range from the single building to the wider ecological region. Several of the principles address the conservation and protection of the natural environment in tandem with suggested reforms for the design and layout of the built landscape. For example, the charter points out that properly conceived metropolitan areas are not independent of natural systems and their limits; i.e., cities cannot exploit resources; generate waste; pollute land, air, and water; and expand with wild abandon. Instead, they are "finite places with geographic boundaries derived from topography, watersheds, coastlines, farmlands, regional parks, and river basins," places that have a "necessary and fragile relationship" to their surrounding agricultural and natural landscapes.[62]

Accordingly, the charter encourages such growth strategies as infill development whenever possible, that is, siting new development in existing areas within the city or an established suburb to avoid further blurring the metropolitan boundaries at the periphery and in the process conserving natural resources and keeping the social fabric of the neighborhood and city from becoming frayed by scattering its citizens far afield.[63] Not surprisingly, transportation alternatives to the automobile are also accented in several of the principles, with the development of pedestrian, bicycle, and public transit systems claimed to yield both environmental and social benefits (of the sort discussed earlier). Furthermore, the charter principles suggest incorporating naturalistic landscape elements (such as parks and community gardens) within neighborhoods and the construction of buildings that are both climatically and topographically appropriate and energy efficient. There is also a call to support the preservation of historic structures and landscapes, suggesting that these features "affirm the evolution and continuity of urban society."[64]

These environmentalist aims in the New Urbanist charter are joined by an assortment of other key design goals, including, as we have discussed, the promotion of dense, mixed-use development, in which a variety of private residences—from single-family units to apartments and townhouses—are interspersed with commercial, public, and other buildings. According to the New Urbanists, this approach will provide a range of affordable housing options for people of all economic circumstances, and the close proximity of residences to shopping, workplaces, and services will lesson the burdens suffered by those who can't afford or otherwise choose not to own a car. Once more, New Urbanists expect this configuration to yield real social and political dividends for the new neighborhoods, since, unlike the dominant suburban residential and land-use pattern (with its demographic homogeneity and single-use zoning), it will bring "diverse ages, races, and incomes into daily interaction, strengthening the personal and civic bonds essential to an authentic community."[65]

In a similar vein, New Urbanists emphasize the need, mentioned earlier, to design inspiring civic architecture and public gathering places and to place them in physically interesting and important sites to bolster community identity and reinforce the "culture of democracy."[66] Architect Andres Duany, one of the pioneers of the movement, has little good to say about the current state of the nation's civic buildings. "It is surely one of the minor mysteries of modern times that civic buildings in America have become cheap to the point of squalor when they were once quite magnificent as a matter of course." Duany in particular bemoans the fact that our post offices, colleges, schools, and town halls are no longer honored with fine architectural materials or form. "The new civic buildings are useful enough," he concedes, but "they are incapable of providing identity or pride for their communities."[67] For New Urbanists, utility is a poor substitute for the aesthetic and communal values generated by architecturally distinctive public and civic buildings located on socially and physically significant sites. One can certainly hear echoes of Josiah Royce's provincialism in Duany's and other New Urbanists' yearning for a prouder civic architecture and a more robust communal spirit.

The pedestrian-oriented neighborhood of the New Urbanists is widely recognized as one of their signature features. In the charter it is reinforced by a number of physical design elements—not only the mixed-use neighborhood but also locating public transit stops so that they are accessible (i.e., within comfortable walking distance) from nearby residences, shops, and workplaces. Along these lines, Peter Calthorpe, one of the movement's founders and probably the most regionally (and ecologically) oriented of New Urbanists, has advocated what he refers to as "transit-oriented development," in which compact, pedestrian-friendly, mixed-use neighborhoods are linked through regional public transit systems. This linkage not only reinforces the dense and mixed neighborhood structure, but also controls growth and conserves wildlife habitat and riparian areas (not to mention provides alternatives to automobile use).[68]

While such developments have and continue to be constructed in metropolitan areas across the United States, Portland, Oregon, is widely considered to be the most successful example of this regional coordination, with its integration of a popular light-rail and bus system, bike paths and walkways, and a famous (and largely effective) urban growth boundary to contain metropolitan development. Portland's approach, including its attempt to bring the built environment into balance with the natural one through the inclusion of greenbelts, parks, and similar features and its efforts to humanize the scale of architecture and reinvigorate public space, has led several observers to note the direct influence of Lewis Mumford's earlier regionalist ideas on the city's land-use reforms over the past three-plus decades, not to mention his legacy for Portland's much-deserved reputation as an icon of progressive planning.[69]

Today, the Congress for the New Urbanism has more than 2,500 members (from twenty countries and forty-nine states), a membership that includes not only architects and planners but also current and former federal and state officials, realtors, citizen-activists, landscape architects, builders, and bankers, among others. The organization's website reports that there are now hundreds of New Urbanist developments under construction or completed in the United States.[70] The public momentum of the New Urbanist movement seems to have grown steadily since the founding of the congress in the early 1990s, and flagship projects like Seaside, Florida, and Kentlands, Maryland, have attracted great visibility and professional comment (both positive and negative). The movement has also made inroads into the public and private development sectors. New Urbanist principles have been embraced, for example,

by the U.S. Department of Housing and Urban Development in their
HOPE VI revitalization program, as well as by the Urban Land Institute,
a large, nonprofit real estate and land development organization.[71]

The reception of New Urbanism among the professional design community, however, has been lukewarm at best (and at worst, downright
hostile). Architectural critics have been particularly scathing in their
remarks about New Urbanists' celebration and employment of neotraditional building styles, suggesting that these predilections stifle creativity and shackle architects to the conservatism and worn-out forms of the
past.[72] New Urbanists like Duany and Plater-Zyberk have replied that
their embrace of traditional building design is not a sentimental exercise
in nostalgia for nostalgia's sake, but an attempt to return to the human-
scaled, functional, and regional styles that characterized the pre-sprawl
landscape. They have also argued that this broad stylistic commitment
need not stifle aesthetic creativity, since it allows the imaginative interpretation of local vernacular forms and site characteristics.

The real problem, many New Urbanists suggest, lies with the mod-
ernist architects who are "violently allergic" to traditional-style architecture and dismiss it out of hand, even as their own avant-garde designs
do little to facilitate human communication and personalization.[73] Architect Daniel Solomon, another co-founder of the Congress for the New
Urbanism, has written that the New Urbanist penchant for traditional
forms is in fact a healthy revolt against the vacuous trendiness of modern
architectural designs. "The willingness of New Urbanists to use architectural style, in some cases even—dare one say it—historical styles, as
a weapon in the struggle against the dreadful tide of homogenization of
places is an affront to the fundamental ethos of orthodox modernism,"
he argues.[74]

Other critics are suspicious of the social and political aspirations of
the New Urbanists. Several commentators, for example, have pointed
out the failure of some New Urbanist projects to become the demo-
graphically pluralistic yet communal enclaves promised by the movement
and sanctioned by its charter.[75] Still, it is clear that New Urbanists are
serious enough about these ends to make them defining features of their
program. Even if New Urbanist projects fail to live up to one or more
of the movement's principles, for example, the charter acts as a critical

normative standard for evaluating their performance, and the principles are also tools that can stimulate further deliberation, self-criticism, and correction as the movement advances and improves its execution of projects.[76] Nevertheless, some detractors, such as Alex Marshall, have faulted New Urbanism for being too utopian, avoiding hard choices about infrastructure and control of growth, and selling an idyllic urban image that bears little resemblance to the complexity and difficulties of real urban experience.[77] While these criticisms may apply to some projects being advanced under the New Urbanist banner, I don't think that they accurately characterize New Urbanism as a whole. As we have seen with Calthorpe's work, New Urbanism has indeed been occupied with regional growth, transportation, and infrastructure issues. Moreover, the increasing number of urban infill projects following New Urbanist principles—projects that also include a range of affordable housing alternatives—suggests that the movement's goals for an "authentically urban" experience are increasingly being met, although perhaps not as often and as significantly as its critics would like.[78]

The environmental credentials of the movement have also been questioned. Some critics have argued, for example, that in practice New Urbanist projects do not, in fact, end up as urban infills, but are built instead on greenfield sites on the suburban fringe, thus contributing further to sprawl development and the loss of natural areas and farmland.[79] Others, even New Urbanist sympathizers, have noted that New Urbanists often do not go far enough in integrating ecological principles in their projects, including their traditional neglect of green building practices and their failure in some cases to link new developments to convenient transportation systems (which, as we have seen, is a hallmark of the New Urbanist design philosophy).[80] While it is certainly true that environmentalist concerns among the New Urbanist thinkers vary in their scope and intensity, and that these ideals are not always fully realized in practice, environmental commitments do play a prominent role in the New Urbanist charter, as we have seen. Furthermore, although greenfield developments may have been more prominent in the early years of the movement, as mentioned earlier New Urbanists can point today to scores of successful infill projects, including Crawford Square in Pittsburgh, the Vermont Village Plaza in South Central

Los Angeles, and the much-heralded Fruitvale station area in Oakland, California.[81]

There are also promising signs that ecological design principles are now playing a much greater role in New Urbanist projects. This is evidenced by the recent commendation of two infill buildings—the Chicago Center for Green Technology and the Natural Resource Defense Council's Robert Redford Building in Santa Monica, California, designed by New Urbanist architects—that have received platinum ratings from the U.S. Green Building Council.[82] Indeed, perhaps because of some of the earlier criticisms, New Urbanists seem to be addressing environmentalist concerns more deliberately and seriously of late. The Twelfth Congress, held in Chicago in June 2004, for example, not only included a plenary session devoted to "The Sustainable City," but also a discussion about amending the charter to clarify the relationship of New Urbanism to environmental issues and concerns. And the increasingly ubiquitous phrase "green urbanism," which has been bandied about recently among some New Urbanists and their allies, clearly suggests a more overt connection with green architecture, urban ecology, conservation of nature and other environmentalist issues and initiatives.[83]

In *Suburban Nation*, Duany, Plater-Zyberk, and Speck note the logical connections between the environmentalist and New Urbanist movements, suggesting that both sides may benefit from a closer conceptual and tactical alliance:

Environmentalists are beginning to understand the compatibility of these two agendas. Now that they have achieved some significant victories in the protection of flora and fauna, they are extending their purview a bit higher up the evolutionary tree, to the protection and projection of the traditional human habitat: the neighborhood. Environmentalists have already begun to mount an attack against sprawl, as they recognize the dangers posed to farms and forests by low-density, automobile-oriented growth. The Sierra Club has launched an official anti-sprawl campaign. . . . Of course, environmentalists have always been concerned with the survival of the human species, but only lately have they recognized that the neighborhood itself is a part of the ecosystem, an organic outgrowth of human needs. If all the energy and goodwill of the environmental movement can now be applied within the urban boundary, the results will be dramatic.[84]

Just as New Urbanists can take lessons from the organizational power and political commitment of environmentalists, the latter can learn from

New Urbanists that the city and the neighborhood are an important part of a truly comprehensive environmentalist agenda. Given the growing environmental thrust of New Urbanism, as well as the increasing number of calls for a more urban agenda in environmentalism, the establishment of a strong philosophical, strategic, and tactical relationship between the New Urbanist and environmental movements would seem to be both pragmatically appealing and intellectually compelling for both camps.

The New Urbanist movement offers an interesting and potentially potent mix of architectural, environmental, and social-political elements, all of which are intended to counteract what its supporters see as the devastating impacts of sprawl development on the natural and built environments and its toll on the social, political, and economic life of communities. It is a broad and humanistic environmental vision; new Urbanists believe that our communities should be attractive, equitable, diverse, human-scaled, and pedestrian-oriented places that are solicitous of nature, while also reinforcing neighborhood pride and a common sense of place and civic identity. It is also a pragmatic and pluralistic vision; environmental values and ends (e.g., protection of natural areas, energy efficiency, and improved air quality) are secured hand-in-hand with social improvements (e.g., aesthetic enhancement, improvements in pedestrian health and safety, and development of a sense of community and civic spirit). There would appear, in fact, to be an intriguing convergence of environmentalist commitments (which may even include intrinsic value-of-nature positions) and various social values in the New Urbanist argument for creating compact, pedestrian-friendly, mixed-use, communities that are also sensitive to the rhythms and values of the natural world.[85]

The charter's emphasis on the provision of public space and its encouragement of interaction and communication among citizens of all ethnic and socioeconomic backgrounds underscores as well the civic intentions of the movement, in which physical planning and design are used as tools to foster the development of what New Urbanists see as authentic community life in an era of privatization and placeless sprawl landscapes. As we have seen, in their criticisms and prescriptions for a reformed physical and social environment, New Urbanists resurrect many of the arguments of Mumford, MacKaye, and their regionalist colleagues in the 1920s and 1930s, especially the ideals of integrating urban forms in the natural world and creating a human-scaled communal environment appropriate to a democratic political culture. We can also see shades of John Dewey's democratic thought in the New Urbanist emphasis on the local face-to-face community and their concerns about providing a means for a democratic public to recognize itself as a common enterprise, one that all citizens have a material and social interest in promoting and sustaining. Like Wes Jackson's vision for sustainable agricultural communities, New Urbanists seek a revitalized citizenry and sense of the common good in contemporary American society, a political end that they hope to serve, as does Jackson, by restructuring the landscape to make it more encouraging of these broader civic goals.

Lessons of Practice

The two movements discussed in this chapter offer some important lessons for the intellectual and practical prospects of a third way environmentalism. I think both show that anthropocentric and nonanthropocentric, cultural and natural values can indeed intersect and reinforce each other in practice. Therefore, any desire on the part of environmentalists to narrow the moral conversation to any single ethical position (whatever it may be) does not capture the complexity of concrete moral experience, nor does it recognize how multiple value commitments and goals may converge in supporting common land-use and environmental reform efforts. In my reading, the Natural Systems Agriculture and New Urbanist programs appeal to both traditional environmental concerns (which may hinge on either instrumental and/or intrinsic value arguments), and to more socially oriented ones (e.g., improved human health, economic stability, the restoration of community and local civic life).

This leads to a second lesson, which is really an extension of the first. I think these two cases show how in practical experience, environmental values are frequently intertwined with broader civic and political commitments. Unfortunately, the flight of certain types of environmentalism from the perceived evils of anthropocentrism has had the effect of insulating it from human social and political experience. Instead of developing something akin to a "land civics" that links environmental values and land conservation to the ideals of public life, citizenship, and community health and identity, the more nonanthropocentrically inclined strains of environmentalism have focused on more isolated and foundational ethics-of-nature questions.[86] An environmental ethic is, in such a view, seen as a moral "corrective" to the political realm, one able to replace social decision making and democratic will with universal directives, such as those requiring citizens to recognize duties to the natural environment, to uphold obligations to promote nature's intrinsic value, and so on.

I think that this situation is regrettable for a number of reasons, not least because of the moral and conceptual fragmentation it promotes in human experience and the gulf it tends to create between our political and environmental commitments. Even from a narrow ideological environmentalist perspective, however, it doesn't make much sense. To my mind, one of the political and policy strengths of the New Urbanists is their inclusive, "big tent" philosophy. The New Urbanist agenda has a place, not only for architectural and planning reformers, but also for environmentalists, housing advocates, landscape architects and engineers, business leaders, real estate developers, public officials, and others interested in healthy, livable, and successful communities that also have the potential to reduce the human ecological footprint. By adopting an integrative and inclusive platform, one that addresses issues pertaining to the built and natural environments as well as the social, economic, and political vitality of such communities, New Urbanists appeal to a potentially powerful democratic coalition of groups and interests, thus building a large constituency for their goals of reforming design and land use.

While New Urbanists often struggle internally over the commitments of the movement and its strategic focus (e.g., whether they should emphasize the individual building and block, the neighborhood, or the region in their projects), they are ultimately a practice-oriented, pragmatic movement committed to building more livable communities, places that respect environmental constraints and human social, cultural, and economic needs. These in-house debates therefore do not immobilize them; they do not keep them from carrying out important and much-needed projects. Alternatively, there is often the sense in more doctrinaire forms of environmentalism (for example those that have developed within such fields as academic environmental ethics and politics and radical ecocentric activism) that we must first settle on one or another metaphysical position and its corresponding general theory of environmental value; that is, that we must change our worldview and adopt a certain ethical stance regarding the value of nature and our duties toward it before we can address matters of environmental practice and policy.

Finally, these two third way movements place humans and their values, intentions, and actions squarely within the environment, accepting the role of human agency but also directing it into nature-affirming channels. Both movements, for example, reject the prevailing land-use assumptions and decisions of our time. Jackson's Natural Systems Agriculture is offered as a rebuke to the dominant industrial agricultural paradigm of the past century, while New Urbanists advance their plans and design projects as a response to the social and environmental abuses of low-density, automobile-dependent, suburban sprawl. Neither program, that is, takes an uncritical or acquiescent view of the effects of human activity on the landscape; both recognize the multiple pathologies and maladaptive character of many of our conventional land-use philosophies and practices. At the same time, however, neither movement is willing to relinquish human responsibility for the character of development and the impact of our modifications of the built and natural environments. While Natural Systems Agriculture and New Urbanist proponents seek a more harmonious relationship between human society and the landscape, they view this goal as arising, not out of grand philosophical invention or the revelation of a universal ethical principle, but from a more modest quarter: the steady improvement and intelligent refinement of proper land-use and design techniques and practices.

It is, admittedly, something less than a heroic conclusion, but I think it is an important and refreshing one for environmentalists to hear, especially given the various ideological temptations of certain strains of nonanthropocentrism and dogmatic, "nature first" varieties of environmentalism. In the end, by not removing human values and actions from the land, third way movements such as Natural Systems Agriculture and

New Urbanism show how it is possible (just as their third way prede-
cessors did) to pragmatically reconcile human needs, ideals, and ambi-
tions with maintaining the health of the environment. They suggest a
more humanistic, pluralistic, and civic-minded agenda for environmentalism and land-use' reform, an integrative social and political agenda
that is just as concerned with the inner city, the subdivision, and the
wheat field as it is with the wolf, the mountain wilderness, and the
old-growth forest.

7

Conclusion: Environmental Ethics as Civic Philosophy

In this book I have offered a new reading of some of the intellectual foundations of American environmentalism. In doing so, I have drawn attention to the wider political and social context of environmental values, placing the latter within a larger discussion about such ends as the revitalization of democratic citizenship, the conservation of regional culture and community identity, and the constitution of the public interest. As I said at the outset, I believe that the philosophies of Liberty Hyde Bailey, Lewis Mumford, Benton MacKaye, and Aldo Leopold offer an important and persuasive counterpoint to the anthropocentrism versus ecocentrism, use versus preservation narrative that has historically dominated discussions of the development of American environmental thought. While they are not the only figures to think and write in this alternative vein, their work offers some of the most powerful statements of what I see as a lost third way tradition in environmentalism. Bailey, Mumford, MacKaye, and Leopold form a remarkable intellectual "hub" within the conservation and regional planning community in the first half of the twentieth century. We can also see evidence of their legacy in the landscape today, most notably in the reform projects of neoagrarians like Wes Jackson and the architects and planners of the New Urbanism.

Among other things, I hope that my recovery of this civic pragmatist tradition can help clear the philosophical ground for a rethinking of some of the ethical assumptions and agendas of contemporary environmentalism. Unlike the approach of Bailey, Mumford, MacKaye, and Leopold, many environmental philosophers and activists today seem to want to circle their moral wagons around a pure and unadulterated nonanthropocentrism rather than accommodate the complex of cultural and

natural values that always intermingle in human experience. The notion
of a greater public interest in a healthy and well-planned landscape, the
sort of ideal that motivated the third way thinkers discussed in this book,
is in these strict nonanthropocentric views eclipsed by the much narrower
discussion of nature's interest. In such a view, the goal of ethical discourse about the environment is typically seen as the radical moral con-
version of the citizenry, the wholesale replacement of an unseemly
anthropocentrism with a nature-affirming philosophical outlook.

This impulse to effect sweeping nonanthropocentric moral reform
within the academic field of environmental ethics was established at its
intellectual founding. The late 1960s and early 1970s saw the rise of
applied ethics as a practical philosophical movement devoted to exploring the moral questions raised by a host of social practices, including
those within biomedicine, business, and engineering contexts. Unlike
these other approaches in practical ethics, however, many of the new
environmental ethicists cleaved from the very beginning to the view that
the conventional Western ethical and political tradition was of little use
in helping us face mounting environmental problems, such as pollution
of air and water, the degradation of land, the loss of species and wildlands, overpopulation, and resource scarcity.

This belief was reinforced during the field's critical period by influential arguments such as those of historian Lynn White, Jr., whose essay,
"The Historical Roots of our Ecologic Crisis," was briefly discussed in
the previous chapter.[1] Of particular significance was White's plea in this
paper for a return to "fundamentals," a rethinking of the humanist
"axioms" of Western culture so that a less destructive and more benign
human–nature relationship might be realized. White's call for a radical
new anti-anthropocentric worldview had a profound impact on the subsequent development of environmental ethics. The prominent ecocentric
philosopher J. Baird Callicott, for example, has observed that White's
"Historical Roots" essay is the "seminal paper in environmental ethics,"
and that following its publication in 1967, "The agenda for a future environmental philosophy thus was set."[2]

While this may be overstating things a bit, it certainly did not take
long for the embrace of nonanthropocentrism (and the denunciation of
moral humanism) to become the default position in environmental

ethical writing.[3] One of the conclusions that emerged from this line of argument was that our environmental policies, politics, and practices, if they are to be truly principled and morally "correct," must be justified by nonanthropocentric ethical arguments, i.e., by claims to nature's intrinsic value. In 1973, for example, the Australian philosopher Richard Routley (later Sylvan) published his pioneering paper, "Is There a Need for a New, an Environmental Ethic?," an essay that introduced his now well-known hypothetical "last man" scenario as a kind of moral litmus test to separate anthropocentrists from nonanthropcentrists. As Routley wrote, according to the traditional moral commitments of Western civilization, the last man surviving the collapse of the world system would be committing no wrong if he set about destroying every species of animal and plant on Earth. Because only humans have value in traditional Western ethics, nature is viewed as essentially valueless (in itself). Therefore, we have no established moral tradition that will allow us to authoritatively condemn the destruction of nature on the grounds that it destroys nonhuman intrinsic value.[4] Routley's paper was intended as a strong rebuke of the Western philosophical tradition, particularly the "human chauvinism" he found in its exclusive concern for the interests of humans. Since Routley's essay is considered to be one of the most important and foundational statements in environmental ethics, a separatist precedent was thus established at the field's inception. Indeed, many influential nonanthropocentric philosophers writing in the field's early years implied (when they did not come right out and say it) that those who do not adopt the nature-centered worldview and a commitment to intrinsic natural value do not hold any environmental ethic worthy of the name.[5]

Although a strong strain of nonanthropocentrism took hold in environmental ethics at its inception and soon grew to dominate the scholarly discourse, it is important to remember that other, more humanistic, voices have always been audible amid the nonanthropocentric chorus. John Passmore's *Man's Responsibility for Nature*, published a year after Routley's paper, was one of the first book-length treatments of environmental ethics and is significant in part for its rejection of the notion, common among nonanthropocentric environmental theorists, that Western philosophical thought had little of value to contribute to the resolution of ecological problems.⁶ The conventional (anthropocentric) ethical tradition, Passmore wrote, with its sensitivity to the consequences of human actions and its stock of moral principles prescribing the advancement of genuine and enduring human interests (i.e., interests beyond immediate physical and material gratification), had more ethical resources at its disposal than the new environmental "mystics" and "primitivists" (his terms) either understood or fully appreciated.

This denial of the need to inject nonanthropocentric principles into the discussion of human relations to nature would gain further play in environmental ethics as the field developed over the ensuing decades. For example, in the mid-1980s, Bryan Norton introduced what he termed "weak anthropocentrism" to the discussion, a broadly humanistic view that distinguished between the purely economic values of "strong" anthropocentrism (a stance Norton rejected) and a "weaker" (i.e., less consumptive) variant of instrumentalism in which the direct experience of nature was seen as providing the means to criticize ecologically "irrational" commitments and could encourage the formation of normative ideals affirming human harmony with the environment.⁷

This same period also saw the emergence of a related set of important discussions in moral and political theory about our duties to future generations and the scope and content of (human) intergenerational justice, conversations that would develop into what we might refer to as "normative sustainability theory" in environmental ethics and policy studies by the mid-1990s.⁸ Finally (although this is by no means a complete survey of humanistic approaches in the field), the anthropocentric strain in environmental ethics received a major boost from the coalescence of "environmental pragmatism" in the mid-1990s, a movement that, as we have seen in this book, highlights the moral and political resources residing in an established (i.e., humanistic) tradition for discussions in environmental ethics.⁹

Despite the pedigree and growing number of humanistic (or humanistic-leaning) ideas in the field, it is safe to say that nonanthropocentrism is still the prevailing philosophical posture in environmental ethics. It is also true that many of the field's contributors remain committed to the eradication of anthropocentric claims and arguments from environmental ethical and policy discourse. For example, Holmes Rolston, one of the leading voices in academic environmental ethics and the most articulate advocate of the ecocentric program writing today, has stated that "Both anthropocentric and anthropogenic values have to come to an end before we can be the best persons. We have to discover intrinsic natural values."[10] Laura Westra, another nonanthropocentric environmental philosopher, has likewise put forth an ecocentric "principle of integrity" that she suggests should serve as the authoritative standard for environmental action, a principle that can even override the democratic will of citizens.[11] And Eric Katz has argued that anthropocentric environmentalist approaches are imperialistic and ultimately devastating to the goals of environmental protection. "An anthropocentric worldview," he writes, "leads logically to the destruction of the nonhuman natural world."[12]

Given such sentiments, it is perhaps not surprising that Leo Marx, the distinguished cultural historian and author of the classic study of the American pastoral tradition, *The Machine in the Garden*,[13] felt compelled to label ecocentric environmentalists "the puritans of today's environmental movement" in an essay published in the *New York Review of Books* a few years back.[14] While Marx was specifically referring to the deep ecologists, his observations are just as fitting for the more mainstream thinkers in environmental ethics who, even if they do not explicitly identify themselves with the deep ecology movement, nevertheless have embraced a similar radical vision of reform focused on the impassioned defense of the intrinsic value of nature and the rejection of all varieties of humanistic outlooks. Whether or not this vision reflects a puritanical attitude, it is certainly clear that many writers in the field today hold exceedingly strong—often proudly uncompromising—convictions about the moral course of environmentalism. It must be centered on protecting nature for its own good rather than for its contribution to human values and interests, and we must work to dismantle all forms of humanism and stop the vulgar instrumentalization of nature that reduces wild species and ecosystems to mere means in the service of human-defined ends.

By focusing so intently on the question of the independent moral standing of nature and the overthrow of anthropocentrism, however, I would argue that the field of environmental ethics has ironically undercut its ability to promote what are presumably its wider social and policy goals. Indeed, I think the ideological approach dominating much of nonanthropocentric environmental ethics today has seriously compromised the field's ability to play a meaningful role in the development of broad-based environmental reform movements and policy coalitions. The almost knee-jerk rejection of all things human by many strong nonanthropocentrists has found ethicists (and their activist counterparts) turning their backs on many of the moral and political commitments that underpin most public policy arguments, not to mention American political culture more generally. Furthermore, and most distressingly, I think it puts them at odds with the public, who we know is often motivated by long-term human interests, such as a concern for the well-being of future generations.[15] And it is an attitude that finds environmental ethicists parting company with an earlier generation of environmental thinkers, including the revered Aldo Leopold, who did not believe that caring for nature required the purging of humanistic values from our environmental discourse.

This is unfortunate because the field does have the potential to contribute to a larger and more useful discussion about the value of nature as part of the moral and political commitments of a "good" society. Unlike the strong nonanthropcentrists in environmental ethics, I do not believe that we need to completely dismantle humanism, nor do I think that an unyielding "nature-first" philosophy must necessarily be the foundation of an effective and principled environmentalism and, by extension, a morally defensible environmental politics. Instead, I would suggest that we learn from the third way thinkers examined in the previous chapters and seek a more integrative and pluralistic environmental ethics, one in which our many and often disparate environmental values, including intrinsic natural values, are seen as products of shared human experience, welded solidly to the frame of our established moral and political traditions.

This does not mean that a concern for nature's good has no moral bearing. Bailey and Leopold certainly show us how arguments about intrinsic value can occupy a significant place in our environmental valuations, and that these may even be pragmatically necessary for achieving certain environmental ends, such as conservation of rural life and land health (ends that in turn promote additional cultural and civic values). Yet both Bailey and Leopold (as well as Mumford and MacKaye) also teach us that human moral, social, and political values have an important role in justifying the environmentalist agenda, and that an environmental ethic that seeks to play one type of valuing off the other rather than accepting their mutually reinforcing character in experience denies the essential continuity of nature and culture. It also fails to take advantage of the powerful connections between them that can generate social action on behalf of important environmentalist objectives.

To get us past this kind of adversarial and dualistic way of thinking about environmental values and goals, in this book I have attempted to contextualize environmental ethics by examining its character and development within specific historical, intellectual, and geographic settings, including places (e.g., agrarian and urban landscapes), movements (e.g., nature study, regional planning), and philosophical traditions (e.g., classic American philosophy and pragmatism) that have traditionally not been focal points of environmental ethical narratives. The result, I hope, has been a more expansive reading of the philosophical and political bases of environmental thought, an analysis that avoids the trap of trying to shoehorn the work of important environmental writers into the confines of narrow anthropocentric or pure nonanthropocentric compartments.

As mentioned earlier, I also think that the tradition advanced in the preceding chapters offers historical justification and a further elaboration of the emerging pragmatic approach within environmental ethics, providing this movement with a philosophical "usable past" (as Mumford's compatriot Waldo Frank might have put it). The recent turn to pragmatism by a number of environmental philosophers is by no means an unprecedented or unusual move within environmental thought. Instead, it is a recovery of a significant, though largely lost moral tradition in the story of American environmentalism. I believe that this contextualist reading makes for a more interdisciplinary approach to environmental ethics and that it reorients the discussion in a way that maximizes the public potential of the field by revealing the historical and intellectual depth of the civic pragmatist vision.

On this last point, I would argue that the adoption of a more democratic style and public orientation in environmental ethics has never been more necessary, nor more timely. In the past decade or so we have seen the rapid growth of what are variously referred to as "collaborative resource management," "community conservation," or "grassroots ecosystem management" approaches, dynamic forms of social action in which citizens share responsibility for environmental planning, decision making, and management with a range of local, state, and federal agencies.[16] Supporters of these efforts argue that they promise more equitable and effective implementation of environmental plans and policies, and that they can improve overall environmental governance. These models are also praised for their ability to encourage social learning, trust, and mutual understanding among citizens, activities that can build social capital and civic capacity within local communities. While they are not a panacea for all of our contemporary environmental ills, and are subject to all the distortions and frustrations of democratic politics, these citizen-led movements clearly offer a vital role for the public in the environmental planning and policy arena, and perhaps signify an intriguing shift toward a wider "civic environmentalism" within various sectors of the environmental movement.[17]

I think that environmental ethics today stands at a crossroads with respect to the intellectual and institutional development of American environmentalism. On the one hand, it has a great opportunity to help environmental activists, professionals, and citizens articulate and justify their efforts within these emerging place-based and civic-spirited movements for environmental reform. In order to do so, however, I believe that the field needs to change. Specifically, I think it must get rid of its "puritanical" baggage (as Leo Marx might put it) if it is truly serious about taking part in what is increasingly a socially diverse, geographically varied, and politically dynamic planning and policy discussion. Pleas for radical nonanthropocentric reform may well have appeared philosophically warranted (and strategically necessary) to the first generation of environmental theorists and advocates howling in the ethical wilderness in the early 1970s. Yet given the mainstreaming of American environmental values and the rise of an extensive (though certainly far from complete) environmental policy regime over the past several decades, as well as this more recent ascendance of citizen-led environmental coalitions focused as much on pressing social and civic issues as on environmentalist concerns (traditionally understood), I believe we find ourselves in a very different sort of historical moment than that faced by environmental philosophers and advocates in the early 1970s.

What we need now, I would argue, are not environmental puritans, but rather environmental civic philosophers; that is, ethicists, political theorists, and social critics who are deeply concerned with understanding the diverse environmental values and commitments of citizens and who seek to connect this normative inquiry, not just to widely supported environmental policy and planning goals, but also to the other social and moral ideals and agendas of the democratic community.[18] I wholeheartedly agree with the political theorist Benjamin Barber, for example, who has suggested that the environmental movement today would do well to develop a robust civic philosophy able to articulate a shared notion of the public interest in a healthy and sustainable environment. "Nowadays," Barber observes, "rather than developing a discussion on behalf of the civic good, environmentalists often feel compelled to engage defensively in strident, unlistening polemics focused as much on their own moral self-righteousness as on the common good, or, say, the rights of hikers and bird-watchers deployed as counterweights to the rights of snowmobilers and loggers." As a result, he concludes, "In the face of adversarial interest politics, the public good that might bring together loggers and bird-watchers in a community of concern about sustainable environments goes missing."[19]

I would hope that the third way environmentalism I have reclaimed in this volume could help to set the historical and intellectual stage for this new kind of civic philosophical program in environmental thought and practice. Ultimately, I believe it is a tradition that points toward a transformed environmental politics, one that can unite nature conservationists and regional planners, wilderness advocates and rural reformers, New Urbanist supporters and boosters of sustainable agriculture, and environmental reform more generally, with a wider social and political criticism.

Notes

Chapter 1

1. The literature on deep ecology is vast. Two authoritative statements are those by Bill Devall and George Sessions, *Deep Ecology: Living as if Nature Mattered* (Salt Lake City, UT: Gibbs Smith, 1985); and Arne Naess, *Ecology, Community and Lifestyle: Outline of an Ecosophy*. Translated and revised by David Rothenberg (Cambridge: Cambridge University Press, 1989).

2. The classic discussion of the Muir–Pinchot debate over damming Hetch Hetchy appears in Roderick Nash's highly influential *Wilderness and the American Mind* (New Haven: Yale University Press, 2001, 4th ed.). For a new and detailed history of the Hetch Hetchy dispute, see Robert W. Righter, *The Battle over Hetch Hetchy: America's Most Controversial Dam and the Birth of Modern Environmentalism* (Oxford: Oxford University Press, 2005). An interesting revisionist interpretation of the Hetch Hetchy battle, one that also attempts to reduce the philosophical distance between Pinchot and Muir, may be found in Bryan G. Norton, *Toward Unity among Environmentalists* (Oxford: Oxford University Press, 1991), chapter 2. Finally, a more flattering account of Pinchot as an environmental thinker may be found in Char Miller's fine biography, *Gifford Pinchot and the Making of Modern Environmentalism* (Washington, DC: Island Press, 2001).

3. Aldo Leopold, *A Sand County Almanac* (Oxford: Oxford University Press, 1949; reprinted 1989).

4. Robert Gottlieb is one of the few scholars to have folded the tradition of regional planning into the narrative of American environmentalism. See Gottlieb, *Forcing the Spring: The Transformation of the American Environmental Movement* (Washington, DC: Island Press, 1993), and his more recent *Environmentalism Unbound: Exploring New Pathways to Change* (Cambridge, MA: MIT Press, 2001).

5. Although my use of the phrase "third way" is not intended to evoke the political centrism made famous by Tony Blair and the Clinton-Gore administration, the general pragmatic attempt to carve out a more moderate position between

two polar extremes—whether strong liberalism and conservatism or anthro-pocentrism and nonanthropocentrism—runs though both understandings. I should also say that my employment of this designation differs from that of schol-ars such as Christopher H. Schroeder, who has identified a "third way environ-mentalism" reflective of an environmental politics ("ecologism") that stands as an alternative to traditional neoliberal and socialist ideologies. See Christopher H. Schroeder, "Third Way Environmentalism," *University of Kansas Law Review* 48 (2000): 801–827. Given that Schroeder's ecologism roughly equates to deep ecology, the distinction between his approach and the civic pragmatist tradition I advance in this book should be quite obvious.

6. See Richard Poirier, *Poetry and Pragmatism* (Cambridge, MA: Harvard Uni-versity Press, 1992); Giles Gunn, *Thinking Across the American Grain: Ideol-ogy, Intellect, and the New Pragmatism* (Chicago: University of Chicago Press, 1992); Raymond Carney, *The Films of John Cassavetes: Pragmatism, Mod-ernism, and the Movies* (Cambridge: Cambridge University Press, 1994); and the papers collected in Morris Dickstein, ed., *The Revival of Pragmatism: New Essays on Social Thought, Law, and Culture* (Durham, NC: Duke University Press, 1998).

7. For example, see Michael Brint and William Weaver, eds., *Pragmatism in Law and Society* (Boulder, CO: Westview Press, 1991); Richard Posner, *Law, Prag-matism, and Democracy* (Cambridge, MA: Harvard University Press, 2003). See also the relevant essays in Dickstein, ed., *The Revival of Pragmatism*.

8. Notable readings on the implications of pragmatism for politics and political theory include Charles Anderson, *Pragmatic Liberalism* (Chicago: University of Chicago Press, 1990); Matthew Festenstein, *Pragmatism and Political Theory: From Dewey to Rorty* (Chicago: University of Chicago Press, 1997); Jurgen Habermas, *Between Facts and Norms: Contributions to a Discourse Theory of Law and Democracy* (Cambridge, MA: MIT Press, 1998); Stanley Fish, *The Trouble with Principle* (Cambridge, MA: Harvard University Press, 1999); and Richard Rorty, *Achieving our Country: Lefitist Thought in Twentieth Century America* (Cambridge, MA: Harvard University Press, 1999). See also Posner, *Law, Pragmatism, and Democracy*. Historical studies of American pragmatism that emphasize its political dimension almost always focus on the work of John Dewey, for good reason. See especially Robert B. Westbrook, *John Dewey and American Democracy* (Ithaca, NY: Cornell University Press, 1991); and Alan Ryan, *John Dewey and the High Tide of American Liberalism* (New York: W. W. Norton, 1995). Noteworthy attempts to claim other classic American philosophers (i.e., William James, Josiah Royce, and Charles Sanders Peirce, respectively) as vital social and political thinkers include Joshua I. Miller, *Demo-cratic Temperament: The Legacy of William James* (Lawrence: University Press of Kansas, 1997); Jacquelyn Ann K. Kegley, *Genuine Individuals and Genuine Communities: A Roycean Public Philosophy* (Nashville, TN: Vanderbilt Univer-sity Press, 1997); and James Hoopes, *Community Denied: The Wrong Turn of Pragmatic Liberalism* (Ithaca, NY: Cornell University Press, 1998).

9. Louis Menand, *The Metaphysical Club: A Story of Ideas in America*. (New York: Farrar, Straus, and Giroux, 2001).

10. I do not mean to suggest that this cursory overview characterizes all of what travels under the name of pragmatism today, or that it applies equally to every historical thinker in the tradition. It does, however, describe what I believe are widely accepted aspects of pragmatic thought, ideas that I will frequently return to as I discuss the works of the third way environmental thinkers in this book.

11. Richard J. Bernstein, *The New Constellation: The Ethical-Political Horizons of Modernity/Postmodernity* (Cambridge, MA: MIT Press, 1992), pp. 335–336.

12. For example, this conclusion is strongly supported by the results of a series of public opinion studies I have conducted with my colleagues on the environmental values, ethics, and policy attitudes of New England residents. See Ben A. Minteer and Robert E. Manning, "Pragmatism in Environmental Ethics: Democracy, Pluralism, and the Management of Nature," *Environmental Ethics* 21 (1999): 191–207, and "Convergence in Environmental Values: An Empirical and Conceptual Defense," *Ethics, Place and Environment*, 3 (2000): 47–60; Robert E. Manning, William A. Valliere, and Ben A. Minteer, "Values, Ethics, and Attitudes Toward National Forest Management: An Empirical Study," *Society and Natural Resources* 12 (1999): 421–436; and Ben A. Minteer, Elizabeth A. Corley, and Robert E. Manning, "Environmental Ethics beyond Principle? The Case for a Pragmatic Contextualism," *Journal of Agricultural and Environmental Ethics* 17 (2004): 131–156.

13. Adolf G. Gundersen, *The Environmental Promise of Democratic Deliberation* (Madison: University of Wisconsin Press, 1995).

14. Elizabeth Anderson, "Pragmatism, Science, and Moral Inquiry," in Richard W. Fox and Robert B. Westbrook, eds., *In Face of the Facts: Moral Inquiry in American Scholarship* (Washington, DC: Woodrow Wilson Center and Cambridge University Press, 1998), pp. 10–39; quote on p. 20.

15. Ben A. Minteer, "No Experience Necessary?: Foundationalism and the Retreat from Culture in Environmental Ethics," *Environmental Values* 7 (1998): 333–348.

16. This characterization is perhaps less apt for the work of William James, which is widely interpreted as displaying a strong individualistic stance. Yet as Joshua Miller suggests, James seems to have hewed to a version of individualism that did not deny a broader understanding of the common good. See Miller, *Democratic Temperament*.

17. See, e.g., John Dewey, *Liberalism and Social Action* in volume 11 of *John Dewey: The Later Works*, Jo Ann Boydston, ed. (Carbondale: Southern Illinois University Press, 1987 [orig. 1935]), pp. 1–65; and Dewey, *Freedom and Culture*, in volume 13 of *John Dewey: The Later Works*, Jo Ann Boydston, ed. (Carbondale: Southern Illinois University Press, 1988 [orig. 1939]), pp. 63–172. An excellent discussion of this aspect of Dewey's work and its place within the liberal tradition of public discourse may be found in James Gouinlock, *Excellence in*

Public Discourse: John Stuart Mill, John Dewey, and Social Intelligence (New York: Teachers College Press, 1986).

18. John Dewey, *The Public and Its Problems*, in volume 2 of *John Dewey: The Later Works*, Jo Ann Boydston, ed. (Carbondale: Southern Illinois University Press, 1984 [orig. 1927]); *Ethics*, in volume 7 of *John Dewey: The Later Works*, Jo Ann Boydston, ed. (Carbondale: Southern Illinois University Press, 1989 [orig. 1932]). For more on the relationship between Dewey's theory of inquiry and his notion of democracy, see Hilary Putnam, *Renewing Philosophy* (Cambridge, MA: Harvard University Press, 1992); Robert B. Westbrook, "Pragmatism and Democracy: Reconstructing the Logic of John Dewey's Faith," in Dickstein, ed., *The Revival of Pragmatism*, pp. 128–140; and Ben A. Minteer, "Deweyan Democracy and Environmental Ethics," in *Democracy and the Claims of Nature: Critical Perspectives for a New Century*, Ben A. Minteer and Bob Pepperman Taylor, eds. (Lanham, MD: Rowman & Littlefield, 2002), pp. 33–48.

19. An important anthology of early pragmatist work in environmental ethics is Andrew Light and Eric Katz, eds., *Environmental Pragmatism* (London: Routledge, 1996). For more recent efforts to explore the implications of pragmatic thought for discussions of environmental ethics, see Ben A. Minteer, "Intrinsic Value for Pragmatists?" *Environmental Ethics* 22 (2001): 57–75, and "Environmental Philosophy and the Public Interest: A Pragmatic Reconciliation," *Environmental Values* 14 (2005): 37–60. Bryan Norton has done more than anyone else in the field to develop the pragmatic point of view within environmental philosophy. For a good overview of his work in this vein, see the relevant essays in his 2003 collection, *Searching for Sustainability: Interdisciplinary Essays in the Philosophy of Conservation Biology* (Cambridge: Cambridge University Press). Norton continues to develop his pragmatist approach to environmental philosophy and management in his new book, *Sustainability: A Philosophy of Adaptive Ecosystem Management* (Chicago: University of Chicago Press, 2005).

20. See Daniel A. Farber, *Eco-Pragmatism: Making Sensible Environmental Decisions in an Uncertain World* (Chicago: University of Chicago Press, 1999).

21. Pragmatism has been especially attractive to environmental (or environmentally oriented) economists working within the traditions of institutional and evolutionary economics. See, e.g., Geoffrey Hodgson, "Economics, Environmental Policy and the Transcendence of Utilitarianism," in John Foster, ed., *Valuing Nature: Economics, Ethics and Environment* (London: Routledge, 1997), pp. 48–63; and Juha Hiedanpää and Daniel W. Bromley, "Environmental Policy as a Process of Reasonable Valuing," in Daniel W. Bromley and Jouni Paavola, eds., *Economics, Ethics, and Environmental Policy: Contested Choices* (Oxford, UK: Blackwell, 2002), pp. 69–84.

22. Good examples of pragmatist-inspired approaches in this area include Kai N. Lee, *Compass and Gryoscope* (Washington, DC: Island Press, 1993); and Norton, *Sustainability*.

23. Readers interested in the more disciplinary discussion of pragmatism in environmental ethics should consult the literature described in note 19.

24 Lewis Mumford, *The Golden Day* (New York: Boni and Liveright, 1926).

25. J. Baird Callicott and Michael P. Nelson, eds., *The Great New Wilderness Debate* (Athens: University of Georgia Press, 1998).

26. John Brinckerhoff Jackson, *Discovering the Vernacular Landscape* (New Haven, CT: Yale University Press, 1986), p. 8.

27. Simon Schama, *Landscape and Memory* (New York: Random House, 1996), p. 18.

Chapter 2

1. The historian Roderick Nash is one of the few scholars to have explicitly acknowledged Bailey's significance in the development of environmental thought. Nash suggests, in fact, that it was to Bailey (as well as Albert Schweitzer) that Aldo Leopold owed his "most direct intellectual debt." See Roderick Frazier Nash, *Wilderness and the American Mind* (New Haven, CT: Yale University Press, 2001, 4th ed.), p. 194 as well as his history of environmental ethics, *The Rights of Nature* (Madison: University of Wisconsin Press, 1989).

2. L. H. Bailey, *The Holy Earth* (New York: Charles Scribner's Sons, 1915).

3. Asa Gray, *Field, Forest, and Garden Botany* (New York: Ivision, Blackman, Taylor, 1868).

4. Andrew Denny Rodgers III, *Liberty Hyde Bailey. A Story of American Plant Sciences* (New York: Hafner, 1965), pp. 3–12.

5. Margaret Beattie Bogue, "Liberty Hyde Bailey, Jr. and the Bailey Family Farm," *Agricultural History* 63 (1989): 26–48.

6. Philip Dorf, *Liberty Hyde Bailey: An Informal Biography* (Ithaca, NY: Cornell University Press, 1956), pp. 42–45; Rodgers, *Liberty Hyde Bailey*, pp. 79–80.

7. Rodgers, *Liberty Hyde Bailey*, p. 81.

8. Rodgers, *Liberty Hyde Bailey*, p. 86.

9. Rodgers, *Liberty Hyde Bailey*, p. 90.

10. George H. M. Lawrence, "Horticulture," in Joseph Ewan, ed., *A Short History of Botany in the United States* (New York: Hafner, 1969), pp. 132–145.

11. Andrew Denny Rodgers III, *American Botany 1873–1892* (Princeton, NJ: Princeton University Press, 1944), pp. 248–249.

12. Gould P. Colman, *Education & Agriculture. A History of the New York State College of Agriculture at Cornell University* (Ithaca, NY: Cornell University Press, 1963), p. 172.

13. Colman, *Education & Agriculture*.

14. David B. Danbom, *The Resisted Revolution* (Ames: Iowa State University Press, 1979).

15. L. H. Bailey, *The Country-Life Movement in the United States* (New York: Macmillan, 1915), p. 20.

16. L. H. Bailey, *The Outlook to Nature* (New York: Macmillan, 1911), p. 73.

17. Bailey, *The Country-Life Movement*, p. 16.

18. Danbom, *The Resisted Revolution*, pp. 29–36.

19. Danbom, *The Resisted Revolution*, pp. 36–40.

20. L. H. Bailey, *The State and the Farmer* (St. Paul: Minnesota Extension Service, University of Minnesota, 1996 [orig. 1908]), pp. 30–48.

21. Dorf, *Liberty Hyde Bailey*, pp. 150–151.

22. William L. Bowers, *The Country Life Movement in America* (Port Washington, NY: Kennikat Press, 1974), p. 25.

23. *Report of the Country Life Commission* (1909). Available at http://library.cornell.edu/gifcache/chla/mono/unit1053/00003.TIF6.gif, p. 23.

24. *Report of the Country Life Commission*, pp. 13–14.

25. *Report of the Country Life Commission*, pp. 17–18.

26. *Report of the Country Life Commission*, pp. 49–50.

27. Bailey, *State and Farmer*, p. 37.

28. *Report of the Country Life Commission*, pp. 50–51.

29. *Report of the Country Life Commission*, p. 59.

30. *Report of the Country Life Commission*, p. 60.

31. Bowers, *The Country Life Movement in America*, p. 27.

32. Bowers, *The Country Life Movement in America*, pp. 128–129.

33. Danbom, *The Resisted Revolution*, pp. 81–85. For a more positive assessment of the Country Life Commission and its reformist vision, see Scott J. Peters and Paul A. Morgan, "The Country Life Commission: Reconsidering a Milestone in American Agricultural History." *Agricultural History* 78 (2004): 289–316.

34. L. H. Bailey, *The Nature-Study Idea* (New York: Doubleday, Page, 1903).

35. Danbom, *The Resisted Revolution*, p. 56.

36. Colman, *Education & Agriculture*, pp. 129–132.

37. Bailey, *The Nature-Study Idea*, p. 33.

38. Bailey, *The Nature-Study Idea*, p. 59.

39. Bailey, *The Nature-Study Idea*, p. 35.

40. Bailey, *Outlook to Nature*, p. 86.

41. Bailey, *The Nature-Study Idea*, p. 7.

42. Bailey, *The Nature-Study Idea*, p. 15.

43. Bailey, *The Nature-Study Idea*, p. 15.

44. Bailey, *The Nature-Study Idea*, p. 15.

45. Bailey, *Outlook to Nature*, p. 34.

46. Bailey, *The Nature-Study Idea*, p. 7.

47. Bailey, *The Nature-Study Idea*, p. 18.

48. Bailey, *The Nature-Study Idea*, p. 32.

49. William L. Bowers has also noted this sympathy between Bailey's and Dewey's educational reform proposals. See Bowers, *The Country Life Movement in America*, pp. 60–61.

50. John Dewey, "The Bearings of Pragmatism Upon Education," in volume 4 of *John Dewey: The Middle Works*, Jo Ann Boydston, ed. (Carbondale: Southern Illinois University Press [orig. 1908–1909]), pp. 178–191; quote on p. 185 (emphasis in original).

51. John Dewey (with Evelyn Dewey), *Schools of To-Morrow*, in volume 8 of *John Dewey: The Middle Works*, Jo Ann Boydston, ed. (Carbondale: Southern Illinois University Press, 1979 [orig. 1915]), pp. 205–405; quote on p. 266.

52. Dewey, "The Bearings of Pragmatism," p. 188.

53. Dewey, "The Bearings of Pragmatism," p. 188.

54. John Dewey, *The School and Society*, in volume 1 of *John Dewey: The Middle Works*, Jo Ann Boydston, ed. (Carbondale: Southern Illinois University Press, 1976 [orig. 1899]), pp. 1–109; quote on p. 46.

55. Dewey, *School and Society*, p. 19.

56. Dewey, *School and Society*, p. 19.

57. Dewey, *School and Society*, p. 55.

58. John Dewey, "The School as a Social Centre," in volume 2 of *John Dewey: The Middle Works*, Jo Ann Boydston, ed. (Carbondale: Southern Illinois University Press, 1976 [orig. 1902]), pp. 80–93; quote on p. 93.

59 John Dewey, *Democracy and Education: An Introduction to the Philosophy of Education*, in volume 9 of *John Dewey: The Middle Works*, Jo Ann Boydston, ed. (Carbondale: Southern Illinois University Press, 1980 [orig. 1916]).

60. Bailey, *The Nature-Study Idea*, p. 55.

61. Bailey, *The Nature-Study Idea*, p. 58.

62. Bailey, *Outlook to Nature*, p. 128.

63. Bailey, *Outlook to Nature*, p. 129.

64. Bailey, *The Nature-Study Idea*, p. 60.

65. Bailey, *Outlook to Nature*, pp. 66–67.

66. Dewey, *School and Society*, p. 8; emphasis in original.

67. Dewey, *Schools of To-Morrow*, p. 268.

68. Robert B. Westbrook, *John Dewey and American Democracy* (Ithaca, NY: Cornell University Press, 1991), p. 97.

69. John Dewey, "Plan of Organization of the University Primary School," in volume 5 of *John Dewey: The Early Works*, Jo Ann Boydston, ed. (Carbondale: Southern Illinois University Press, 1972 [orig. n.d./1895?]), pp. 223–243.

70. John Dewey, "A Pedagogical Experiment," in volume 5 of *John Dewey: The Early Works*, Jo Ann Boydston, ed. (Carbondale: Southern Illinois University Press, 1972 [orig. 1896]), pp. 244–246; quote on p. 245.

71. Larry D. Hickman, "The Edible Schoolyard: Agrarian Ideals and Our Industrial Milieu," in Paul B. Thompson and Thomas C. Hilde, eds., *The Agrarian Roots of Pragmatism* (Nashville, TN: Vanderbilt University Press, 2000), pp. 195–205 (see esp. p. 198).

72. Dewey, *Schools of To-Morrow*, p. 269.

73. Dewey, *Schools of To-Morrow*, p. 269.

74. Dewey, *Schools of To-Morrow*, p. 272.

75. John Dewey, "The Moral Significance of the Common School Studies," in volume 4 of *John Dewey: The Middle Works*, Jo Ann Boydston, ed. (Carbondale: Southern Illinois University Press, 1977 [orig. 1909]), pp. 205–213; quote on p. 211.

76. Ann M. Keppel, "The Myth of Agrarianism in Rural Educational Reform, 1890–1914," *History of Education Quarterly* 2 (1962): 100–112.

77. Peter J. Schmitt, *Back to Nature: The Arcadian Myth in Urban America* (Baltimore: Johns Hopkins University Press, 1990), p. 84.

78. Bailey, *The Country-Life Movement*, p. 58.

79. Bailey, *The Country-Life Movement*, pp. 59–60.

80. Bailey, *Holy Earth*, p. 11.

81. Bailey, *The Country-Life Movement*, p. 184.

82. Bailey, *The Country-Life Movement*, p. 184.

83. Bailey, *The Country-Life Movement*, p. 178.

84. Bailey, *The Country-Life Movement*, p. 193.

85. Bailey, *The Country-Life Movement*, p. 188.

86. Bailey, *The Country-Life Movement*, p. 188.

87. Bailey, *Holy Earth*, p. 73.

88. Bailey, *The Nature-Study Idea*, p. 100.

89. Bailey, *The Nature-Study Idea*, p. 97.

90. Bailey, *The Nature-Study Idea*, p. 109.

91. Bailey, *The Nature-Study Idea*, p. 110.

92. Bailey, *The Nature-Study Idea*, p. 110.

93. Bailey, *Outlook to Nature*, p. 88.

94. Bailey, *Outlook to Nature*, p. 88.

95. Bailey, *Holy Earth*, p. 3.

96. Bailey, *Holy Earth*, p. 8.

97. Bailey, *Outlook to Nature*, p. 140.

98. Bailey, *Outlook to Nature*, p. 174.

99. Bailey, *Outlook to Nature*, p. 179.

100. This interpretation is commonly traced to Lynn White, Jr.'s highly influential (and still controversial) discussion of the antienvironmental implications of the Christian dogma of creation in his essay, "The Historical Roots of Our Ecologic Crisis," *Science* 155 (1967): 1203–1207.

101. Bailey, *Holy Earth*, p. 6.

102. Bailey, *Holy Earth*, p. 16.

103. Bailey, *Holy Earth*, p. 18.

104. Bailey, *Holy Earth*, pp. 18–19.

105. Bailey, *Holy Earth*, p. 30; emphasis added.

106. Bailey, *Holy Earth*, p. 24.

107. Bailey, *Holy Earth*, pp. 130–131.

108. Bailey, *Holy Earth*, p. 119.

109. L. H. Bailey, *Ground-Levels in Democracy* (Ithaca, NY: Privately published, 1916).

110. L. H. Bailey, *Universal Service, the Hope of Humanity* (New York: Sturgis and Walton Co., 1918).

111. L. H. Bailey, *What Is Democracy?* (Ithaca, NY: Comstock, 1918).

112. Bailey, *Ground-Levels in Democracy*, pp. 23, 24.

113. Bailey, *Ground-Levels in Democracy*, p. 69.

114. Bailey, *The State and the Farmer*, p. 70.

115. Bailey, *What Is Democracy?*, p. 36.

116. Bailey, *What Is Democracy?*, p. 64. As I discuss in chapter 4, this view about the intellectual and cultural homogenization of modern industrialism was also on the mind of many thinkers during this period, including the philosopher Josiah Royce and Bailey's younger conservation colleague, Benton MacKaye.

117. Bailey, *What Is Democracy?*, p. 76.

118. Bailey, *The State and the Farmer*, p. 29.

119. A small sampling of work addressing stewardship ideas in environmental ethics and ecotheology (some of it critical) would include John Passmore, *Man's Responsibility for Nature: Ecological Problems and Western Traditions* (New York: Charles Scribner's Sons, 1974); Loren Wilkinson, ed. (in collaboration with Peter De Vos, Calvin De Witt, Eugene Dykeman, Vernon Ehlers, Derk Pereboom, and Aileen Van Beilen), *Earthkeeping: Christian Stewardship of*

Natural Resources (Grand Rapids, MI: Eerdman's, 1980); Robin Attfield, *The Ethics of Environmental Concern* (New York: Columbia University Press, 1983); Paul H. Santmire, *The Travail of Nature: The Ambiguous Ecological Promise of Christian Theology* (Philadelphia: Fortress Press, 1985); and Calvin B. DeWitt, *Caring for Creation: Responsible Stewardship of God's Handiwork,* James W. Skillen and Luis E. Lugo, eds. (Grand Rapids, MI: Baker Books, 1998).

120. The stewardship mission of Marsh-Billings-Rockefeller National Historical Park is described in Rolf Diamant, "Reflections on Environmental History with a Human Face: Experiences from a New National Park," *Environmental History* 8 (2003): 628–642. For more on the National Park Service Conservation Study Institute, see http://www.nps.gov/mabi/mabi/csi/.

Chapter 3

1. This almost teleological account of the rise of nonanthropocentrism appears in the work of many environmental philosophers. See, for example, Eric Katz, "The Traditional Ethics of Nature Resource Management," in Richard L. Knight and Sarah F. Bates, eds., *A New Century for Natural Resources Management* (Washington, DC: Island Press, 1995), pp. 101–116; and J. Baird Callicott, "Wither Conservation Ethics?" *Conservation Biology 4* (1990): 15–20.

2. Samuel P. Hays, *Conservation and the Gospel of Efficiency: The Progressive Conservation Movement, 1890–1920* (Cambridge, MA: Harvard University Press, 1959); Roderick Frazier Nash, *Wilderness and the American Mind* (New Haven: Yale University Press, 2001, 4th ed.); Stephen Fox, *John Muir and his Legacy: The American Conservation Movement* (Boston: Little, Brown, 1981).

3. See, for example, Richard Judd, *Common Lands, Common People: The Origins of Conservation in Northern New England* (Cambridge, MA: Harvard University Press, 1997); Robert McCullough, *The Landscape of Community* (Hanover, NH: University of New England Press, 1995); Karl Jacoby, *Crimes Against Nature: Squatters, Poachers, Thieves, and the Hidden History of American Conservation* (Berkeley: University of California Press, 2001); Louis S. Warren, *The Hunter's Game: Poachers and Conservationists in Twentieth-Century America* (New Haven, CT: Yale University Press, 1997).

4. Such alternative interpretations of the environmental thought of Pinchot and Muir may be found in Bryan Norton, *Toward Unity among Environmentalists* (New York: Oxford University Press, 1991); and Bob Pepperman Taylor, *Our Limits Transgressed: Environmental Political Thought in America* (Lawrence: University Press of Kansas, 1992).

5. I should note that Curt Meine (personal communication) has made me more sensitive to the potential historiographic and normative distinctions between "conservation philosophy" and "environmental philosophy." While a sufficiently developed treatment of the differences between the two traditions is beyond the scope of this chapter, I will point out here that I believe Mumford's pragmatic

conservationism was forged in a very different fire than most contemporary environmental philosophy, an intellectual development marked by its traffic with the ideas of the conservation movement *and* American philosophy (not to mention early planning thinkers such as Howard and Geddes). As I suggest, this account would seem to challenge many of the presuppositions of environmental philosophers about the progressive evolution of classic conservation-period philosophy into a full-blown "environmental philosophy" later in the twentieth century.

6. Historians Robert Fishman and John L. Thomas have chronicled the differences between the decentralized, normative "communitarian regionalism" of Mumford and the RPAA and the more mainstream "metropolitan regionalism" of planner Thomas Adams and his allies behind the Regional Plan of New York in the early 1930s. See the papers by Fishman and Thomas in Robert Fishman, ed., *The American Planning Tradition* (Washington, DC: Woodrow Wilson Center Press, 2000).

7. Lewis Mumford, *The Pentagon of Power* (New York: Harcourt Brace Jovanovich, 1964).

8. Ramachandra Guha is one of the few writers who have considered Mumford's relevance for discussions in contemporary environmentalism and environmental philosophy. See his insightful "Lewis Mumford, the Forgotten American Environmentalist: An Essay in Rehabilitation," in David Macauley, ed., *Minding Nature: Philosophers of Ecology* (New York: Guilford Press, 1996), pp. 209–228. My focus in this paper is targeted more to Mumford's regionalism and the pragmatism of his interwar planning theory, whereas Guha devotes more attention in his essay to Mumford's later work on technology and his fit within the tradition of social ecology.

9. Robert Fishman, *Urban Utopias in the Twentieth Century: Ebenezer Howard, Frank Lloyd Wright, and Le Corbusier* (Cambridge, MA: MIT Press, 1982), pp. 29–39.

10. Ebenezer Howard, *Garden Cities of To-Morrow* (Cambridge, MA: MIT Press, 1965 [orig. 1902]).

11. Howard, *Garden Cities of To-Morrow*, pp. 50–57; Peter Hall, *Cities of Tomorrow* (Oxford, UK: Blackwell, 1996, updated ed.), pp. 87–94.

12. Howard, *Garden Cities of To-Morrow*, p. 146.

13. Lewis Mumford, "Introduction," in *Garden Cities of To-Morrow*, p. 33. For more on Howard and his legacy for town and city planning, see Peter Hall and Colin Ward, *Sociable Cities: The Legacy of Ebenezer Howard* (Chichester, UK: Wiley, 1998); and Kermit C. Parsons and David Schuyler, eds., *From Garden City to Green City* (Baltimore: Johns Hopkins University Press, 2002).

14. Helen Meller, *Patrick Geddes: Social Evolutionist and City Planner* (London: Routledge, 1990); Wolker M. Welter, *Biopolis: Patrick Geddes and the City of Life* (Cambridge, MA: MIT Press, 2002).

15. Welter, *Biopolis*, pp. 109–112.

16. Geddes, quoted in Meller, p. 179.

17. Welter, *Biopolis*.

18. Meller, *Patrick Geddes*, p. 134.

19. Geddes's significance for contemporary discussions about the city is the subject of the stimulating collection by Volker M. Welter and James Lawson, eds., *The City after Patrick Geddes* (Oxford, UK: Peter Lang, 2000).

20. See the discussions of the RPAA's regionalist agenda and design principles in Mark Luccarelli, *Lewis Mumford and the Ecological Region* (New York: Guilford Press, 1995), pp. 76–83; and Edward K. Spann, *Designing Modern America: The Regional Planning Association of America and Its Members* (Columbus: Ohio State University Press, 1996).

21. For revealing considerations of the social and environmental aspects of Olmsted's landscape philosophy and his influence in subsequent urban planning, see David Schuyler, *The New Urban Landscape* (Baltimore: Johns Hopkins University Press, 1986); Thomas Bender, *Toward an Urban Vision: Ideas and Institutions in Nineteenth Century America* (Baltimore: Johns Hopkins University Press, 1975), esp. chapter 7; Geoffrey Blodgett, "Frederick Law Olmsted: Landscape Architecture as Conservative Reform," *Journal of American History* 62 (1976): 869–889; George L. Scheper, "The Reformist Vision of Frederick Law Olmsted and the Poetics of Park Design," *New England Quarterly* 62 (1989): 369–402; Ann Whiston Spirn, "Constructing Nature: The Legacy of Frederick Law Olmsted," in William Cronon, ed., *Uncommon Ground: Toward Reinventing Nature* (New York: W. W. Norton, 1996), pp. 91–113; and Charles E. Beveridge and Paul Rocheleau, *Frederick Law Olmsted. Designing the American Landscape* (New York: Universe Publishing, 1998).

22. Lewis Mumford, "The Fourth Migration," reprinted in Carl Sussman, ed., *Planning the Fourth Migration: The Neglected Vision of the Regional Planning Association of America* (Cambridge, MA: MIT Press, 1976), pp. 55–64.

23. Benton MacKaye, *The New Exploration: A Philosophy of Regional Planning* (Harpers Ferry, WV and Urbana-Champaign, IL: The Appalachian Trail Conference and the University of Illinois Press, 1990 [orig. 1928]).

24. Benton MacKaye, "An Appalachian Trail: A Project in Regional Planning," *Journal of the American Institute of Architects* 9 (1921): 3–8.

25. On the more popular front, See Bill Bryson's hilarious account of his attempt to hike the Trail in the bestselling *A Walk in the Woods* (New York: Broadway Books, 1998). Ian Marshall's *Story Line: Exploring the Literature of the Appalachian Trail* (Charlottesville: University Press of Virginia, 1998) is an interesting mélange of "outdoor" literature and ecocriticism, exploring the Trail as both a powerful recreational experience and a fount of regional literature.

26. George Perkins Marsh, *Man and Nature* (New York: Charles Scribner, 1864).

27. Lewis Mumford, *The Brown Decades: A Study of the Arts in America 1865–1895* (New York: Dover, 1971 [orig. 1931]). David Lowenthal, Marsh's

biographer, reports that Mumford's interest in the great Vermont conservationist was originally kindled by Patrick Geddes. Given the influence of Mumford's "rediscovery" of Marsh on our understanding of the conservation tradition, Geddes deserves some credit for keeping the conservation idea burning during this period. See Lowenthal, *George Perkins Marsh: Prophet of Conservation* (Seattle: University of Washington Press, 2000), p. 309.

28. Mumford, *Brown Decades*, p. 34.

29. Mumford, *Brown Decades*, pp. 40–41.

30. Lewis Mumford, *The Culture of Cities* (New York: Harcourt Brace, 1938), p. 360.

31. Lewis Mumford, *Sketches from Life* (Boston: Beacon Press, 1982), p. 166.

32. Mumford, *Culture of Cities*, p. 254. As I discuss in chapter 4, Mumford's concern for the cultural homogenization of the rural province by the metropolis was also shared by Benton MacKaye.

33. Mumford, *Culture of Cities*, p. 255.

34. Mumford, *Sketches from Life*, p. 166.

35. Donald L. Miller, *Lewis Mumford: A Life* (New York: Weidenfield & Nicolson, 1989), pp. 57–60.

36. Mumford, *Sketches from Life*, pp. 156–158.

37. Spann, *Designing Modern America*, p. 46.

38. Fishman, "The Metropolitan Tradition in American Planning," in R. Fishman, ed., *The American Planning Tradition: Culture and Policy* (Washington, DC: Woodrow Wilson Center Press, 2000), pp. 65–85.

39. Lewis Mumford, "Regions—to Live in," in Sussman, ed., *Planning the Fourth Migration*, p. 92, emphasis added.

40. Mumford, "Regions—to Live in," p. 90, emphasis added.

41. Lewis Mumford, "The Theory and Practice of Regionalism (2)," *Sociological Review* 19 (1927): 131–141; quote on p. 140.

42. Mumford, *Culture of Cities*, p. 332.

43. William Cronon, "The Trouble with Wilderness; or, Getting Back to the Wrong Nature," in William Cronon, ed., *Uncommon Ground: Rethinking the Human Place in Nature* (New York: W. W. Norton, 1996), pp. 69–90.

44. Mumford, *Culture of Cities*, p. 303.

45. Mumford, *Culture of Cities*, p. 302.

46. Mumford, *Culture of Cities*, p. 253. A penetrating discussion of Mumford's commitment to organicism and resistance to the machine may be found in Leo Marx, "Lewis Mumford: Prophet of Organicism," in Thomas P. Hughes and Agatha C. Hughes, eds., *Lewis Mumford: Public Intellectual* (New York: Oxford University Press, 1990), pp.164–180.

47. Mumford, *Culture of Cities*, p. 327.

48. Mumford, quoted in John Friedmann and Clyde Weaver, *Territory and Function: The Evolution of Regional Planning* (Berkeley: University of California Press, 1979), p. 29.

49. Lewis Mumford, *Sketches from Life*, pp. 135–136.

50. Dewey himself would devote a good deal of attention to aesthetic concerns in the 1930s; see, for example, his *Art as Experience*, in volume 10 of *John Dewey: The Later Works*, Jo Ann Boydston, ed. (Carbondale: Southern Illinois University Press, 1987 [orig. 1934]).

51. Lewis Mumford, *The Golden Day* (New York: Boni and Liveright, 1926).

52. John Dewey, "Pragmatic America," in volume 13 of *John Dewey: The Middle Works*, Jo Ann Boydston, ed. (Carbondale: Southern Illinois University Press, 1983 [orig. 1922]), pp. 306–310.

53. See the discussion of the Bourne-Dewey debate in Casey Blake, *Beloved Community: The Cultural Criticism of Randolph Bourne, Van Wyck Brooks, Waldo Frank, and Lewis Mumford* (Chapel Hill: University of North Carolina Press, 1990); and Robert B. Westbrook, *John Dewey and American Democracy* (Ithaca, NY: Cornell University Press, 1991).

54. Mumford, *Golden Day*, pp. 262–263; emphasis in original.

55. Mumford, *Golden Day*, pp. 266–267.

56. Mumford, *Golden Day*, p. 279.

57. Mumford, *Golden Day*, p. 266.

58. John Dewey, "The Pragmatic Acquiescence," in volume 3 of *John Dewey: The Later Works*, Jo Ann Boydston, ed. (Carbondale: Southern Illinois University Press, 1984 [orig. 1927]), pp. 145–151; quote on pp. 150–151.

59. Lewis Mumford, "The Pragmatic Acquiescence: A Reply," *New Republic* 59 (1927): 250–251. Reprinted in Gail Kennedy, ed., *Pragmatism and American Culture* (Boston: D. C. Heath, 1950), pp. 54–57. Quote taken from Kennedy, p. 56.

60. Mumford, "Pragmatic Acquiescence," in Kennedy, p. 56.

61. Robert Westbrook, "Lewis Mumford, John Dewey, and the 'Pragmatic Acquiescence'," in T. P. Hughes and A. C. Hughes, eds., *Lewis Mumford: Public Intellectual* (New York: Oxford University Press, 1990), pp. 301–322.

62. John Dewey, *Experience and Nature* in volume 1 of *John Dewey: The Later Works*, Jo Ann Boydston, ed. (Carboudale: Southern Illinois University Press, 1981 [orig. 1925]).

63. Dewey, *Art as Experience*.

64. John Dewey, *A Common Faith*, in volume 9 of *John Dewey: The Later Works*, Jo Ann Boydston, ed. (Carbondale: Southern Illinois University Press, 1986 [orig. 1934]), pp. 1–58. The aesthetic, cultural, and religious dimensions of Dewey's thought are explored in Thomas M. Alexander, *John Dewey's Theory of Art, Experience, and Nature* (Albany: State University of New York Press,

1987); Steven C. Rockefeller, *John Dewey: Religious Faith and Democratic Humanism* (New York: Columbia University Press, 1991); and Michael Eldridge, *Transforming Experience: John Dewey's Cultural Instrumentalism* (Nashville, TN: Vanderbilt University Press, 1998). Victor Kestenbaum, *The Grace and the Severity of the Ideal. John Dewey and the Transcendent* (Chicago: University of Chicago Press, 2002), makes an interesting argument for the role of the ideal and transcendent goods in his philosophical system.

65. See especially John Dewey, *Ethics*, in volume 7 of *John Dewey: The Later Works*, Jo Ann Boydston, ed. (Carbondale: Southern Illinois University Press, 1985 [orig. 1932]); and John Dewey, *Human Nature and Conduct*, in volume 14 of *John Dewey: The Middle Works*, Jo Ann Boydston, ed. (Carbondale: Southern Illinois University Press, 1983 [orig. 1922]). For a good discussion of Dewey's ethical theory that emphasizes its creative and imaginative character, see Steven Fesmire's *John Dewey and Moral Imagination: Pragmatism in Ethics* (Bloomington: Indiana University Press, 2003).

66. Lewis Mumford, letter to Patrick Geddes, March 7, 1926. In *Lewis Mumford and Patrick Geddes: The Correspondence*, Frank G. Novak, Jr., ed. (London: Routledge, 1995), p. 242.

67. Casey Blake, *Beloved Community*, p. 226.

68. Casey Blake, *Beloved Community*, p. 226.

69. Mumford, *Culture of Cities*, p. 384.

70. See John Dewey, *Logic: The Theory of Inquiry*, in volume 12 of *John Dewey: The Later Works*, Jo Ann Boydston, ed. (Carbondale: Southern Illinois University Press, 1986 [orig. 1938]).

71. Dewey, *Logic.*

72. Mumford, *Culture of Cities*, pp. 376–380.

73. John Dewey, *Liberalism and Social Action*, in volume 11 of *John Dewey: The Later Works*, Jo Ann Boydston, ed. (Carbondale: Southern Illinois University Press, 1987 [orig. 1935]), pp. 1–65; quote on p. 36.

74. Mumford, *Culture of Cities*, pp. 378–379.

75. Mumford, *Culture of Cities*, pp. 380–381; emphasis added.

76. See C. S. Holling, *Adaptive Environmental Assessment and Management* (London: Wiley, 1978); Carl J. Walters, *Adaptive Management of Renewable Resources* (New York: Macmillan, 1986); Kai Lee, *Compass and Gyroscope: Integrating Science and Politics for the Environment* (Washington, DC: Island Press, 1993); Lance H. Gunderson, C. S. Holling, and Stephen S. Light, eds., *Barriers and Bridges to the Renewal of Ecosystems and Institutions* (New York: Columbia University Press, 1995). Bryan Norton has written extensively about the pragmatist underpinnings of the methods of contemporary adaptive management. See Norton, "Integration or Reduction: Two Approaches to Environmental Values," in Andrew Light and Eric Katz, eds., *Environmental Pragmatism* (London: Routledge, 1996), pp. 105–138; Norton, "Pragmatism, Adaptive

Management, and Sustainability," *Environmental Values* 8 (1999): 451–466; and *Sustainability: A Philosophy of Adaptive Ecosystem Management* (Chicago: University of Chicago Press, 2005).

77. Mumford, *Culture of Cities*, p. 377.

78. John Dewey, *The Public and Its Problems*, in volume 2 of *John Dewey: The Later Works*, Jo Ann Boydston, ed. (Carbondale: Southern Illinois University Press, 1984 [orig. 1927]), quote on p. 364.

79. Dewey develops this line of argument in numerous works, including *The Public and Its Problems* and *Liberalism and Social Action*.

80. For a revealing analysis of Dewey's and Mill's liberalism and their understanding of public deliberation, see James Gouinlock's *Excellence in Public Discourse: John Stewart Mill, John Dewey, and Social Intelligence* (New York: Teachers College Press, 1986).

81. Dewey, *Liberalism and Social Action*, p. 56.

82. Dewey, *The Public and Its Problems*, p. 328.

83. Dewey, *The Public and Its Problems*, p. 331.

84. Mumford, *Culture of Cities*, p. 380.

85. Mumford, *Culture of Cities*, p. 384

86. Mumford, *Culture of Cities*, p. 387.

87. Mumford, *Culture of Cities*, p. 386.

88. Dewey, *The Public and Its Problems*, p. 370.

89. On this I clearly disagree with John Friedmann's conclusion that Mumford's intellectual foundations were not pragmatic, even if Friedmann recognizes that Mumford expressed a Deweyan approach to social learning in the 1930s. See Friedmann, *Planning in the Public Domain: From Knowledge to Action* (Princeton, NJ: Princeton University Press, 1987), pp. 198–200. I think Friedmann misses the pragmatic logic of Mumford's planning method and the degree to which Mumford's social democratic commitments mirrored Dewey's own. Friedmann's characterization of Dewey as a technocrat who favored the opinion of experts in planning and policy argument is, I suspect, the primary culprit in this misreading. In fact, Dewey was much more of a "radical" democrat than Friedmann suggests. See Westbrook, *John Dewey and American Democracy*, for one of the more compelling discussions of Dewey's strong democratic credentials.

90. Donald Worster, *A River Running West: The Life of John Wesley Powell* (New York: Oxford University Press, 2001), p. 552.

91. Thomas P. Hughes, *Human-Built World* (Chicago: University of Chicago Press, 2004).

Chapter 4

1. J. Baird Callicott and Michael P. Nelson, eds., *The Great New Wilderness Debate* (Athens: University of Georgia Press, 1998).

2. Larry Anderson, *Benton MacKaye: Conservationist, Planner, and Creator of the Appalachian Trail* (Baltimore: Johns Hopkins University Press, 2002). In addition to Anderson's book, several other fine treatments of MacKaye's environmental thought have appeared over the past decade. See especially the discussions of MacKaye in Robert McCullough, *The Landscape of Community. A History of Communal Forests in New England* (Hanover, NH: University Press of New England, 1995); Mark Luccarelli, *Lewis Mumford and the Ecological Region. The Politics of Planning* (New York: Guilford Press, 1995); Edward K. Spann, *Designing Modern America: The Regional Planning Association of America and Its Members* (Columbus: Ohio State University Press, 1996); Keller Easterling, *Organization Space: Landscapes, Highways, and Houses in America* (Cambridge, MA: MIT Press, 1999); Paul S. Sutter, *Driven Wild: How the Fight Against Automobiles Launched the Modern Wilderness Movement* (Seattle: University of Washington Press, 2002); and Matthew Dalbey, *Regional Visionaries and Metropolitan Boosters: Decentralization, Regional Planning, and Parkways During the Interwar Years* (Boston: Kluwer Academic Publishers, 2002). This beginnings of this quasi-renaissance in MacKaye scholarship were in hindsight kicked off by Tony Hiss's discussion of MacKaye in his widely read book, *The Experience of Place* (New York: Random House, 1990).

3. For a more detailed analysis of this contextualist trend in conservation and environmental history and philosophy, see Ben A. Minteer and Robert E. Manning, eds., *Reconstructing Conservation: Finding Common Ground* (Washington, DC: Island Press, 2003).

4. See Andrew Light and Eric Katz, eds., *Environmental Pragmatism* (London: Routledge, 1996) for a description of this revisionist and pluralist stance within environmental ethics.

5. Josiah Royce, *The Religious Aspect of Philosophy* (Boston: Houghton Mifflin, 1885).

6. Josiah Royce, *The World and the Individual* (New York: Macmillan, 1900–1901).

7. Josiah Royce, *The Philosophy of Loyalty* (New York: Macmillan, 1908).

8. Josiah Royce, *The Problem of Christianity* (New York: Macmillan, 1913).

9. As John Clendenning writes, Royce used to remark that he had started his philosophical career as a "very pure pragmatist," and considered his mature philosophy as a form of "Absolute pragmatism." John Clendenning, *The Life and Thought of Josiah Royce* (Nashville, TN: Vanderbilt University Press, 1999, rev. ed.), p. 286.

10. For a perceptive examination of the similarities between Royce and Dewey's understanding of community, see the essay by John E. Smith, "The Value of

Community: Dewey and Royce," in his *America's Philosophical Vision* (Chicago: University of Chicago Press, 1992), pp. 139–152.

11. Josiah Royce, *Race Questions, Provincialism, and Other American Problems* (New York: Macmillan, 1908).

12. Josiah Royce, *The Basic Writings of Josiah Royce*, John J. McDermott, ed., vol. 2 (Chicago: University of Chicago Press, 1969), p. 1067.

13. Royce, *Basic Writings*, p. 1069.

14. Royce, *Basic Writings*, p. 1070.

15. Royce, *Basic Writings*, p. 1088.

16. See, e.g., Martha Nussbaum (with respondents) in Joshua Cohen, ed., *For Love of Country. Debating the Limits of Patriotism* (Boston: Beacon Press, 1996).

17. Royce, *Basic Writings*, vol. 2, p. 1072.

18. For a creative attempt to apply Royce's communitarianism to modern problems of the family, education, and medicine, see Jacquelyn Ann K. Kegley, *Genuine Individuals and Genuine Communities: A Roycean Public Philosophy* (Nashville, TN: Vanderbilt University Press, 1997).

19. Royce, *Basic Writings*, p. 1074.

20. John Dewey, *The Public and Its Problems*, in volume 2 of *John Dewey: The Later Works*, Jo Ann Boydston, ed. (Carbondale: Southern Illinois University Press, 1984 [orig. 1927]), p. 296.

21. Gustave Le Bon, *The Crowd: A Study of the Popular Mind* (London: T. F. Unwin, 1897, 2nd ed.).

22. Royce, *Basic Writings*, p. 1079.

23. John J. McDermott, "Josiah Royce's Philosophy of the Community: The Danger of the Detached Individual," in Marcus Singer, ed., *American Philosophy* (Cambridge: Cambridge University Press, 1985), pp. 153–176; quote on p. 172.

24. R. Jackson Wilson has observed that "As the absolute dwindled [in Royce's philosophical system], Royce's emphasis on working forms of community grew. In the end the absolute practically disappeared from his thought and was replaced by the community." Wilson, *In Quest of Community. Social Philosophy in the United States, 1860–1920* (New York: Wiley, 1968), p. 165.

25. Josiah Royce, *The Hope of the Great Community* (New York: Macmillan, 1916).

26. Royce, *Hope of the Great Community*, pp. 51–52.

27. I borrow the term *political technology* in this sense from Michael Eldridge, *Transforming Experience. John Dewey's Cultural Instrumentalism* (Nashville, TN: Vanderbilt University Press, 1998).

28. Paul Bryant, "The Quality of the Day: The Achievement of Benton MacKaye" (Ph.D. dissertation, University of Illinois, 1965), passim.

29. Bryant, "The Quality of the Day," p. 55.

30. Anderson, *Benton MacKaye*, p. 31.

31. Shaler was also a polygenist, a racist, and an anti-Semite, thus making his legacy for contemporary environmentalism uneven, to put it mildly. See David N. Livingstone, *Nathaniel Southgate Shaler and the Culture of American Science* (Tuscaloosa: University of Alabama Press, 1987).

32. Livingstone, *Nathaniel Southgate Shaler*, p. 196.

33. Anderson, *Benton MacKaye*, p. 32.

34. Bryant, "Quality of the Day," pp. 58–59.

35. Indeed, MacKaye appears to have had a keen interest in the philosophical and political arguments of the day. As Paul Bryant and Larry Anderson write in their biographical accounts, MacKaye's room at Harvard during his tenure as a forestry instructor became the regular meeting place for the Harvard Socialist Club, a group that included such present and future public intellectual luminaries as Lincoln Steffens and Walter Lippmann (see Bryant, "Quality of the Day," p. 84 and Anderson, *Benton MacKaye*, pp. 59–60). This leads me to conclude that MacKaye would have been in an intellectual environment attuned to Royce's ideas, especially since MacKaye had spent time in the philosopher's classroom. I am, of course, aware that such backward-looking attributions of intellectual debts are often quite difficult to make, and must be offered with great caution and humility. Nevertheless, I think that it is reasonable to make such an attribution here, particularly given the details of MacKaye's biography. More significantly, I believe that my discussion of their shared concerns about the threats to American provincialism and their more general communitarian commitments provides a persuasive, even if indirect, argument for this intriguing philosophical influence.

36. Benton MacKaye, *Employment and Natural Resources* (Washington, DC: Government Printing Office, 1919).

37. Despite the endorsement of publications like the *New Republic*, MacKaye's recolonization plans were lost with the postwar shrinkage of government programs. As he himself put it, "Washington went down like a circus tent." Quoted in Edward K. Spann, *Designing Modern America*, p. 5.

38. Anderson, *Benton MacKaye*, pp. 143–145.

39. Benton MacKaye, "An Appalachian Trail: A Project in Regional Planning," *Journal of the American Institute of Architects* 9 (1921): 3–8; quote on p. 3.

40. Mackaye, "An Appalachian Trail," quote on p. 3.

41. MacKaye, "An Appalachian Trail," p. 5.

42. Bryan G. Norton, *Why Preserve Natural Variety?* (Princeton, NJ: Princeton University Press, 1987), p. 189.

43. Bob Pepperman Taylor, *America's Bachelor Uncle. Thoreau and the American Polity* (Lawrence: University Press of Kansas, 1996), p. 90.

44. Henry David Thoreau, *Walden*, collected in *Henry David Thoreau* (New York: Library of America, 1985), p. 575.

45. My characterization of Thoreau as a politically engaged thinker and social critic owes much to the work of Bob Pepperman Taylor, who has advanced this alternative reading of the poet of Walden Pond in a number of publications, including *Our Limits Transgressed: Environmental Political Thought in America* (Lawrence: University Press of Kansas, 1992), and especially the aforementioned *America's Bachelor Uncle*.

46. Thoreau, *Walden*, p. 551.

47. Walter Benn Michaels, "Walden's False Bottoms," *Glyph* 1 (1977): 132–149.

48. For a fuller discussion of this critical thought in Thoreau's work, see Taylor, *America's Bachelor Uncle*.

49. Benton MacKaye, "On the Purpose of the Appalachian Trail," unpublished manuscript, MacKaye Family Papers, Dartmouth College Library, box 183, folder 57, p. 2.

50. Benton MacKaye, *The New Exploration: A Philosophy of Regional Planning* (Harpers Ferry, WV, and Urbana-Champaign: The Appalachian Trail Conference and the University of Illinois Press, 1990 [orig. 1928]), p. 166.

51. MacKaye, "On the Purpose," MacKaye Family Papers, Dartmouth College Library, box 183, folder 57, p. 1.

52. MacKaye, Untitled and unpublished manuscript, MacKaye Family Papers, Dartmouth College Library, box 183, folder 30, p. 5.

53. Benton MacKaye, "Our Common Mind," unpublished manuscript, MacKaye Family Papers, Dartmouth College Library, box 183, folder 34, p. 7.

54. Benton MacKaye, "Cultural Aspects of Regionalism," unpublished manuscript, MacKaye Family Papers, Dartmouth College Library, box 184, folder 29, p. 4.

55. Bernard Bailyn, *To Begin the World Anew. The Genius and Ambiguities of the American Founders* (New York: Knopf, 2003), quote on p. 4.

56. Bailyn, *To Begin the World Anew*, pp. 35–36.

57. MacKaye, *The New Exploration*, pp. 118–119; emphasis in original.

58. Benton MacKaye, Address to the Appalachian Trail Conference, Gatlinburg, Tennessee, 1931. MacKaye Family Papers, Dartmouth College Library, box 184, folder 40, p. 4.

59. As Larry Anderson writes, MacKaye continued to hew to a broadly anthropocentric environmentalism in the decades following his early Appalachian Trail work, although by the 1950s he appeared to be more open to alternative justifications for conservation policy, including what Anderson believes was a kind of biocentrism inspired by Aldo Leopold's appropriation of community ecology and Leopold's ideas about wilderness and the goal of land health. While I do not think MacKaye really came all that close to a "pure" biocentric worldview (and

as I write in the next chapter, Leopold's notion of land health possesses a significant humanistic component), I certainly agree that MacKaye's thinking about wilderness, like Leopold's, took on a much more ecological and preservationist policy slant by the early 1950s. See Anderson, *Benton MacKaye*, pp. 325–326.

60. Royce, *Basic Writings*, p. 953.

61. Royce, *Basic Writings*, pp. 1087–1088. A few other scholars have noted the similarities between the RPAA's environmentalist outlook and Royce's understanding of provincialism, although they have not (as I have here) singled out MacKaye as a direct heir to this line of thought. See Christopher Tunnard and Henry Hope Reed, *American Skyline: The Growth and Form of our Cities and Towns* (Boston: Houghton Mifflin, 1955); and John L. Thomas, "Holding the Middle Ground," in Robert Fishman, ed., *The American Planning Tradition* (Washington, DC: Woodrow Wilson Center Press, 2000), pp. 33–63.

62. Historian Robert Hine, in his discussion of the metaphysical influence of the American West on Royce's thought, suggests that Royce actually shared many similarities with biocentric wilderness champion John Muir. As Hine writes, "Royce and Muir were both comfortable with pioneer pragmatism, but like Albert Bierstadt painting a western mountain, they wrapped it in a spiritual glow." Robert Hine, The American West as Metaphysics: A Perspective on Josiah Royce," *Pacific Historical Review* 58 (1989): 267–291; quote on p. 281. While I agree that in terms of deeper metaphysical views, Royce is closer to the transcendentalism of Muir than he is the more materialistic views of MacKaye, Royce's social philosophy is much more in line with MacKaye's communitarianism than it is with Muir's well-known individualism and his disdain for much in American civic life.

63. MacKaye, "An Appalachian Trail," p. 6.

64. MacKaye, "An Appalachian Trail," passim.

65. Benton MacKaye, address to the Appalachian Trail Conference. MacKaye Family Papers, Dartmouth College Library, box 184, folder 40, p. 3.

66. Mark Luccarelli, *Lewis Mumford and the Ecological Region. The Politics of Planning* (New York: Guilford Press, 1995), p. 77.

67. John L. Thomas, "Lewis Mumford, Benton MacKaye, and the Regional Vision," in Thomas P. Hughes and Agatha C. Hughes, eds, *Lewis Mumford, Public Intellectual* (New York: Oxford University Press 1990), pp. 66–99.

68. Spann, *Designing Modern America*, p. 39.

69. Lewis Mumford, "Introduction," in Benton MacKaye, *New Exploration*, p. xv.

70. Aldo Leopold, "The Wilderness and Its Place in Forest Recreational Policy," *Journal of Forestry* 19 (1921): 718–721.

71. See Paul S. Sutter, " 'A Blank Spot on the Map': Aldo Leopold, Wilderness, and U.S. Forest Service Recreational Policy, 1909–1924." *Western Historical*

Quarterly 29 (1998): 187–214, ·quote on p. 213. See also Sutter, *Driven Wild*, Chapter 3.

72. This shift is most clearly described by Curt Meine in his authoritative biography, *Aldo Leopold. His Life and Work* (Madison: University of Wisconsin Press, 1988), especially pp. 340–361.

73. Aldo Leopold, letter to Benton MacKaye, MacKaye Family Papers, Dartmouth College Library, box 167, folder 2.

74. MacKaye, *The New Exploration*, p. 202.

75. MacKaye, Untitled and unpublished manuscript, MacKaye Family Papers, Dartmouth College Library, box 183, folder 30, p. 2.

76. Ronald Foresta, "The Transformation of the Appalachian Trail," *Geographical Review* 77 (1987): 76–85.

77. Robert Gottlieb, *Forcing the Spring: The Transformation of the American Environmental Movement* (Washington, DC: Island Press, 1993), p. 74.

78. Robert Dorman, *Revolt of the Provinces. The Regionalist Movement in America, 1920–1945.* (Chapel Hill: University of North Carolina Press, 1993), pp. 318–319.

79. William Cronon, "The Trouble with Wilderness; or, Getting Back to the Wrong Nature," in W. Cronon, ed., *Uncommon Ground. Rethinking the Human Place in Nature* (New York: W. W. Norton, 1996), pp. 69–90.

80. Cronon, "The Trouble with Wilderness," pp. 80–81.

81. Cronon, "The Trouble with Wilderness," p. 80.

82. Gary Snyder, "Nature as Seen from Kitkitdizze Is No 'Social Construction,'" *Wild Earth* 6 (1996/97): 8–9.

83. Holmes Rolston III, "Nature for Real: Is Nature a Social Construct?" in T. D. J. Chappell, ed, *The Philosophy of the Environment* (Edinburgh: Edinburgh University Press, 1997), pp. 38–64; quote on p. 49.

84. Cronon, "The Trouble with Wilderness," p. 89.

85. Dave Foreman, *Rewilding North America: A Vision for Conservation in the 21st Century* (Washington, DC: Island Press, 2004).

86. Michael Soulé and Reed Noss, "Rewilding and Biodiversity: Complementary Goals for Continental Conservation," *Wild Earth* Fall (1998): 1–11; quote on p. 8.

87. As Foreman writes, the rewilding vision "stands out because it is bold, scientifically credible, practicably achievable, and hopeful. . . . It is bold because it offers a plain alternative to business as usual and is unflinching in daring to say what actually needs to be done to stop our war on nature. By using the best ecological research to set goals and to guide the selection, design, and restoration of protected areas, it is scientifically credible. . . . In taking advantage of the vast experience of the citizen conservation movement to weave a strategy for implementation of the vision, the vision becomes practically achievable." Foreman, *Rewilding North America*, p. 143.

88. Leslie Paul Thiele, *Environmentalism for a New Millennium. The Challenge of Coevolution* (New York: Oxford University Press, 1999).

Chapter 5

1. Aldo Leopold, *A Sand County Almanac* (Oxford, UK: Oxford University Press, 1989 [orig. 1949]).

2. Rachel Carson, *Silent Spring* (Boston: Houghton Mifflin, 1962).

3. Curt Meine, *Aldo Leopold: His Life and Work* (Madison: University of Wisconsin Press, 1988), p. 35.

4. Susan L. Flader, *Thinking Like a Mountain: Aldo Leopold and the Evolution of an Ecological Attitude Toward Deer, Wolves, and Forests* (Madison: University of Wisconsin Press, 1994, reprint ed.), p. 8.

5. Flader, *Thinking Like a Mountain*, pp. 10–12.

6. Flader, *Thinking Like a Mountain*, p. 15.

7. Aldo Leopold, "The Wilderness and Its Place in Forest Recreation Policy," *Journal of Forestry* 19 (1921): 718–721.

8. Meine, *Aldo Leopold*, p. 197.

9. See, for example, Aldo Leopold, "Conserving the Covered Wagon," and "Wilderness as a Form of Land Use," in Susan Flader and J. Baird Callicott, eds., *The River of God and other Essays by Aldo Leopold* (Madison: University of Wisconsin Press, 1991), pp. 128–132 and 134–142, respectively.

10. Flader, *Thinking Like a Mountain*, pp. 16–18.

11. Aldo Leopold, "Some Fundamentals of Conservation in the Southwest." *Environmental Ethics* 8 (1979): 195–220.

12. Meine, *Aldo Leopold*, p. 234.

13. Aldo Leopold, "The Home Builder Conserves," in Flader and Callicott, *River*, pp. 143–147.

14. Meine, *Aldo Leopold*, p. 262.

15. Meine, *Aldo Leopold*, p. 279.

16. Aldo Leopold, *Game Management* (New York: Charles Scribners Sons, 1933).

17. Aldo Leopold, "The Conservation Ethic," in Flader and Callicott, *River*, pp. 181–192.

18. Leopold, "Conservation Ethic," in Falder and Callicott, *River*, p. 183 (emphasis in original).

19. Leopold, "Conservation Ethic," in Falder and Callicott, *River*, p. 182.

20. Meine, *Aldo Leopold*, p. 313.

21. Susan Flader, "Aldo Leopold's Sand Country," in J. Baird Callicott, ed., *A Companion to A Sand County Almanac* (Madison: University of Wisconsin Press, 1987), pp. 40–62.

22. See Paul S. Sutter, *Driven Wild: How the Fight Against Automobiles Launched the Modern Wilderness Movement* (Seattle: University of Washington Press, 2002).

23. Meine, *Aldo Leopold*, pp. 353–356.

24. Aldo Leopold, Unpublished 1947 foreword to *A Sand County Almanac*, in J. Baird Callicott, ed., *A Companion to A Sand County Almanac* (Madison: University of Wisconsin Press, 1987), pp. 281–288; quote on pp. 285–286.

25. Aldo Leopold, "A Biotic View of Land," in Flader and Callicott, *River*, pp. 266–273.

26. Leopold, "A Biotic View," in Flader and Callicott, *River*, pp. 266–267.

27. Leopold, "A Biotic View," in Flader and Callicott, *River*, p 269.

28. Leopold, "A Biotic View," in Flader and Callicott, *River*, pp. 269–270.

29. Charles S. Elton, *Animal Ecology* (Chicago: University of Chicago Press, 2001 [orig. 1926]).

30. Meine, *Aldo Leopold*, p. 284.

31. Arthur G. Tansley, "The Use and Abuse of Vegetational Concepts and Terms," *Ecology* 16: 284–307. For useful historical discussions of the development of ecosystem ecology, see Robert P. McIntosh, *The Background of Ecology: Concept and Theory* (Cambridge: Cambridge University Press, 1985); Joel B. Hagen, *An Entangled Bank: The Origins of Ecosystem Ecology* (New Brunswick, NJ: Rutgers University Press, 1992); and Frank Benjamin Golley, *A History of the Ecosystem Concept in Ecology* (New Haven, CT: Yale University Press, 1996).

32. Meine, *Aldo Leopold*, pp. 458–459.

33. See Meine, *Aldo Leopold*, pp. 437–452.

34. Flader, *Thinking Like a Mountain*, p. 237.

35. This essay appears in Flader and Callicott, *River*, pp. 330–335.

36. Aldo Leopold, "The Ecological Conscience," in Flader and Callicott, *River*, pp. 338–346.

37. Leopold, "Ecological Conscience," in Flader and Callicott, *River*, p. 345.

38. Curt Meine, "Moving Mountains: Aldo Leopold and A Sand County Almanac," in Richard L. Knight and Suzanne Riedel, eds., *Aldo Leopold and the Ecological Conscience* (Oxford: Oxford University Press, 2002), pp. 14–31; cit. p. 25.

39. Leopold, *A Sand County Almanac*, pp. 224–225.

40. Leopold, *A Sand County Almanac*, pp. 214–221.

41. Leopold, *A Sand County Almanac*, p. 223.

42. Leopold, *A Sand County Almanac*, p. 204.

43. See J. Baird Callicott, "The Conceptual Foundations of the Land Ethic," in Callicott, ed., *A Companion to A Sand County Almanac*, pp. 186–217.

44. See Bill Devall and George Sessions, *Deep Ecology: Living as if Nature Mattered:* (Salt Lake City, UT: Gibbs Smith, 1985), esp. pp. 85–86.

45. Max Oelschlaeger, *The Idea of Wilderness: From Prehistory to the Age of Ecology* (New Haven, CT: Yale University Press, 1991), p. 242.

46. Eric Katz, "The Traditional Ethics of Natural Resource Management," in Richard L. Knight and Sarah F. Bates, eds., *A New Century for Natural Resources Management* (Washington, DC: Island Press, 1995), pp. 101–116.

47. Bryan G. Norton, "The Constancy of Leopold's Land Ethic," *Conservation Biology* 2 (1988): 93–102.

48. Norton has continued to make this case for Leopold as pragmatist over the years. In a 1995 paper appearing in *Environmental Ethics*, for example, he argued that Leopold's land ethic should not be read as speaking to the question of the moral status of nature, but is best understood as a practical piece of advice on how to manage the land as a complex ecological system, management that is ultimately justified by an appeal to an array of broadly instrumental values. See Bryan G. Norton, "Why I am Not a Nonanthropocentrist: Callicott and the Failure of Monistic Inherentism," *Environmental Ethics* 17 (1995): 341–358. More recently, Norton has written that Leopold's pragmatism and ecological worldview position him as one of the main precursors to contemporary adaptive ecosystem management. See Bryan G. Norton, "Pragmatism, Adaptive Management, and Sustainability," *Environmental Values* 8 (1999): 451–466; and his forthcoming book, *Sustainability: A Philosophy of Adaptive Ecosystem Management* (Chicago: University of Chicago Press, 2005).

49. Larry A. Hickman, "Nature as Culture: John Dewey's Pragmatic Naturalism," in Andrew Light and Eric Katz, eds., *Environmental Pragmatism* (London: Routledge, 1996), pp. 50–72; quote on p. 61.

50. Hickman, "Nature as Culture," in Light and Katz, *Environmental Pragmatism*, p. 66; emphasis added.

51. See Susan Flader, "Aldo Leopold and the Evolution of a Land Ethic," in Thomas Tanner, ed., *Aldo Leopold: The Man and His Legacy* (Ankeny, IA: Soil Conservation Society of America, 1987), pp. 3–24, p. 22 (footnote).

52. Callicott, "Conceptual Foundations," in Callicott, *Companion to A Sand County Almanac*, p. 214.

53. Bob Pepperman Taylor, "Aldo Leopold's Civic Education," in Ben A. Minteer and Bob Pepperman Taylor, eds., *Democracy and the Claims of Nature: Critical Perspectives for a New Century* (Lanham, MD: Rowman & Littlefield, 2002), pp. 173–187.

54. Taylor, "Aldo Leopold's Civic Education," in Minteer and Pepperman Taylor, *Democracy and the Claims of Nature*, p. 180.

55. Susan Flader, "Building Conservation on the Land: Aldo Leopold and the Tensions of Professionalism and Citizenship," in Ben A. Minteer and Robert E. Manning, eds., *Reconstructing Conservation: Finding Common Ground* (Washington, DC: Island Press, 2003), pp. 115–132.

56. Flader, "Building Conservation," in Minteer and Manning, *Reconstructing Conservation*, pp. 125–127.

57. Aldo Leopold, "The Civic Life of Albuquerque," September 27, 1918. Aldo Leopold Papers, University of Wisconsin-Madison Library.

58. Leopold, "Civic Life," p. 1.

59. Leopold, "Civic Life," p. 3.

60. Leopold, "Civic Life," p. 5.

61. Leopold, "Civic Life," p. 6.

62. For an interesting discussion of the political and civic aspects of the City Beautiful and Social Centers movements, see Kevin Mattson, *Creating a Democratic Public: The Struggle for Urban Participatory Democracy during the Progressive Era* (University Park: Pennsylvania State University Press, 1997).

63. Aldo Leopold, "Pioneers and Gullies," in Flader and Callicott, *River*, pp. 106–113; quote on p. 110.

64. Leopold, "Pioneers and Gullies," in Flader and Callicott, *River*, pp. 112–113; emphasis added.

65. Leopold, "Wilderness as a Form of Land Use," in Flader and Callicott, *River*, pp. 139–140.

66. Aldo Leopold, "Conservation Economics," in Flader and Callicott, *River*, pp. 193–202.

67. Leopold, "Conservation Economics," in Flader and Callicott, *River*, p. 200.

68. Leopold, "Conservation Economics," in Flader and Callicott, *River*, p. 201.

69. Leopold, "Conservation Economics," in Flader and Callicott, *River*, p. 202.

70. Aldo Leopold, "Wilderness," in Flader and Callicott, *River*, pp. 226–229; quote on p. 228.

71. Leopold, "A Biotic View of Land," in Flader and Callicott, *River*, pp. 266–273; quote on p. 266.

72. Aldo Leopold, "Wilderness as a Land Laboratory," in Flader and Callicott, *River*, pp. 287–289.

73. Aldo Leopold, "Conservation: In Whole or in Part?" in Flader and Callicott, *River*, pp. 310–319.

74. "The Land-Health Concept and Conservation," in Callicott and Freyfogle, *Health of the Land*, pp. 218–226.

75. Aldo Leopold, "Biotic Land-Use," in J. Baird Callicott and Eric T. Freyfogle, eds., *For the Health of the Land: Previously Unpublished Essays and Other Writings* (Washington, DC: Island Press, 1999), pp. 198–207; quote on p. 202.

76. Leopold, "Biotic Land-Use," in Callicott and Freyfogle, *Health of the Land*, p. 203.

77. Leopold, "Biotic Land-Use," in Callicott and Freyfogle, *Health of the Land*, p. 205.

78. For more on the notion of ecological resilience, see C. S. Holling, "Resilience and Stability of Ecological Systems," *Annual Review of Ecology and Systematics* 4 (1973): 1–24; and C. S. Holling and Lance H. Gunderson, "Resilience and Adaptive Cycles," in Lance H. Gunderson and C. S. Holling, eds., *Panarchy: Understanding Transformations in Human and Natural Systems* (Washington; DC: Island Press, 2002), pp. 25–62.

79. For contemporary discussions of the paradigm of ecological health, see the essays in Robert Costanza, Bryan G. Norton, and Benjamin D. Haskell, eds., *Ecosystem Health: New Goals for Environmental Management* (Washington, DC: Island Press, 1992); and David Rapport, Robert Costanza, Paul R. Epstein, Connie Gaudet, and Richard Levins, eds., *Ecosystem Health* (Malden, MA: Blackwell, 1998). Eric Freyfogle has written extensively about Aldo Leopold and the normative and legal implications of his notion of land health for current discussions in American land use and property law. See his *Bounded People, Boundless Lands: Envisioning a New Land Ethic* (Washington, DC: Island Press, 1998), and *The Land We Share: Private Property and the Common Good* (Washington, DC: Island Press, 2003).

80. Leopold, "Conservation: In Whole or in Part?" in Flader and Callicott, *River*, p. 310.

81. A point also made by J. Baird Callicott. See Callicott, *Beyond the Land Ethic: More Essays in Environmental Philosophy* (Albany: State University of New York Press, 1999), p. 342.

82. Leopold, "Conservation: In Whole or in Part?" in Flader and Callicott, *River*, p. 316.

83. Leopold, "Conservation: In Whole or in Part?" in Flader and Callicott, *River*, p. 315.

84. Leopold, "Conservation: In Whole or in Part?" in Flader and Callicott, *River*, p. 317.

85. Leopold, "Conservation: In Whole or in Part?" in Flader and Callicott, *River*, p. 319.

86. Aldo Leopold, "Planning for Wildlife," in Callicott and Freyfogle, *For the Health of the Land*, pp. 193–198; quote on p. 194.

87. Aldo Leopold, "Land-Use and Democracy," in Flader and Callicott, *River*, pp. 295–300; quote on p. 300.

88. Aldo Leopold, "The Land-Health Concept and Conservation," in Callicott and Freyfogle, *For the Health of the Land*, pp. 218–226; quote on p. 224.

89. Leopold, "The Land-Health Concept," in Callicott and Freyfogle, *For the Health of the Land*, p. 225; emphasis added.

90. Aldo Leopold, "Economics, Philosophy and Land," November 23, 1938. Aldo Leopold Papers, University of Wisconsin-Madison Library, p. 6.

91. Leopold, *Sand County Almanac*, p. 204.

92. Leopold, *Sand County Almanac*, p. 221.

93. Leopold, *Sand County Almanac*, p. 223.

94. Leopold, *Sand County Almanac*, p. viii.

95. Aldo Leopold, "A Criticism of the Booster Spirit," in Flader and Callicott, *River*, pp. 98–105; quote on p. 105.

96. Leopold, "The Conservation Ethic," in Flader and Callicott, *River*, p. 188.

97. Aldo Leopold, "Land Pathology," in Flader and Callicott, *River*, pp. 212–217; quote on p. 217.

98. Aldo Leopold, "The Farmer as a Conservationist," in Flader and Callicott, *River*, pp. 255–265; quote on p. 259.

99. Leopold, *Sand County Almanac*, p. ix.

100. Leopold, "Biotic Land-Use," in Callicott and Freyfogle, *Health of the Land*, pp. 206–207.

101. Leopold, *Sand County Almanac*, p. vii.

102. Leopold, *Sand County Almanac*, pp. 46, 100.

103. Leopold, "Wilderness as a Form of Land Use," in Flader and Callicott, *River*, p. 142.

104. For more on this point, see Bob Pepperman Taylor's discussion of Leopold as a democratic thinker in his aforementioned "Aldo Leopold's Civic Education," in Minteer and Taylor, *Democracy and the Claims of Nature*.

105. John Dewey, *The Public and Its Problems*, in volume 2 of *John Dewey: The Later Works*, Jo Ann Boydston, ed. (Carbondale: Southern Illinois University Press, 1984 [orig. 1927]), p. 314.

106. Flader, *Thinking Like a Mountain*, p. 225.

107. Leopold, quoted in Meine, *Aldo Leopold*, p. 488.

108. For more on the nature of ecological services and attempts to understand and measure their value to society and the human economy, see Robert Costanza, Ralph d'Arge, Rudolf de Groot, Stephen Farber, Monica Grasso, Bruce Hannon, Karin Limburg, Shahid Naeem, Robert V. O'Neill, Jose Paruelo, Robert G. Raskin, Paul Sutton, and Marjan van den Belt, "The Value of the World's Ecosystem Services and Natural Capital," *Nature* 387 (1997): 253–260; Gretchen C. Daily, ed., *Nature's Services: Societal Dependence on Natural Ecosystems* (Washington, DC: Island Press, 1997); Yvonne Baskin, *The Work of Nature: How the Diversity of Life Sustains Us* (Washington, DC: Island Press, 1997); and Geoffrey Heal, *Nature and the Marketplace: Capturing the Value of Ecosystem Services* (Washington, DC: Island Press, 2000).

109. I advance this argument in much greater detail in my paper, "Environmental Philosophy and the Public Interest: A Pragmatic Reconciliation," *Environmental Values* 14 (2005): 37–60.

Chapter 6

1. For example, Robert Elliot, "Faking Nature," *Inquiry* 25 (1982): 81–93; Eric Katz, "The Big Lie: Human Restoration of Nature," *Research in Philosophy and Technology* 12 (1992): 231–241.

2. Andrew Light, "Ecological Restoration and the Culture of Nature: A Pragmatic Perspective," in Paul H. Gobster and R. Bruce Hull, eds., *Restoring Nature: Perspectives form the Social Sciences and Humanities* (Washington, DC: Island Press, 2000), pp. 49–70; and "Restoring Ecological Citizenship," in Ben A. Minteer and Bob Pepperman Taylor, eds., *Democracy and the Claims of Nature: Critical Perspectives for a New Century* (Lanham, MD: Rowman & Littlefield, 2002), pp. 153–172.

3. Eric Higgs, *Nature by Design: People, Natural Process, and Ecological Restoration* (Cambridge, MA: MIT Press, 2003); William Jordan III, *The Sunflower Forest: Ecological Restoration and the New Communion with Nature* (Berkeley: University of California Press, 2003).

4. Margaret Palmer, Emily Bernhardt, Elizabeth Chornesky, Scott Collins, Andrew Dobson, Clifford Duke, Barry Gold, Robert Jacobson, Charon Kingsland, Rhonda Kranz, Michael Mappin, M. Luisa Martinez, Fiorenza Micheli, Jennifer Morse, Michael Pace, Mercedes Pascual, Stephen Palumbi, O. J. Reichman, Ashley Simons, Alan Townsend, and Monica Turner, "Ecology for a Crowded Planet," *Science* 304 (2004): 1251–1252; quote on p. 1252.

5. Michael L. Rosenzweig, *Win-Win Ecology: How Earth's Species can Survive in the Midst of Human Enterprise* (Oxford: Oxford University Press, 2003).

6. Paul B. Thompson, *The Spirit of the Soil: Agriculture and Environmental Ethics* (London: Routledge, 1995).

7. Donald VanDeVeer and Christine Pierce, eds., *The Environmental Ethics & Policy Book: Philosophy Ecology, Economics* (Belmont, CA: Thomson Wadsworth, 2003, 3rd ed.)

8. Deane Curtin, "Making Peace with the Earth: Indigenous Agriculture and the Green Revolution," *Environmental Ethics* 17 (1995): 59–73; Michaelle L. Browers, "Jefferson's Land Ethic: Environmentalist Ideas in *Notes on the State of Virginia*," *Environmental Ethics* 21 (1999): 43–57; Peter S. Wenz: "Pragmatism in Practice: The Efficiency of Sustainable Agriculture," *Environmental Ethics* 21 (1999): 391–400; John L. Paterson, "Conceptualizing Stewardship in Agriculture within the Christian Tradition," *Environmental Ethics* 25 (2003): 43–58; and Kimberly Smith, "Black Agrarianism and the Foundations of Black Environmental Thought," *Environmental Ethics* 26 (2004): 267–286.

9. Lynn White, Jr., "The Historical Roots of Our Ecologic Crisis," *Science* 155 (1967): 1203–1207.

10. White, "Historical Roots," p. 1205.

11. See Paul B. Thompson, "Expanding the Conservation Tradition: The Agrarian Vision," in Ben A. Minteer and Robert E. Manning, eds., *Reconstructing Conservation: Finding Common Ground* (Washington, DC: Island Press, 2003), pp. 77–92; and James A. Montmarquet, *The Idea of Agrarianism: From Hunter-Gatherer to Agrarian Radical in Western Culture* (Moscow: University of Idaho Press, 1989).

12. Thompson, "Expanding the Conservation Tradition," p. 83.

13. See, for example, the essays in Eric T. Freyfogle, ed., *The New Agrarianism: Land, Culture, and the Community of Life* (Washington, DC: Island Press, 2001); and Norman Wirzba, ed., *The Essential Agrarian Reader: The Future of Culture, Community, and the Land* (Lexington: University Press of Kentucky, 2003).

14. Randal S. Beeman and James A. Pritchard, *A Green and Permanent Land: Ecology and Agriculture in the Twentieth Century* (Lawrence: University Press of Kansas, 2001).

15. As Beeman and Pritchard note, however, the rhetoric of "sustainable agriculture" has also been coopted by the agricultural establishment, which generally tends to dilute the movement's ecological and social elements. See their *A Green and Permanent Land*, esp. pp. 146–153.

16. Beeman and Pritchard, *A Green and Permanent Land*, chapter 5.

17. Evan Eisenberg, "Back to Eden," *Atlantic Monthly*, November (1989): 57–89.

18. Eisenberg, "Back to Eden," p. 59.

19. Judith D. Soule and Jon K. Piper, *Farming in Nature's Image: An Ecological Approach to Agriculture* (Washington, DC: Island Press, 1992); Stuart L. Pimm, "In Search of Perennial Solutions," *Nature* 389 (1997): 126–127.

20. Wes Jackson, "Nature as the Measure for a Sustainable Agriculture," in VanDeVeer and Pierce, *Environmental Ethics & Policy*, pp. 508–515.

21. For general discussions of some of the results of The Land Institute's experimental projects, see Soule and Piper, *Farming in Nature's Image*, pp. 180–192; Janine M. Benyus, *Biomimicry: Innovation Inspired by Nature* (New York: Perennial/HarperCollins, 2002, reissue), pp. 27–35; and Wes Jackson, "Natural Systems Agriculture: A Truly Radical Alternative," *Agriculture, Ecosystems and Environment* 88 (2002) 111–117.

22. Jackson, "Natural Systems Agriculture," pp. 114–115.

23. Wes Jackson, "Aldo Leopold: Central Figure for Prairie Festival 1998," available online at http://www.landinstitute.org.

24. See Wes Jackson, *Becoming Native to this Place* (Washington, DC: Counterpoint, 1996), esp. chapter 2.

25. Jackson, "Nature as the Measure for a Sustainable Agriculture," pp. 508–509.

26. Wes Jackson, *New Roots for Agriculture* (San Francisco: Friends of the Earth, 1980).

27. Jackson, *New Roots*, p. 141.

28. Jackson, *Altars of Unhewn Stone: Science and the Earth* (San Francisco: North Point Press, 1987), p. 6.

29. Jackson, "Nature as the Measure," in VanDeVeer and Pierce, *Environmental Ethics & Policy*, p. 509.

30. Jackson, "Nature as the Measure," in VanDeVeer and Price, *Environmental Ethics & Policy*, p. 512.

31. Jackson, "Nature as the Measure," in VanDeVeer and Price, *Environmental Ethics & Policy*.

32. Jackson, "Natural Systems Agriculture," p. 113.

33. Jackson, *Altars of Unhewn Stone*, p. 35.

34. Jackson, *Altars of Unhewn Stone*, p. 114.

35. Jackson, *Altars of Unhewn Stone*, p. 114.

36. Jackson, *Altars of Unhewn Stone*, p. 36.

37. Jackson, *Altars of Unhewn Stone*, pp. 12–13.

38. Wes Jackson, "Matfield Green," in William Vitek and Wes Jackson, eds., *Rooted in the Land: Essays on Community and Place* (New Haven, CT: Yale University Press, 1996) pp. 95–103; quotes on pp. 96, 101.

39. See Morton White and Lucia White, *The Intellectual Versus the City* (Cambridge, MA: MIT Press/Harvard University Press, 1962); and John J. McDermott, "Nature Nostalgia and the City: An American Dilemma," in his *The Culture of Experience: Philosophical Essays in the American Grain* (New York: New York University Press, 1976), pp. 179–204.

40. See Warwick Fox, "Introduction: Ethics and the Built Environment," in Warwick Fox, ed., *Ethics and the Built Environment* (London: Routledge, 2000), pp. 1–12; and Andrew Light, "The Urban Blind Spot in Environmental Ethics," *Environmental Politics* 10 (2001): 7–35. Other environmental philosophers who have explored urban and suburban themes in the field include Dale Jamieson, "The City Around Us," in Tom Regan, ed., *Earthbound: New Introductory Essays in Environmental Ethics* (Philadelphia: Temple University Press, 1984), pp. 38–73; Alastair S. Gunn, "Rethinking Communities: Environmental Ethics in an Urbanized World," *Environmental Ethics* 20 (1998): 341–360; Roger J. H. King, "Environmental Ethics and the Built Environment," *Environmental Ethics* 22 (2000): 115–131; and Robert Kirkman, "Reasons to Dwell on (if Not Necessarily in) the Suburbs," *Environmental Ethics* 26 (2004): 77–96.

41. Alastair S. Gunn, "Rethinking Communities," p. 341.

42. Gunn, "Rethinking Communities," pp. 355; 360. See Ian McHarg, *Design with Nature* (Garden City, NY: Anchor, 1969).

43. This is one of the primary goals of the Fox volume, *Ethics and the Built Environment*.

44. A good introduction to the various elements of the New Urbanist program is Peter Katz, *The New Urbanism: Toward an Architecture of Community* (New York: McGraw-Hill, 1994).

45. See especially Peter Calthorpe, *The Next American Metropolis: Ecology, Community, and the American Dream* (New York: Princeton Architectural Press, 1993); and Peter Calthorpe and William Fulton, *The Regional City: Planning for the End of Sprawl* (Washington, DC: Island Press, 2001).

46. Jane Jacobs, *The Death and Life of Great American Cities* (New York: Vintage Books, 1992 [orig. 1961]).

47. Joel Garreau, *Edge City: Life on the New Frontier* (New York: Anchor Books, 1991). Urban historian Dolores Hayden has recently coined the more comprehensive phrase "edge nodes" to refer to both the larger edge cities chronicled by Garreau and smaller growth nodes that display a similar pattern of sprawl. See her *Building Suburbia: Green Fields and Urban Growth, 1820–2000* (New York: Pantheon Books, 2003), esp. chapter 8.

48. Kenneth T. Jackson, *Crabgrass Frontier: The Suburbanization of the United States* (New York: Oxford University Press, 1985).

49. Jackson, *Crabgrass Frontier*, p. 204.

50. See Adam Rome, *The Bulldozer in the Countryside: Suburban Sprawl and the Rise of American Environmentalism* (Cambridge: Cambridge University Press, 2001), chapter 1; and Hayden, *Building Suburbia*, chapter 7.

51. Jackson, *Crabgrass Frontier*, p. 217.

52. Jackson, *Crabgrass Frontier*, p. 249. See also Owen D. Gutfreund, *Twentieth-Century Sprawl: Highways and the Reshaping of the American Landscape* (Oxford: Oxford University Press, 2004).

53. Andres Duany, Elizabeth Plater-Zyberk, and Jeff Speck, *Suburban Nation: The Rise of Sprawl and the Decline of the American Dream* (New York: North Point Press, 2000).

54. Duany et al., *Suburban Nation*, p. 60.

55. Christopher Lasch, *The Revolt of the Elites and the Betrayal of Democracy* (New York: W. W. Norton, 1995), pp. 117–128.

56. James Howard Kunstler, *Geography of Nowhere. The Rise and Decline of America's Man-Made Landscape* (New York: Simon and Schuster, 1993).

57. James Howard Kunstler, *Home from Nowhere: Remaking our Everyday World for the 21st Century* (New York: Simon & Schuster, 1996).

58. Kunstler, *Home from Nowhere*, pp. 54–57.

59. Kunstler, *Home from Nowhere*, p. 5.

60. Congress for the New Urbanism, *Charter of the New Urbanism* (New York: McGraw-Hill, 2000), p. v.

61. Congress, *Charter*, p. v.

62. Congress, *Charter*, pp. 23, 29.

63. Congress, *Charter*, p. 35.

64. Congress, *Charter*, pp. 113, 155; quote on p. 173.

65. Congress, *Charter*, p. 89.

66. Congress, *Charter*, p. 161.

67. Andres Duany, in Congress, *Charter*, p. 161.

68. Calthorpe, *The Next American Metropolis*, p. 43.

69. Carl J. Abbot, "The Capital of Good Planning: Metropolitan Portland Since 1970," in Robert Fishman, ed., *The American Planning Tradition* (Washington, DC: Woodrow Wilson Center Press, 2000), pp. 241–261. See also Martha J. Bianco, "Robert Moses and Lewis Mumford: Competing Paradigms of Growth in Portland, Oregon," *Planning Perspectives* 16 (2001): 95–114.

70. These and the preceding figures appear on the Congress for the New Urbanism web site, which can be accessed at http://www.cnu.org.

71. Daniel Solomon, *Global City Blues* (Washington, DC: Island Press, 2003), pp. 212–213.

72. See, for example, Ada Louise Huxtable, *The Unreal America: Architecture and Illusion* (New York: New Press, 1997); and Peter G. Rowe, *Civic Realism* (Cambridge, MA: MIT Press, 1997).

73. Duany, Plater-Zyberk, and Speck, *Suburban Nation*, pp. 209–210.

74. Solomon, *Global City Blues*, p. 102.

75. These sorts of criticisms may be found in Alex Krieger, "Arguing the 'Against' Position: New Urbanism as a Means of Building and Rebuilding our Cities," in The Seaside Institute, *The Seaside Debates: A Critique of the New Urbanism* (New York: Rizzoli, 2002), pp. 51–58; Ute Angelika Lehrer and Richard Milgrom, "New (Sub)Urbanism: Countersprawl or Repackaging the Product," *Capitalism, Nature, Socialism* 7 (1996): 49–64; and Peter Marcuse, "The New Urbanism: The Dangers so Far," *DISP* 140 (2000): 4–6.

76. The New Urbanist reflexivity and openness to internal criticism and the ongoing dialogue about the movement's principles and practices is captured nicely in Seaside Institute, *The Seaside Debates*.

77. Alex Marshall, *How Cities Work: Suburbs, Sprawl, and the Roads Not Taken* (Austin: University of Texas Press, 2000).

78. See Cliff Ellis, "The New Urbanism: Critiques and Rebuttals," *Journal of Urban Design* 7 (2002): 261–291.

79. For example, Marcuse, "The New Urbanism"; Lehrer and Milgrom, "New (Sub)Urbanism."

80. Timothy Beatley and Kristy Manning, *The Ecology of Place: Planning for Environment, Economy, and Community* (Washington, DC: Island Press), p. 116.

81. See Katz, *The New Urbanism*; Calthorpe, *The Regional City*; and Seaside Institute, *The Seaside Debates* for a survey of these and other New Urbanist projects. A thoughtful discussion of the social and environmental dimensions of the Fruitvale Transit project may be found in William A. Shutkin, *The Land That Could Be: Environmentalism and Democracy in the Twenty-First Century* (Cambridge, MA: MIT Press, 2001), chapter 5.

82. Congress for the New Urbanism, "Making Environmentalism More Urban," press release, April 27, 2004. Available at http://www.cnu.org.

83. Congress for the New Urbanism, "Board Explores Clarifying Charter," press release, March 4, 2004. Available at http://www.cnu.org.

84. Duany, Plater-Zyberk, and Speck, *Suburban Nation*, pp. 150–151.

85. Here the New Urbanist projects provide implicit support for environmental philosopher Bryan Norton's convergence hypothesis, which predicts that nonanthropocentric and broad (i.e., long-sighted and pluralistic) anthropocentric positions tend to lead to the same policies in practice. See Norton, *Toward Unity among Environmentalists* (Oxford: Oxford University Press, 1991).

86. I see this conclusion as being quite compatible with William Shutkin's development of a civic environmentalism. See Shutkin, *The Land That Could Be*. My focus, however, unlike Shutkin's, is more on the philosophical dimension of this discussion.

Chapter 7

1. Lynn White, Jr., "The Historical Roots of Our Ecologic Crisis," *Science* 155 (1967): 1203–1207.

2. J. Baird Callicott, *Beyond the Land Ethic: More Essays in Environmental Philosophy* (Albany: State University of New York Press, 1999), pp. 40–41.

3. For early work along these lines in the 1970s and 1980s, see Richard Routley, "Is There a Need for a New, an Environmental Ethic?" in *Proceedings of the Fifteenth World Congress of Philosophy*, vol. 1, Bulgarian Organizing Committee, ed. (Sophia, Bulgaria: Sophia Press), pp. 205–210; Holmes Rolston III, "Is There an Ecological Ethic?" *Ethics* 85 (1975): 93–109; Tom Regan, "The Nature and Possibility of an Environmental Ethic," *Environmental Ethics* 3 (1981): 19–34; Paul W. Taylor, *Respect for Nature* (Princeton, NJ: Princeton University Press, 1986); Holmes Rolston III, *Philosophy Gone Wild: Essays in Environmental Ethics* (Buffalo, NY: Prometheus Books, 1986) and *Environmental Ethics: Duties to and Values in the Natural World* (Philadelphia: Temple University Press, 1988); J. Baird Callicott, *In Defense of the Land Ethic* (Albany: State University of New York Press, 1989).

4. Routley, "Is There a Need for a New, an Environmental Ethic?"

5. Examples of this view may be found in Routley, "Is There a Need for a New, an Environmental Ethic?"; Rolston, "Is There an Ecological Ethic?"; and Regan, "The Nature and Possibility of an Environmental Ethic."

6. John Passmore, *Man's Responsibility for Nature* (New York: Charles Scribner's Sons, 1974).

7. Bryan G. Norton, "Environmental Ethics and Weak Anthropocentrism," *Environmental Ethics* 6 (1984): 131–148.

8. For early work on intergenerational justice and duties to future generations, see Richard I. Sikora and Brian M. Barry, eds., *Obligations to Future Generations* (Philadelphia: Temple University Press, 1978); Ernest Patridge, ed., *Responsibilities to Future Generations: Environmental Ethics* (Buffalo, NY: Prometheus Books, 1981); Bryan G. Norton, "Environmental Ethics and the Rights of Future Generations," *Environmental Ethics* 4 (1982): 319–337; Douglas MacLean and Peter Brown, eds., *Energy and the Future* (Totowa, NJ: Rowman & Littlefield, 1983); Annette Baier, "For the Sake of Future Generations," in Tom Regan, ed., *Earthbound: New Introductory Essays in Environmental Ethics* (New York: Random House, 1984), pp. 214–246; and Edith Brown Weiss, *In Fairness to Future Generations: International Law, Common Patrimony, and Intergenerational Equity* (Dobbs Ferry, NY: Transnational Publishers, 1989). For efforts to tease out the normative dimensions of sustainability and sustainable development, see Herman E. Daly and John B. Cobb, Jr., *For the Common Good* (Boston, Beacon Press, 1989); Wilfred Beckerman, "Sustainable Development: Is It a Useful Concept?" *Environmental Values* 3 (1994): 191–209; Mary Midgley, "Sustainability and Moral Pluralism," *Ethics and the Environment* 1 (1996): 41–54; John Foster, ed., *Valuing Nature? Ethics, Economics, and the Environment* (London: Routledge, 1997); Andrew Dobson, ed., *Fairness and Futurity: Essays on Environmental Sustainability and Social Justice* (Oxford: Oxford University Press, 1999); and Bryan G. Norton, *Searching for Sustainability: Interdisciplinary Essays in the Philosophy of Conservation Biology* (Cambridge: Cambridge University Press, 2003).

9. Andrew Light and Eric Katz, eds., *Environmental Pragmatism* (London: Routledge, 1996).

10. Holmes Rolston III, *Conserving Natural Value* (New York: Columbia University Press, 1994), p. 166.

11. Laura Westra, *An Environmental Proposal for Ethics: The Principle of Integrity* (Lanham, MD: Rowman & Littlefield, 1994).

12. Eric Katz, *Nature as Subject: Human Obligation and Natural Community* (Lanham, MD: Rowman & Littlefield, 1997), p. 183.

13. Leo Marx, *The Machine in the Garden. Technology and the Pastoral Ideal in America* (New York: Oxford University Press, 1964).

14. Leo Marx, "The Struggle over Thoreau," *New York Review of Books* (June 24, 1999): 60.

15. High levels of public concern for future generations have been revealed in a number of public opinion studies. See Ben A. Minteer and Robert E. Manning, "Pragmatism in Environmental Ethics: Democracy, Pluralism, and the Management of Nature," *Environmental Ethics* 21 (1999): 191–207; "Convergence in Environmental Values: An Empirical and Conceptual Defense," *Ethics, Place and Environment*, 3 (2000): 47–60; and Willett Kempton, James S. Boster, and Jennifer A. Hartley, *Environmental Values in American Culture* (Cambridge, MA: MIT Press, 1996).

16. See, e.g., Daniel A. Mazmanian and Michael E. Kraft, eds., *Toward Sustainable Communities: Transition and Transformations in Environmental Policy* (Cambridge, MA: MIT Press, 1999); Philip Brick, Donald Snow, and Sarah Van De Wetering, eds., *Across the Great Divide: Explorations in Collaborative Conservation and the American West* (Washington, DC: Island Press, 2000); William A. Shutkin, *The Land that Could Be*: *Environmentalism and Democracy in the Twenty-First Century* (Cambridge, MA: MIT Press, 2000); Julia M. Wondolleck and Steven L. Yaffee, *Making Collaboration Work: Lessons from Innovation in Resource Management* (Washington, DC: Island Press, 2000); Robert Gottlieb, *Environmentalism Unbound: Exploring New Pathways to Change* (Cambridge, MA: MIT Press, 2001); Ben A. Minteer and Robert E. Manning, eds., *Reconstructing Conservation: Finding Common Ground* (Washington, DC: Island Press, 2003); Edward P. Webber, *Bringing Society Back In: Grassroots Ecosystem Management, Accountability, and Sustainable Communities* (Cambridge, MA: MIT Press, 2003); and Paul A. Sabatier, Will Focht, Mark Lubell, Zev Trachtenberg, Arnold Vedlitz, and Marty Matlock, eds., *Swimming Upstream: Collaborative Approaches to Watershed Management* (Cambridge, MA: MIT Press, 2005).

17. Shutkin, *The Land That Could Be.*

18. See Bryan Norton and Ben Minteer, "From Environmental Ethics to Environmental Public Philosophy: Ethicists and Economists, 1973–2010," in Tom Tietenberg and Henk Folmer, eds., *International Yearbook of Environmental and Resource Economics 2002/2003* (Cheltenham, UK: Edward Elgar 2002), pp. 373–407. Andrew Light and Avner de-Shalit make a sympathetic case for a public environmental philosophy in the introduction to their anthology, *Moral and Political Reasoning in Environmental Practice* (Cambridge, MA: MIT Press, 2003), pp. 1–27.

19. Benjamin R. Barber, *A Place for Us: How to Make Society Civil and Democracy Strong* (New York: Hill and Wang, 1998).

Bibliography

Abbot, Carl J. "The Capital of Good Planning: Metropolitan Portland Since 1970," in *The American Planning Tradition*, Robert Fishman, ed. Washington, DC: Woodrow Wilson Center Press, 2000.

Alexander, Thomas M. *John Dewey's Theory of Art, Experience, and Nature.* Albany: State University of New York Press, 1987.

Anderson, Charles. *Pragmatic Liberalism.* Chicago: University of Chicago Press, 1990.

Anderson, Elizabeth. "Pragmatism, Science, and Moral Inquiry," in *In Face of the Facts: Moral Inquiry in American Scholarship*, Richard W. Fox and Robert B. Westbrook, eds. Washington, DC: Woodrow Wilson Center and Cambridge University Press, 1998.

Anderson, Larry. *Benton MacKaye: Conservationist, Planner, and Creator of the Appalachian Trail.* Baltimore: Johns Hopkins University Press, 2002.

Attfield, Robin. *The Ethics of Environmental Concern.* New York: Columbia University Press, 1983.

Baier, Annette "For the Sake of Future Generations," in *Earthbound: New Introductory Essays in Environmental Ethics*, Tom Regan, ed. New York: Random House, 1984.

Bailey, L. H. *The Nature-Study Idea.* New York: Doubleday, Page, 1903.

Bailey, L. H. *The Outlook to Nature.* New York: Macmillan, 1911.

Bailey, L. H. *The Country-Life Movement in the United States.* New York: Macmillan, 1915 (reprint; orig. 1911).

Bailey, L. H. *The Holy Earth.* New York: Charles Scribner's Sons, 1915.

Bailey, L. H. *Ground-Levels in Democracy.* Ithaca, NY: Privately published, 1916.

Bailey, L. H. *What Is Democracy?* Ithaca, NY: Comstock, 1918.

Bailey, L. H. *Universal Service, The Hope of Humanity.* New York: Sturgis and Watton Co., 1918.

Bailey, L. H. *The State and the Farmer*. St. Paul: Minnesota Extension Service, University of Minnesota, 1996 (orig. 1908).

Bailyn, Bernard. *To Begin the World Anew. The Genius and Ambiguities of the American Founders*. New York: Knopf, 2003.

Barber, Benjamin R. *A Place for Us: How to Make Society Civil and Democracy Strong*. New York: Hill and Wang, 1998.

Baskin, Yvonne. *The Work of Nature: How the Diversity of Life Sustains Us*. Washington, DC: Island Press, 1997.

Beatley, Timothy, and Kristy Manning. *The Ecology of Place: Planning for Environment, Economy, and Community*. Washington, DC: Island Press.

Beckerman, Wilfred. "Sustainable Development: Is it a Useful Concept?" *Environmental Values* 3 (1994): 191–209.

Beeman, Randal S., and James A. Pritchard. *A Green and Permanent Land: Ecology and Agriculture in the Twentieth Century*. Lawrence: University Press of Kansas, 2001.

Bender, Thomas. *Toward an Urban Vision: Ideas and Institutions in Nineteenth Century America*. Baltimore: Johns Hopkins University Press, 1975.

Benyus, Janine M. *Biomimicry: Innovation Inspired by Nature*. New York: Perennial/HarperCollins, 2002 (reissue).

Bernstein, Richard J. *The New Constellation: The Ethical-Political Horizons of Modernity/Postmodernity*. Cambridge, MA: MIT Press, 1992.

Beveridge, Charles E., and Paul Rocheleau. *Frederick Law Olmsted. Designing the American Landscape*. New York: Universe Publishing, 1998.

Bianco, Martha J. "Robert Moses and Lewis Mumford: Competing Paradigms of Growth in Portland, Oregon," *Planning Perspectives* 16 (2001): 95–114.

Blake, Casey. *Beloved Community: The Cultural Criticism of Randolph Bourne, Van Wyck Brooks, Waldo Frank, and Lewis Mumford*. Chapel Hill: University of North Carolina Press, 1990.

Blodgett, Geoffrey. "Frederick Law Olmsted: Landscape Architecture as Conservative Reform," *Journal of American History* 62 (1976): 869–889.

Bogue, Margaret Beattie. "Liberty Hyde Bailey, Jr. and the Bailey Family Farm," *Agricultural History* 63 (1989): 26–48.

Bowers, William L. *The Country Life Movement in America*. Port Washington, NY: Kennikat Press, 1974.

Brick, Philip, Donald Snow, and Sarah Van De Wetering, eds. *Across the Great Divide: Explorations in Collaborative Conservation and the American West*. Washington, DC: Island Press, 2000.

Brint, Michael, and William Weaver, eds. *Pragmatism in Law and Society*. Boulder, CO: Westview Press, 1991.

Browers, Michaelle L. "Jefferson's Land Ethic: Environmentalist Ideas in Notes on the State of Virginia," *Environmental Ethics* 21 (1999): 43–57.

Bryant, Paul. "The Quality of the Day: The Achievement of Benton MacKaye." Unpublished Ph. D. dissertation, University of Illinois, 1965.

Bryson, Bill. *A Walk in the Woods*. New York: Broadway Books, 1998.

Callicott, J. Baird. "The Conceptual Foundations of the Land Ethic," in *A Companion to A Sand County Almanac*, J. Baird Callicott, ed. Madison: University of Wisconsin Press, 1987.

Callicott, J. Baird. *In Defense of the Land Ethic*. Albany: State University of New York Press, 1989.

Callicott, J. Baird. "Wither Conservation Ethics?" *Conservation Biology* 4 (1990): 15–20.

Callicott, J. Baird. *Beyond the Land Ethic: More Essays in Environmental Philosophy*. Albany: State University of New York Press, 1999.

Callicott, J. Baird, and Michael P. Nelson, eds. *The Great New Wilderness Debate*. Athens: University of Georgia Press, 1998.

Calthorpe, Peter. *The Next American Metropolis: Ecology, Community, and the American Dream*. New York: Princeton Architectural Press, 1993.

Calthorpe, Peter, and William Fulton. *The Regional City: Planning for the End of Sprawl*. Washington, DC: Island Press, 2001.

Carney, Raymond. *The Films of John Cassavetes: Pragmatism, Modernism, and the Movies*. Cambridge: Cambridge University Press, 1994.

Carson, Rachel. *Silent Spring* Boston: Houghton Mifflin, 1962.

Clendenning, John. *The Life and Thought of Josiah Royce*. Nashville, TN: Vanderbilt University Press, 1999 (rev. ed.).

Colman, Gould P. *Education & Agriculture. A History of the New York State College of Agriculture at Cornell University*. Ithaca, NY: Cornell University Press, 1963.

Congress for the New Urbanism. *Charter of the New Urbanism*. New York: McGraw-Hill, 2000.

Congress for the New Urbanism. "Making Environmentalism More Urban," press release, April 27, 2004. Available at http://www.cnu.org.

Congress for the New Urbanism. "Board Explores Clarifying Charter," press release, March 4, 2004. Available at http://www.cnu.org.

Costanza, Robert, Bryan G. Norton, and Benjamin D. Haskell, eds. *Ecosystem Health: New Goals for Environmental Management*. Washington, DC: Island Press, 1992.

Costanza, Robert, et al. "The Value of the World's Ecosystem Services and Natural Capital," *Nature* 387 (1997): 253–260.

Cronon, William. "The Trouble with Wilderness; or, Getting Back to the Wrong Nature," in *Uncommon Ground: Rethinking the Human Place in Nature*, William Cronon, ed. New York: W. W. Norton, 1996.

Curtin, Deane. "Making Peace with the Earth: Indigenous Agriculture and the Green Revolution," *Environmental Ethics* 17 (1995): 59–73.

Daily, Gretchen C., ed. *Nature's Services: Societal Dependence on Natural Ecosystems*. Washington, DC: Island Press, 1997.

Dalbey, Matthew. *Regional Visionaries and Metropolitan Boosters: Decentralization, Regional Planning, and Parkways During the Interwar Years*. Boston: Kluwer Academic Publishers, 2002.

Daly, Herman E., and John B. Cobb, Jr. *For the Common Good*. Boston: Beacon Press, 1989.

Danbom, David B. *The Resisted Revolution*. Ames: Iowa State University Press, 1979.

Devall, Bill, and George Sessions. *Deep Ecology: Living as if Nature Mattered*. Salt Lake City, UT: Gibbs Smith, 1985.

Dewey, John. "Plan of Organization of the University Primary School," in volume 5 of *John Dewey: The Early Works*, Jo Ann Boydston, ed. Carbondale: Southern Illinois University Press, 1972 (orig. n.d./1895?).

Dewey, John. "A Pedagogical Experiment," in volume 5 of *John Dewey: The Early Works*, Jo Ann Boydston, ed. Carbondale: Southern Illinois University Press, 1972 (orig. 1896).

Dewey, John. *The School and Society*, in volume 1 of *John Dewey: The Middle Works*, Jo Ann Boydston, ed. Carbondale: Southern Illinois University Press, 1976 (orig. 1899).

Dewey, John. "The School as a Social Centre," in volume 2 of *John Dewey: The Middle Works*, Jo Ann Boydston, ed. Carbondale: Southern Illinois University Press, 1976 (orig. 1902).

Dewey, John. "The Bearings of Pragmatism Upon Education," in volume 4 of *John Dewey: The Middle Works*, Jo Ann Boydston, ed. Carbondale: Southern Illinois University Press, 1977 (orig. 1908–1909).

Dewey, John. "The Moral Significance of the Common School Studies," in volume 4 of *John Dewey: The Middle Works*, Jo Ann Boydston, ed. Carbondale: Southern Illinois University Press, 1977 (orig. 1909).

Dewey, John (with Evelyn Dewey). *Schools of To-Morrow*, in volume 8 of *John Dewey: The Middle Works*, Jo Ann Boydston, ed. Carbondale: Southern Illinois University Press, 1979 (orig. 1915).

Dewey, John. *Democracy and Education: An Introduction to the Philosophy of Education*, in volume 9 of *John Dewey: The Middle Works*, Jo Ann Boydston, ed. Carbondale: Southern Illinois University Press, 1980 (orig. 1916).

Dewey, John. "Pragmatic America," in volume 13 of *John Dewey: The Middle Works*, Jo Ann Boydston, ed. Carbondale: Southern Illinois University Press, 1983 (orig. 1922).

Dewey, John. *Human Nature and Conduct*, in volume 14 of *John Dewey: The Middle Works*, Jo Ann Boydston, ed. Carbondale: Southern Illinois University Press, 1983 (orig. 1922).

Dewey, John. *Experience and Nature*, in volume 1 of *John Dewey: The Later Works*, Jo Ann Boydston, ed. Carbondale: Southern Illinois University Press, 1981 (orig. 1925).

Dewey, John. *The Public and Its Problems*, in volume 2 of *John Dewey: The Later Works*, Jo Ann Boydston, ed. Carbondale: Southern Illinois University Press, 1984 (orig. 1927).

Dewey, John. "The Pragmatic Acquiescence," in volume 3 of *John Dewey: The Later Works*, Jo Ann Boydston, ed. Carbondale: Southern Illinois University Press, 1984 (orig. 1927).

Dewey, John. *Ethics*, in volume 7 of *John Dewey: The Later Works*, Jo Ann Boydston, ed. Carbondale: Southern Illinois University Press, 1985 (orig. 1932).

Dewey, John. *A Common Faith*, in volume 9 of *John Dewey: The Later Works*, Jo Ann Boydston, ed. Carbondale: Southern Illinois University Press, 1986 (orig. 1934).

Dewey, John. *Art as Experience*, in volume 10 of *John Dewey: The Later Works*, Jo Ann Boydston, ed. Carbondale: Southern Illinois University Press, 1987 (orig. 1934).

Dewey, John. *Liberalism and Social Action*, in volume 11 of *John Dewey: The Later Works*, Jo Ann Boydston, ed. Carbondale: Southern Illinois University Press, 1987 (orig. 1935).

Dewey, John. *Logic: The Theory of Inquiry*, in volume 12 of *John Dewey: The Later Works*, Jo Ann Boydston, ed. Carbondale: Southern Illinois University Press, 1986 (orig. 1938).

Dewey, John. *Freedom and Culture*, in volume 13 of *John Dewey: The Later Works*, Jo Ann Boydston, ed. Carbondale: Southern Illinois University Press, 1988 (orig. 1939).

DeWitt, Calvin B. *Caring for Creation: Responsible Stewardship of God's Handiwork*. James W. Skillen and Luis E. Lugo, eds. Grand Rapids, MI: Baker Books, 1998.

Diamant, Rolf. "Reflections on Environmental History with a Human Face: Experiences from a New National Park," *Environmental History* 8 (2003): 628–642.

Dickstein, Morris, ed. *The Revival of Pragmatism: New Essays on Social Thought, Law, and Culture*. Durham, NC: Duke University Press, 1998.

Dobson, Andrew, ed. *Fairness and Futurity: Essays on Environmental Sustainability and Social Justice*. Oxford: Oxford University Press, 1999.

Dorf, Philip. *Liberty Hyde Bailey: An Informal Biography*. Ithaca, NY: Cornell University Press, 1956.

Dorman, Robert. *Revolt of the Provinces. The Regionalist Movement in America, 1920–1945*. Chapel Hill: University of North Carolina Press, 1993.

Duany, Andres, Elizabeth Plater-Zyberk, and Jeff Speck. *Suburban Nation: The Rise of Sprawl and the Decline of the American Dream*. New York: North Point Press, 2000.

Easterling, Keller. *Organization Space: Landscapes, Highways, and Houses in America*. Cambridge, MA: MIT Press, 1999.

Eisenberg, Evan. "Back to Eden," *Atlantic Monthly*, November (1989): 57–89.

Eldridge, Michael. *Transforming Experience: John Dewey's Cultural Instrumentalism*. Nashville, TN: Vanderbilt University Press, 1998.

Elliot, Robert. "Faking Nature," *Inquiry* 25 (1982): 81–93.

Ellis, Cliff. "The New Urbanism: Critiques and Rebuttals," *Journal of Urban Design* 7 (2002): 261–291.

Elton, Charles S. *Animal Ecology*. Chicago: University of Chicago Press, 2001 (orig. 1926).

Farber, Daniel A. *Eco-Pragmatism: Making Sensible Environmental Decisions in an Uncertain World*. Chicago: University of Chicago Press, 1999.

Fesmire, Steven. *John Dewey and Moral Imagination: Pragmatism in Ethics*. Bloomington: Indiana University Press, 2003.

Festenstein, Matthew. *Pragmatism and Political Theory: From Dewey to Rorty*. Chicago: University of Chicago Press, 1997.

Fish, Stanley. *The Trouble with Principle*. Cambridge, MA: Harvard University Press, 1999.

Fishman, Robert. *Urban Utopias in the Twentieth Century: Ebenezer Howard, Frank Lloyd Wright, and Le Corbusier*. Cambridge, MA: MIT Press, 1982.

Fishman, Robert. "The Metropolitan Tradition in American Planning," in *The American Planning Tradition: Culture and Policy*, Robert Fishman, ed. Washington, DC: Woodrow Wilson Center Press, 2000.

Fishman, Robert, ed. *The American Planning Tradition: Culture and Policy*. Washington, DC: Woodrow Wilson Center Press, 2000.

Flader, Susan. "Aldo Leopold's Sand Country," in *A Companion to A Sand County Almanac*, J. Baird Callicott, ed. Madison: University of Wisconsin Press, 1987.

Flader, Susan. "Aldo Leopold and the Evolution of a Land Ethic," in *Aldo Leopold: The Man and His Legacy*, Thomas Tanner, ed. Ankeny, IA: Soil Conservation Society of America, 1987.

Flader, Susan. *Thinking Like a Mountain: Aldo Leopold and the Evolution of an Ecological Attitude Toward Deer, Wolves, and Forests*. Madison: University of Wisconsin Press, 1994 (reprint; orig. 1979).

Flader, Susan. "Building Conservation on the Land: Aldo Leopold and the Tensions of Professionalism and Citizenship," in *Reconstructing Conservation: Finding Common Ground*, Ben A. Minteer and Robert E. Manning, eds. Washington, DC: Island Press, 2003.

Foreman, Dave. *Rewilding North America: A Vision for Conservation in the 21st Century*. Washington, DC: Island Press, 2004.

Foresta, Ronald. "The Transformation of the Appalachian Trail," *Geographical Review* 77 (1987): 76–85.

Foster, John, ed. *Valuing Nature? Ethics, Economics, and the Environment.* London: Routledge, 1997.

Fox, Stephen. *John Muir and His Legacy: The American Conservation Movement.* Boston: Little, Brown, 1981.

Fox, Warwick. "Introduction: Ethics and the Built Environment," in *Ethics and the Built Environment,* Warwick Fox, ed. London: Routledge, 2000.

Freyfogle, Eric T. *Bounded People, Boundless Lands: Envisioning a New Land Ethic* Washington, DC: Island Press, 1998.

Freyfogle, Eric T. *The Land We Share: Private Property and the Common Good.* Washington, DC: Island Press, 2003.

Freyfogle, Eric T., ed. *The New Agrarianism: Land, Culture, and the Community of Life.* Washington, DC: Island Press, 2001.

Friedmann, John. *Planning in the Public Domain: From Knowledge to Action.* Princeton, NJ: Princeton University Press, 1987.

Friedmann, John, and Clyde Weaver. *Territory and Function: The Evolution of Regional Planning.* Berkeley: University of California Press, 1979.

Garreau, Joel. *Edge City: Life on the New Frontier.* New York: Anchor Books, 1991.

Golley, Frank Benjamin. *A History of the Ecosystem Concept in Ecology.* New Haven, CT: Yale University Press, 1996.

Gottlieb, Robert. *Forcing the Spring: The Transformation of the American Environmental Movement.* Washington, DC: Island Press, 1993.

Gottlieb, Robert. *Environmentalism Unbound: Exploring New Pathways to Change.* Cambridge, MA: MIT Press, 2001.

Gouinlock, James. *Excellence in Public Discourse: John Stuart Mill, John Dewey, and Social Intelligence.* New York: Teachers College Press, 1986.

Gray, Asa. *Field, Forest, and Garden Botany.* New York: Ivison, Blackman, Taylor, 1868.

Guha, Ramachandra. "Lewis Mumford, the Forgotten American Environmentalist: An Essay in Rehabilitation," in *Minding Nature: Philosophers of Ecology,* David Macauley, ed. New York: Guilford Press, 1996.

Gundersen, Adolf G. *The Environmental Promise of Democratic Deliberation.* Madison: University of Wisconsin Press, 1995.

Gunderson, Lance H., C. S. Holling, and Stephen S. Light, eds. *Barriers and Bridges to the Renewal of Ecosystems and Institutions.* New York: Columbia University Press, 1995.

Gunn, Alastair S. "Rethinking Communities: Environmental Ethics in an Urbanized World," *Environmental Ethics* 20 (1998): 341–360.

Gunn, Giles. *Thinking Across the American Grain: Ideology, Intellect, and the New Pragmatism.* Chicago: University of Chicago Press, 1992.

Gutfreund, Owen D. *Twentieth-Century Sprawl: Highways and the Reshaping of the American Landscape.* Oxford: Oxford University Press, 2004.

Habermas, Jurgen. *Between Facts and Norms: Contributions to a Discourse Theory of Law and Democracy.* Cambridge, MA: MIT Press, 1998.

Hagen, Joel B. *An Entangled Bank: The Origins of Ecosystem Ecology.* New Brunswick, NJ: Rutgers University Press, 1992.

Hall, Peter. *Cities of Tomorrow.* Oxford: Blackwell, 1996 (updated ed.)

Hall, Peter, and Colin Ward. *Sociable Cities: The Legacy of Ebenezer Howard.* Chichester, UK: Wiley, 1998.

Hayden, Dolores. *Building Suburbia: Green Fields and Urban Growth, 1820–2000* New York: Pantheon Books, 2003.

Hays, Samuel P. *Conservation and the Gospel of Efficiency: The Progressive Conservation Movement, 1890–1920.* Cambridge, MA: Harvard University Press, 1959.

Heal, Geoffrey. *Nature and the Marketplace: Capturing the Value of Ecosystem Services.* Washington, DC: Island Press, 2000.

Hickman, Larry A. "Nature as Culture: John Dewey's Pragmatic Naturalism," in *Environmental Pragmatism,* Andrew Light and Eric Katz, eds. London: Routledge, 1996.

Hickman, Larry A. "The Edible Schoolyard: Agrarian Ideals and Our Industrial Milieu," in *The Agrarian Roots of Pragmatism,* Paul B. Thompson and Thomas C. Hilde, eds. Nashville, TN: Vanderbilt University Press, 2000.

Hiedanpää, Juha, and Daniel W. Bromley, "Environmental Policy as a Process of Reasonable Valuing," in *Economics, Ethics, and Environmental Policy: Contested Choices,* Daniel W. Bromley and Jouni Paavola, eds. Oxford: Blackwell, 2002.

Higgs, Eric. *Nature by Design: People, Natural Process, and Ecological Restoration* Cambridge, MA: MIT Press, 2003.

Hine, Robert. "The American West as Metaphysics: A Perspective on Josiah Royce," *Pacific Historical Review* 58 (1989): 267–291.

Hiss, Tony. *The Experience of Place.* New York: Random House, 1990.

Hodgson, Geoffrey. "Economics, Environmental Policy and the Transcendence of Utilitarianism," in *Valuing Nature: Economics, Ethics and Environment,* John Foster, ed. London: Routledge, 1997.

Holling, C. S. "Resilience and Stability of Ecological Systems," *Annual Review of Ecology and Systematics* 4 (1973): 1–24.

Holling, C. S. *Adaptive Environmental Assessment and Management.* London: Wiley, 1978.

Holling, C. S. and Lance H. Gunderson, "Resilience and Adaptive Cycles," in *Panarchy: Understanding Transformations in Human and Natural Systems,* Lance H. Gunderson and C. S. Holling, eds. Washington, DC: Island Press, 2002.

Hoopes, James. *Community Denied: The Wrong Turn of Pragmatic Liberalism.* Ithaca, NY: Cornell University Press, 1998.

Howard, Ebenezer. *Garden Cities of To-Morrow.* Cambridge, MA: MIT Press, 1965 (orig. 1902).

Hughes, Thomas P. *Human-Built World.* Chicago: University of Chicago Press, 2004.

Hughes, Thomas P. and Agatha C. Hughes, eds. *Lewis Mumford: Public Intellectual.* New York: Oxford University Press, 1990.

Huxtable, Ada Louise. *The Unreal America: Architecture and Illusion.* New York: New Press, 1997.

Jackson, John Brinckerhoff. *Discovering the Vernacular Landscape.* New Haven, CT: Yale University Press, 1986.

Jackson, Kenneth T. *Crabgrass Frontier: The Suburbanization of the United States.* New York: Oxford University Press, 1985.

Jackson, Wes. *New Roots for Agriculture.* San Francisco: Friends of the Earth, 1980.

Jackson, Wes. *Altars of Unhewn Stone: Science and the Earth.* San Francisco: North Point Press, 1987.

Jackson, Wes. *Becoming Native to this Place.* Washington, DC: Counterpoint, 1996.

Jackson, Wes. "Matfield Green," in *Rooted in the Land: Essays on Community and Place,* William Vitek and Wes Jackson, eds. New Haven, CT: Yale University Press, 1996.

Jackson, Wes. "Aldo Leopold: Central Figure for Prairie Festival 1998" Available at http://www.landinstitute.org.

Jackson, Wes. "Nature as the Measure for a Sustainable Agriculture," in *The Environmental Ethics & Policy Book*, Donald VanDeVeer and Christine Pierce, eds. Belmont, CA: Thomson Wadsworth, 2003 (3rd ed.).

Jackson, Wes. "Natural Systems Agriculture: A Truly Radical Alternative," *Agriculture, Ecosystems and Environment* 88 (2002) 111–117.

Jacobs, Jane. *The Death and Life of Great American Cities.* New York: Vintage Books, 1992 (orig. 1961).

Jacoby, Karl. *Crimes Against Nature: Squatters, Poachers, Thieves, and the Hidden History of American Conservation.* Berkeley: University of California Press, 2001.

Jamieson, Dale. "The City Around Us," in *Earthbound: New Introductory Essays in Environmental Ethics,* Tom Regan, ed. Philadelphia: Temple University Press, 1984.

Jordan, William III. *The Sunflower Forest: Ecological Restoration and the New Communion with Nature*. Berkeley: University of California Press, 2003.

Judd, Richard. *Common Lands, Common People: The Origins of Conservation in Northern New England*. Cambridge, MA: Harvard University Press, 1997.

Katz, Eric. "The Big Lie: Human Restoration of Nature," *Research in Philosophy and Technology* 12 (1992): 231–241.

Katz, Eric. "The Traditional Ethics of Nature Resource Management," in *A New Century for Natural Resources Management*, Richard L. Knight and Sarah F. Bates, eds. Washington, DC: Island Press, 1995.

Katz, Eric. *Nature as Subject: Human Obligation and Natural Community*. Lanham, MD: Rowman & Littlefield, 1997.

Katz, Peter. *The New Urbanism: Toward an Architecture of Community*. New York: McGraw-Hill, 1994.

Kegley, Jacquelyn Ann K. *Genuine Individuals and Genuine Communities: A Roycean Public Philosophy*. Nashville, TN: Vanderbilt University Press, 1997.

Kempton, Willett, James S. Boster, and Jennifer A. Hartley. *Environmental Values in American Culture*. Cambridge, MA: MIT Press, 1996.

Keppel, Ann M. "The Myth of Agrarianism in Rural Educational Reform, 1890–1914," *History of Education Quarterly* 2 (1962): 100–112.

Kestenbaum, Victor. *The Grace and the Severity of the Ideal. John Dewey and the Transcendent*. Chicago: University of Chicago Press, 2002.

King, Roger J. H. "Environmental Ethics and the Built Environment," *Environmental Ethics* 22 (2000): 115–131.

Kirkman, Robert. "Reasons to Dwell on (if Not Necessarily in) the Suburbs," *Environmental Ethics* 26 (2004): 77–96.

Krieger, Alex. "Arguing the 'Against' Position: New Urbanism as a Means of Building and Rebuilding our Cities," in *The Seaside Debates: A Critique of the New Urbanism*, The Seaside Institute. New York: Rizzoli, 2002.

Kunstler, James Howard. *Geography of Nowhere: The Rise and Decline of America's Man-made Landscape*. New York: Simon and Schuster, 1993.

Kunstler, James Howard. *Home from Nowhere: Remaking our Everyday World for the 21ˢᵗ Century*. New York: Simon & Schuster, 1996.

Lasch, Christopher. *The Revolt of the Elites and the Betrayal of Democracy*. New York: W. W. Norton, 1995.

Lawrence, George H. M. "Horticulture," in *A Short History of Botany in the United States,* Joseph Ewan, ed. New York: Hafner, 1969.

Le Bon, Gustave. *The Crowd; A Study of the Popular Mind*. London; T. F. Unwin, 1897 (2nd ed.).

Lee, Kai N. *Compass and Gryoscope: Integrating Science and Politics for the Environment*. Washington, DC: Island Press, 1993.

Lehrer, Ute Angelika, and Richard Milgrom. "New (Sub)Urbanism: Counter-sprawl or Repackaging the Product," *Capitalism, Nature, Socialism* 7 (1996): 49–64.

Leopold, Aldo. "The Civic Life of Albuquerque," September 27, 1918. Aldo Leopold Papers, University of Wisconsin-Madison Library.

Leopold, Aldo. "The Wilderness and Its Place in Forest Recreational Policy," *Journal of Forestry* 19 (1921): 718–721.

Leopold, Aldo. *Game Management.* New York: Charles Scribner's Sons, 1933.

Leopold, Aldo. "Economics, Philosophy and Land," November 23, 1938. Aldo Leopold Papers, University of Wisconsin-Madison Library.

Leopold, Aldo. *A Sand County Almanac.* Oxford: Oxford University Press, 1989 (orig. 1949).

Leopold, Aldo. 1947 Foreword to *A Sand County Almanac,* in *A Companion to A Sand County Almanac,* J. Baird Callicott, ed. Madison: University of Wisconsin Press, 1987.

Leopold, Aldo. "Some Fundamentals of Conservation in the Southwest." *Environmental Ethics* 8 (1979): 195–220.

Leopold, Aldo. *The River of the Mother of God and other Essays by Aldo Leopold,* Susan L. Flader and J. Baird Callicott, eds. Madison: University of Wisconsin Press, 1991.

Leopold, Aldo. "A Criticism of the Booster Spirit," in *The River of the Mother of God and other Essays by Aldo Leopold,* Susan L. Flader and J. Baird Callicott, eds. Madison: University of Wisconsin Press, 1991.

Leopold, Aldo. "Pioneers and Gullies," in *The River of the Mother of God and other Essays by Aldo Leopold,* Susan L. Flader and J. Baird Callicott, eds. Madison: University of Wisconsin Press, 1991.

Leopold, Aldo. "Conserving the Covered Wagon," in *The River of the Mother of God and other Essays by Aldo Leopold,* Susan L. Flader and J. Baird Callicott, eds. Madison: University of Wisconsin Press, 1991.

Leopold, Aldo. "Wilderness as a form of Land Use," in *The River of the Mother of God and other Essays by Aldo Leopold,* Susan L. Flader and J. Baird Callicott, eds. Madison: University of Wisconsin Press, 1991.

Leopold, Aldo. "The Home Builder Conserves," in *The River of the Mother of God and other Essays by Aldo Leopold,* Susan L. Flader and J. Baird Callicott, eds. Madison: University of Wisconsin Press, 1991.

Leopold, Aldo. "The Conservation Ethic," in *The River of the Mother of God and other Essays by Aldo Leopold,* Susan L. Flader and J. Baird Callicott, eds. Madison: University of Wisconsin Press, 1991.

Leopold, Aldo. "Conservation Economics," in *The River of the Mother of God and other Essays by Aldo Leopold,* Susan L. Flader and J. Baird Callicott, eds. Madison: University of Wisconsin Press, 1991.

Leopold, Aldo. "Land Pathology," in *The River of the Mother of God and other Essays by Aldo Leopold*, Susan L. Flader and J. Baird Callicott, eds. Madison: University of Wisconsin Press, 1991.

Leopold, Aldo. "Wilderness," in *The River of the Mother of God and other Essays by Aldo Leopold*, Susan L. Flader and J. Baird Callicott, eds. Madison: University of Wisconsin Press, 1991.

Leopold, Aldo. "The Farmer as a Conservationist," in *The River of the Mother of God and other Essays by Aldo Leopold*, Susan L. Flader and J. Baird Callicott, eds. Madison: University of Wisconsin Press, 1991.

Leopold, Aldo. "A Biotic View of Land," in *The River of the Mother of God and other Essays by Aldo Leopold*, Susan L. Flader and J. Baird Callicott, eds. Madison: University of Wisconsin Press, 1991.

Leopold, Aldo. "Wilderness as a Land Laboratory," in *The River of the Mother of God and other Essays by Aldo Leopold*, Susan L. Flader and J. Baird Callicott, eds. Madison: University of Wisconsin Press, 1991.

Leopold, Aldo. "Land-Use and Democracy," in *The River of the Mother of God and other Essays by Aldo Leopold*, Susan L. Flader and J. Baird Callicott, eds. Madison: University of Wisconsin Press, 1991.

Leopold, Aldo. "Conservation: In Whole or in Part?," in *The River of the Mother of God and other Essays by Aldo Leopold*, Susan L. Flader and J. Baird Callicott, eds. Madison: University of Wisconsin Press, 1991.

Leopold, Aldo. "The Ecological Conscience," in *The River of the Mother of God and other Essays by Aldo Leopold*, Susan L. Flader and J. Baird Callicott, eds. Madison: University of Wisconsin Press, 1991.

Leopold, Aldo. *For the Health of the Land: Previously Unpublished Essays and Other Writings*, J. Baird Callicott and Eric T. Freyfogle, eds. Washington, DC: Island Press, 1999.

Leopold, Aldo. "Planning for Wildlife," in *For the Health of the Land: Previously Unpublished Essays and Other Writings*, J. Baird Callicott and Eric T. Freyfogle, eds. Washington, DC: Island Press, 1999.

Leopold, Aldo. "Biotic Land-Use," in *For the Health of the Land: Previously Unpublished Essays and Other Writings*, J. Baird Callicott and Eric T. Freyfogle, eds. Washington, DC: Island Press, 1999.

Leopold, Aldo. "The Land-Health Concept and Conservation," *For the Health of the Land: Previously Unpublished Essays and Other Writings*, J. Baird Callicott and Eric T. Freyfogle, eds. Washington, DC: Island Press, 1999.

Light, Andrew. "Ecological Restoration and the Culture of Nature: A Pragmatic Perspective," in *Restoring Nature: Perspectives from the Social Sciences and Humanities*, Paul H. Gobster and R. Bruce Hull, eds. Washington, DC: Island Press, 2000.

Light, Andrew. "The Urban Blind Spot in Environmental Ethics," *Environmental Politics* 10 (2001): 7–35.

Light, Andrew. Restoring Ecological Citizenship," in *Democracy and the Claims of Nature: Critical Perspectives for a New Century,* Ben A. Minteer and Bob Pepperman Taylor, eds. Lanham, MD: Rowman & Littlefield, 2002.

Light, Andrew, and Eric Katz, eds. *Environmental Pragmatism.* London: Routledge, 1996.

Light, Andrew, and Avner de-Shalit, eds. *Moral and Political Reasoning in Environmental Practice.* Cambridge, MA: MIT Press, 2003.

Livingstone, David N. *Nathaniel Southgate Shaler and the Culture of American Science.* Tuscaloosa: University of Alabama Press, 1987.

Lowenthal, David. *George Perkins Marsh: Prophet of Conservation.* Seattle: University of Washington Press, 2000.

Luccarelli, Mark. *Lewis Mumford and the Ecological Region. The Politics of Planning.* New York: Guilford Press, 1995.

MacKaye, Benton. *Employment and Natural Resources.* Washington, DC: Government Printing Office, 1919.

MacKaye, Benton. "An Appalachian Trail: A Project in Regional Planning," *Journal of the American Institute of Architects* 9 (1921): 3–8.

MacKaye, Benton. "Our Common Mind," unpublished manuscript, MacKaye Family Papers, Dartmouth College Library, box 183, folder 34.

MacKaye, Benton. "On the Purpose of the Appalachian Trail," Unpublished manuscript, MacKaye Family Papers, Dartmouth College Library, box 183, folder 57.

MacKaye, Benton. "Cultural Aspects of Regionalism," unpublished manuscript, MacKaye Family Papers, Dartmouth College Library, box 184, folder 29.

MacKaye, Benton. Address to the Appalachian Trail Conference, Gatlinburg, Tennessee, 1931. MacKaye Family Papers, Dartmouth College Library, box 184, folder 40.

MacKaye, Benton. *The New Exploration: A Philosophy of Regional Planning.* Harpers Ferry, WV and Urbana-Champaign, IL: The Appalachian Trail Conference and the University of Illinois Press, 1990 (orig. 1928).

MacLean, Douglas, and Peter Brown, eds. *Energy and the Future.* Totowa, NJ: Rowman & Littlefield, 1983.

Manning, Robert E., William A. Valliere, and Ben A. Minteer, "Values, Ethics, and Attitudes Toward National Forest Management: An Empirical Study," *Society and Natural Resources* 12 (1999): 421–436.

Marcuse, Peter. "The New Urbanism: The Dangers So Far," *DISP* 140 (2000): 4–6.

Marsh, George Perkins. *Man and Nature.* New York, Charles Scribner, 1864.

Marshall, Alex. *How Cities Work: Suburbs, Sprawl, and the Roads Not Taken.* University of Texas Press, 2000.

Marshall, Ian. *Story Line: Exploring the Literature of the Appalachian Trail.* Charlottesville: University Press of Virginia, 1998.

Marx, Leo. *The Machine in the Garden. Technology and the Pastoral Ideal in America.* New York: Oxford University Press, 1964.

Marx, Leo. "Lewis Mumford: Prophet of Organicism," in *Lewis Mumford: Public Intellectual,* Thomas P. Hughes and Agatha C. Hughes, eds. Oxford: Oxford University Press, 1990.

Marx, Leo. "The Struggle over Thoreau," *New York Review of Books,* June 24, 1999, pp. 60–64.

Mattson, Kevin. *Creating a Democratic Public: The Struggle for Urban Participatory Democracy during the Progressive Era.* University Park: Pennsylvania State University Press, 1997.

Mazmanian, Daniel A., and Michael E. Kraft, eds. *Toward Sustainable Communities: Transition and Transformations in Environmental Policy.* Cambridge, MA: MIT Press, 1999.

McCullough, Robert. *The Landscape of Community. A History of Communal Forests in New England.* Hanover, NH: University of New England Press, 1995.

McDermott, John J. "Nature Nostalgia and the City: An American Dilemma," in *The Culture of Experience: Philosophical Essays in the American Grain.* New York: New York University Press, 1976.

McDermott, John J. *The Culture of Experience: Philosophical Essays in the American Grain.* New York: New York University Press, 1976.

McDermott, John J. "Josiah Royce's Philosophy of the Community: The Danger of the Detached Individual," in *American Philosophy,* Marcus Singer, ed. Cambridge: Cambridge University Press, 1985.

McHarg, Ian. *Design with Nature.* Garden City, NY: Anchor, 1969.

McIntosh, Robert P. *The Background of Ecology: Concept and Theory.* Cambridge: Cambridge University Press, 1985.

Meine, Curt. *Aldo Leopold. His Life and Work.* Madison: University of Wisconsin Press, 1988.

Meine, Curt. "Moving Mountains: Aldo Leopold and A Sand County Almanac," in *Aldo Leopold and the Ecological Conscience,* Richard L. Knight and Suzanne Riedel, eds. Oxford: Oxford University Press, 2002.

Meller, Helen. *Patrick Geddes: Social Evolutionist and City Planner.* London: Routledge, 1990.

Menand, Louis. *The Metaphysical Club: A Story of Ideas in America.* New York: Farrar, Straus, and Giroux, 2001.

Michaels, Walter Benn. "Walden's False Bottoms," *Glyph* 1 (1977): 132–149.

Midgley, Mary. "Sustainability and Moral Pluralism," *Ethics and the Environment* 1 (1996): 41–54.

Miller, Char. *Gifford Pinchot and the Making of Modern Environmentalism.* Washington, DC: Island Press, 2001.

Miller, Donald L. *Lewis Mumford: A Life.* New York: Weidenfield & Nicolson, 1989.

Miller, Joshua I. *Democratic Temperament: The Legacy of William James.* Lawrence: University Press of Kansas, 1997.

Minteer, Ben A. "No Experience Necessary?: Foundationalism and the Retreat from Culture in Environmental Ethics," *Environmental Values* 7 (1998): 333–348.

Minteer, Ben A. "Intrinsic Value for Pragmatists?" *Environmental Ethics* 22 (2001): 57–75.

Minteer, Ben A. "Deweyan Democracy and Environmental Ethics," in *Democracy and the Claims of Nature: Critical Perspectives for a New Century,* Ben A. Minteer and Bob Pepperman Taylor, eds. Lanham, MD: Rowman & Littlefield, 2000.

Minteer, Ben A. "Environmental Philosophy and the Public Interest: A Pragmatic Reconciliation," *Environmental Values* 14 (2005): 37–60.

Minteer, Ben A., Elizabeth A. Corley, and Robert E. Manning, "Environmental Ethics beyond Principle? The Case for a Pragmatic Contextualism," *Journal of Agricultural and Environmental Ethics* 17 (2004): 131–156.

Minteer, Ben A., and Robert E. Manning. "Pragmatism in Environmental Ethics: Democracy, Pluralism, and the Management of Nature," *Environmental Ethics* 21 (1999): 191–207.

Minteer, Ben A., and Robert E. Manning. "Convergence in Environmental Values: An Empirical and Conceptual Defense," *Ethics, Place and Environment,* 3 (2000): 47–60.

Minteer, Ben A., and Robert E. Manning, eds. *Reconstructing Conservation: Finding Common Ground.* Washington, DC: Island Press, 2003.

Montmarquet, James A. *The Idea of Agrarianism: From Hunter-Gatherer to Agrarian Radical in Western Culture.* Moscow: University of Idaho Press, 1989.

Mumford, Lewis. "Regions—to Live in," in *Planning the Fourth Migration: The Neglected Vision of the Regional Planning Association of America,* Carl Sussman, ed. Cambridge, MA: MIT Press, 1976 (orig. 1925).

Mumford, Lewis. "The Fourth Migration," in *Planning the Fourth Migration: the Neglected Vision of the Regional Planning Association of America,* Carl Sussman, ed. Cambridge, MA: MIT Press, 1976 (orig. 1925).

Mumford, Lewis. Letter to Patrick Geddes, March 7, 1926, in *Lewis Mumford and Patrick Geddes: The Correspondence,* Frank G. Novak, Jr., ed. London: Routledge, 1995.

Mumford, Lewis. *The Golden Day.* New York: Boni and Liveright, 1926.

Mumford, Lewis. "The Theory and Practice of Regionalism (2)," *Sociological Review* 19 (1927): 131–141.

Mumford, Lewis. "The Pragmatic Acquiescence: A Reply," *New Republic* 59 (1927): 250–251. Reprinted in *Pragmatism and American Culture*, Gail Kennedy, ed. Boston: D. C. Heath, 1950.

Mumford, Lewis. *The Brown Decades: A Study of the Arts in America 1865–1895*. New York: Dover, 1971 (orig. 1931).

Mumford, Lewis. *The Culture of Cities*. New York: Harcourt Brace, 1938.

Mumford, Lewis. *The Pentagon of Power*. New York: Harcourt Brace Jovanovich, 1964.

Mumford, Lewis. *Sketches from Life*. Boston: Beacon Press, 1982.

Naess, Arne. *Ecology, Community and Lifestyle: Outline of an Ecosophy*. Translated and revised by David Rothenberg. Cambridge: Cambridge University Press, 1989.

Nash, Roderick Frazier. *The Rights of Nature: A History of Environmental Ethics*. Madison: University of Wisconsin Press, 1989.

Nash, Roderick Frazier. *Wilderness and the American Mind*. New Haven, CT: Yale University Press, 2001 (4th ed.).

Norton, Bryan G. "Environmental Ethics and the Rights of Future Generations," *Environmental Ethics* 4 (1982): 319–337.

Norton, Bryan G. "Environmental Ethics and Weak Anthropocentrism," *Environmental Ethics* 6 (1984): 131–148.

Norton, Bryan G. *Why Preserve Natural Variety?* Princeton, NJ: Princeton University Press, 1987.

Norton, Bryan G. "The Constancy of Leopold's Land Ethic," *Conservation Biology* 2 (1988): 93–102.

Norton, Bryan G. *Toward Unity among Environmentalists*. Oxford: Oxford University Press, 1991.

Norton, Bryan G. "Why I Am Not a Nonanthropocentrist: Callicott and the Failure of Monistic Inherentism," *Environmental Ethics* 17 (1995): 341–358.

Norton, Bryan G. "Integration or Reduction: Two Approaches to Environmental Values," in Andrew Light and Eric Katz, eds., *Environmental Pragmatism*. London: Routledge, 1996.

Norton, Bryan G. "Pragmatism, Adaptive Management, and Sustainability," *Environmental Values* 8 (1999): 451–466.

Norton, Bryan G. *Searching for Sustainability: Interdisciplinary Essays in the Philosophy of Conservation Biology*. Cambridge: Cambridge University Press, 2003.

Norton, Bryan G. *Sustainability: A Philosophy of Adaptive Ecosystem Management*. Chicago: University of Chicago Press, 2005.

Norton, Bryan, and Ben Minteer. "From Environmental Ethics to Environmental Public Philosophy: Ethicists and Economists, 1973–2010," in *International*

Yearbook of Environmental and Resource Economics 2002/2003, Tom Tietenberg and Henk Folmer, eds. Cheltenham, UK: Edward Elgar, 2002.

Nussbaum, Martha et al., *For Love of Country. Debating the Limits of Patriotism.* Boston: Beacon Press, 1996.

Oelschlaeger, Max. *The Idea of Wilderness: From Prehistory to the Age of Ecology.* New Haven, CT: Yale University Press, 1991.

Palmer, Margaret et al. "Ecology for a Crowded Planet," *Science* 304 (2004): 1251–1252.

Parsons, Kermit C., and David Schuyler, eds. *From Garden City to Green City: The Legacy of Ebenezer Howard.* Baltimore: Johns Hopkins University Press, 2002.

Patridge, Ernest, ed. *Responsibilities to Future Generations: Environmental Ethics.* Buffalo, NY: Prometheus Books, 1981.

Passmore, John. *Man's Responsibility for Nature: Ecological Problems and Western Traditions.* New York: Charles Scribner's Sons, 1974.

Paterson, John L. "Conceptualizing Stewardship in Agriculture within the Christian Tradition," *Environmental Ethics* 25 (2003): 43–58.

Pimm, Stuart L. "In Search of Perennial Solutions," *Nature* 389 (1997): 126–127.

Poirier, Richard. *Poetry and Pragmatism.* Cambridge, MA: Harvard University Press, 1992.

Posner, Richard. *Law, Pragmatism, and Democracy.* Cambridge, MA: Harvard University Press, 2003.

Putnam, Hilary. *Renewing Philosophy.* Cambridge, MA: Harvard University Press, 1992.

Rapport, David, Robert Costanza, Paul R. Epstein, Connie Gaudet, and Richard Levins, eds., *Ecosystem Health.* Malden, MA: Blackwell, 1998.

Regan, Tom. "The Nature and Possibility of an Environmental Ethic," *Environmental Ethics* 3 (1981): 19–34.

Report of the Country Life Commission. Available at http://library.cornell.edu/gifcache/chla/mono/unit1053/00003.TIF6.gif (orig. 1909).

Righter, Robert W. *The Battle over Hetch Hetchy: America's Most Controversial Dam and the Birth of Modern Environmentalism.* Oxford: Oxford University Press, 2005.

Rockefeller, Steven C. *John Dewey: Religious Faith and Democratic Humanism.* New York: Columbia University Press, 1991.

Rodgers, Andrew Denny III. *American Botany 1873–1892.* Princeton, NJ: Princeton University Press, 1944.

Rodgers, Andrew Denny III. *Liberty Hyde Bailey. A Story of American Plant Sciences.* New York: Hafner, 1965.

Rolston, Holmes III. "Is There an Ecological Ethic?" *Ethics* 85 (1975): 93–109.

Rolston, Holmes III. *Philosophy Gone Wild: Essays in Environmental Ethics.* Buffalo, NY: Prometheus Books, 1986.

Rolston, Holmes III. *Environmental Ethics: Duties to and Values in the Natural World.* Philadelphia: Temple University Press, 1988.

Rolston, Holmes III. *Conserving Natural Value.* New York: Columbia University Press, 1994.

Rolston, Holmes III. "Nature for Real: Is Nature a Social Construct?" in *The Philosophy of the Environment*, T.D.J. Chappell, ed. Edinburgh: Edinburgh University Press, 1997.

Rome, Adam. *The Bulldozer in the Countryside: Suburban Sprawl and the Rise of American Environmentalism.* Cambridge: Cambridge University Press, 2001.

Rorty, Richard. *Achieving our Country: Lefitist Thought in Twentieth Century America.* Cambridge, MA: Harvard University Press, 1999.

Rosenzweig, Michael L. *Win-Win Ecology: How Earth's Species can Survive in the Midst of Human Enterprise.* Oxford: Oxford University Press, 2003.

Routley, Richard. "Is There a Need for a New, an Environmental Ethic?" in *Proceedings of the Fifteenth World Congress of Philosophy*, vol. 1, Bulgarian Organizing Committee, ed. Sophia, Bulgaria: Sophia Press, 1973.

Royce, Josiah. *The Religious Aspect of Philosophy.* Boston: Houghton Mifflin, 1885.

Royce, Josiah. *The World and the Individual.* New York: Macmillan, 1900–1901.

Royce, Josiah. *The Philosophy of Loyalty.* New York: Macmillan, 1908.

Royce, Josiah. *Race Questions, Provincialism, and Other American Problems.* New York: Macmillan, 1908.

Royce, Josiah. *The Problem of Christianity.* New York: Macmillan, 1913.

Royce, Josiah. *The Hope of the Great Community.* New York: Macmillan, 1916.

Royce, Josiah. *The Basic Writings of Josiah Royce*, vol. 2, John J. McDermott, ed. Chicago: University of Chicago Press, 1969.

Rowe, Peter G. *Civic Realism.* Cambridge, MA: MIT Press, 1997.

Ryan, Alan. *John Dewey and the High Tide of American Liberalism.* New York: W. W. Norton, 1995.

Sabatier, Paul A., Will Focht, Mark Lubell, Zev Trachtenberg, et al., eds. *Swimming Upstream: Collaborative Approaches to Watershed Management.* Cambridge, MA: MIT Press, 2005.

Santmire, Paul H. *The Travail of Nature: The Ambiguous Ecological Promise of Christian Theology.* Philadelphia: Fortress Press, 1985.

Schama, Simon. *Landscape and Memory.* New York: Random House, 1996.

Schmitt, Peter J. *Back to Nature: The Arcadian Myth in Urban America.* Baltimore: Johns Hopkins University Press, 1990 (reprint ed.).

Scheper, George L. "The Reformist Vision of Frederick Law Olmsted and the Poetics of Park Design," *New England Quarterly* 62 (1989): 369–402.

Schroeder, Christopher H. "Third Way Environmentalism," *University of Kansas Law Review* 48 (2000): 801–827.

Schuyler, David. *The New Urban Landscape*. Baltimore: Johns Hopkins University Press, 1986.

Shutkin, William A. *The Land That Could Be: Environmentalism and Democracy in the Twenty-First Century*. Cambridge, MA: MIT Press, 2000.

Sikora, Richard I., and Brian M. Barry, eds. *Obligations to Future Generations*. Philadelphia: Temple University Press, 1978.

Smith, John E. *America's Philosophical Vision*. Chicago: University of Chicago Press, 1992.

Smith, Kimberly. "Black Agrarianism and the Foundations of Black Environmental Thought," *Environmental Ethics* 26 (2004): 267–286.

Solomon, Daniel. *Global City Blues*. Washington, DC: Island Press, 2003.

Soule, Judith D., and Jon K. Piper, *Farming in Nature's Image: An Ecological Approach to Agriculture*. Washington, DC: Island Press, 1992.

Soulé, Michael, and Reed Noss. "Rewilding and Biodiversity: Complementary Goals for Continental Conservation," *Wild Earth* Fall (1998): 1–11.

Snyder, Gary. "Nature as Seen from Kitkitdizze Is No 'Social Construction,'" *Wild Earth* 6 (1996/97): 8–9.

Spann, Edward K. *Designing Modern America: The Regional Planning Association of America and Its Members*. Columbus: Ohio State University Press, 1996.

Spirn, Ann Whiston. "Constructing Nature: The Legacy of Frederick Law Olmsted," in *Uncommon Ground: Toward Reinventing Nature,* William Cronon, ed. New York: W. W. Norton, 1996.

Sutter, Paul S. *Driven Wild: How the Fight Against Automobiles Launched the Modern Wilderness Movement*. Seattle: University of Washington Press, 2002.

Tansley, Arthur G. "The Use and Abuse of Vegetational Concepts and Terms," *Ecology* 16: 284–307.

Taylor, Bob Pepperman. *Our Limits Transgressed: Environmental Political Thought in America*. Lawrence: University Press of Kansas, 1992.

Taylor, Bob Pepperman. *America's Bachelor Uncle. Thoreau and the American Polity*. Lawrence: University Press of Kansas, 1996.

Taylor, Bob Pepperman. "Aldo Leopold's Civic Education," in *Democracy and the Claims of Nature: Critical Perspectives for a New Century,* Ben A. Minteer and Bob Pepperman Taylor, eds. Lanham, MD: Rowman & Littlefield, 2002.

Taylor, Paul W. *Respect for Nature*. Princeton, NJ: Princeton University Press, 1986.

Thiele, Leslie Paul. *Environmentalism for a New Millennium. The Challenge of Coevolution.* New York: Oxford University Press, 1999.

Thomas, John L. "Lewis Mumford, Benton MacKaye, and the Regional Vision," in *Lewis Mumford: Public Intellectual,* Thomas P. Hughes and Agatha C. Hughes, eds. New York: Oxford University Press, 1990.

Thomas, John L. "Holding the Middle Ground," in *The American Planning Tradition,* Robert Fishman, ed. Washington, DC: Woodrow Wilson Center Press, 2000.

Thoreau, Henry David. *Walden.* Collected in *Henry David Thoreau.* New York: Library of America, 1985.

Thompson, Paul B. *The Spirit of the Soil: Agriculture and Environmental Ethics.* London: Routledge, 1995.

Thompson, Paul B. "Expanding the Conservation Tradition: The Agrarian Vision," in *Reconstructing Conservation: Finding Common Ground,* Ben A. Minteer and Robert E. Manning, eds. Washington, DC: Island Press, 2003.

Tunnard, Christopher, and Henry Hope Reed. *American Skyline: The Growth and Form of our Cities and Towns.* Boston: Houghton Mifflin, 1955.

Walters, Carl J. *Adaptive Management of Renewable Resources.* New York: Macmillan, 1986.

VanDeVeer, Donald, and Christine Pierce, eds. *The Environmental Ethics & Policy Book: Philosophy Ecology, Economics.* Belmont, CA: Thomson Wadsworth, 2003 (3rd ed.).

Warren, Louis S. *The Hunter's Game: Poachers and Conservationists in Twentieth-Century America.* New Haven, CT: Yale University Press, 1997.

Webber, Edward P. *Bringing Society Back In: Grassroots Ecosystem Management, Accountability, and Sustainable Communities.* Cambridge, MA: MIT Press, 2003.

Weiss, Edith Brown. *In Fairness to Future Generations: International Law, Common Patrimony, and Intergenerational Equity.* Dobbs Ferry, NY: Transnational Publishers, 1989.

Welter, Volker M. *Biopolis: Patrick Geddes and the City of Life.* Cambridge, MA: MIT Press, 2002.

Welter, Volker M., and James Lawson, eds. *The City after Patrick Geddes* Oxford, UK: Peter Lang, 2000.

Wenz, Peter S. "Pragmatism in Practice: The Efficiency of Sustainable Agriculture," *Environmental Ethics* 21 (1999): 391–400.

Westbrook, Robert B. "Lewis Mumford, John Dewey, and the 'Pragmatic Acquiescence,' " in *Lewis Mumford: Public Intellectual,* Thomas P. Hughes and Agatha C. Hughes, eds. New York: Oxford University Press, 1990.

Westbrook, Robert. B. *John Dewey and American Democracy.* Ithaca, NY: Cornell University Press, 1991.

Westbrook, Robert. "Pragmatism and Democracy: Reconstructing the Logic of John Dewey's Faith," in Morris Dickstein, ed., *The Revival of Pragmatism: New Essays on Social Thought, Law, and Culture*. Durham, NC: Duke University Press, 1998.

Westra, Laura. *An Environmental Proposal for Ethics: The Principle of Integrity*. Lanham, MD.: Rowman & Littlefield, 1994.

White, Lynn, Jr. "The Historical Roots of Our Ecologic Crisis," *Science* 155 (1967): 1203–1207.

White, Morton, and Lucia White. *The Intellectual Versus the City*. Cambridge, MA: MIT Press/Harvard University Press, 1962.

Wilkinson, Loren ed. (in collaboration with Peter De Vos, Calvin De Witt, Eugene Dykeman, Vernon Ehlers, Derk Pereboom, and Aileen Van Beilen) *Earthkeeping: Christian Stewardship of Natural Resources*. Grand Rapids, MI: Eerdman's, 1980.

Wilson, R. Jackson. *In Quest of Community. Social Philosophy in the United States, 1860–1920*. New York: Wiley, 1968.

Wirzba, Norman, ed. *The Essential Agrarian Reader: The Future of Culture, Community, and the Land*. Lexington: University Press of Kentucky, 2003.

Wondolleck, Julia M., and Steven L. Yaffee. *Making Collaboration Work: Lessons from Innovation in Resource Management*. Washington, DC: Island Press, 2000.

Worster, Donald. *A River Running West: The Life of John Wesley Powell*. New York: Oxford University Press, 2001.

Index